MW01098003

KÖNEMANN

© 2016 koenemann.com GmbH
www.koenemann.com

Editorial project:
LOFT Publications
Barcelona, Spain

Editorial coordinator: Simone K. Schleifer
Assistant to editorial coordination: Aitana Lleonart Triquell
Art director: Mireia Casanovas Soley
Design and layout coordination: Claudia Martínez Alonso
Editor: Àlex Sánchez Vidiella
Layout: Guillermo Pfaff Puigmartí
Translations: Cillero & de Motta, Mengès (FR)

ISBN 978-3-7419-1400-3

Printed in Spain

LOFT affirms that it possesses all the necessary rights for the publication of this material and has duly paid all royalties related to the authors'
and photographers' rights. LOFT also affirms that it has violated no property rights and has respected common law, all authors' rights and other
rights that could be relevant. Finally, LOFT affirms that this book contains no obscene or slanderous material. The total or partial reproduction
of this book without the authorization of the publishers violates the two rights reserved; any use must be requested in advance. In some cases
it might have been impossible to locate copyright owners of the images published in this book. Please contact the publisher if you are the
copyright owner in such a case.

At this particular time in history when environmental, and social issues have close links to economics, bamboo offers an innovative response to the problems faced by contemporary design. In fact, the current path taken by environmentally aware design foresees the development of new tecnologies and the rediscovery of traditional materials because it is essential to tackle the subject of sustainability not only through energy savings but also through the use of natural materials.

Utilization of this material, like that of other natural products, involves a number of difficulties, among them cultural ones and those related to current building codes.

In the cultural, economic and industrial context of developed countries, bamboo is looked on with suspicion as a strange material that is foreign to local building customs. And it is, as were most of the common and presently used materials that have become accepted over time. Then why shouldn't bamboo be included in this list?

Bamboo is a plant with such special characteristics that it can be considered a strategic element in the specific solution to modern-day problems in fields that go beyond architecture: the severe shrinking of tropical rainforests, effective support for the economies of the the planet's least developed regions, and the application of low-cost building practices that prioritize the environment. It is highly competitive when compared to traditional materials: it is enough to say that owing to its characteristic mechanical strength and extreme light weight, it is now currently known as "organic steel."

In order to be used as building material, a fir tree needs to grow between 12 and 15 years, while an oak needs at least 120 years. Bamboo is ready for use in just three years. It has an excellent shape. It is comparable with carbon fiber in terms of performance, lightness, and strength. It is hollow and light and made up of highly resistant fibers. Not only is bamboo one of the plants that absorbs the greatest amount of CO_2 during its life cycle, it generates 35% more oxygen than trees of the same size, prevents erosion and is particularly prevalent in the world's poorest regions. Also important is the fact that new culms or shoots that grow from a bamboo stem are ready to be cut in between three and five years, without endangering the size of the forest. There is little doubt that this is a highly renewable resource.

What is so incredible is that bamboo still is not in use in Europe and other countries as a common building material.

Importing it from countries where it is mostly grown, particularly in Latin America and Asia, using regular means of commercial and maritime traffic, boosts local economies in those developing countries, especially through the use of microloans.

The current demands for environmentally, economically, and socially sustainable design are leading architects and engineers the world over to invest energy and work in research and experimentation with this material.

The projects illustrated in this book edited by the art historian Àlex Sánchez Vidiella, each in an original way, are evidence of how intelligence and simplicity are all that is needed in order to propose new, perfectly feasible ways of creating environmentally-friendly architecture that will contribute to resolving social, economic, and environmental problems.

This book is an example of the large variety of architecture projects and designs created in bamboo, ranging from the most traditional aesthetics to cutting-edge contemporaneity. Artisans, architects, engineers, designers, and distribution companies around the world have contributed to this ample selection with surprising and striking creations. Special mention should be made of the design section, which features the facet of bamboo that is most familiar to the general public, in addition to other unconventional uses given to this magnificent material.

Bamboo is an age-old material that has returned to the world scene. Its versatility makes it applicable to very different fields, from architecture to industrial design and structural engineering.

Mauricio Cárdenas Laverde
This Colombian architect is the founder of Studio Cárdenas Conscious Design in Milan, Italy, and is the author of a large number of articles and one book on bamboo as a building material. His projects featuring bamboo have recieved major international awards.

Wir befinden uns an einem Scheidepunkt, an dem die Umweltproblematik und soziale Probleme eng mit wirtschaftlichen Aspekten verknüpft sind. Bambus liefert eine innovative Antwort auf die Schwierigkeiten, mit denen heutige Bauprojekte behaftet sind. Umweltbewusstes Bauen bezieht die Entwicklung neuer Technologien und die Wiederentdeckung traditioneller Materialien ein, weshalb das Thema Nachhaltigkeit nicht nur mithilfe der Energieeinsparung, sondern auch über die Verwendung von Naturmaterialien angegangen werden muss.

Der Einsatz dieses Baustoffs und auch anderer Produkte aus der Natur bringt diverse Schwierigkeiten mit sich, wie unter anderem kulturelle Aspekte und die Einhaltung geltender Bauvorschriften.

Im kulturellen, gesellschaftlichen, wirtschaftlichen und industriellen Kontext der Industrieländer wird Bambus mit Argwohn betrachtet und als ungewöhnliches Material im Bauwesen angesehen. Und ja, Bambus ist ungewöhnlich, genau wie der Großteil der mittlerweile weit verbreiteten Baumaterialien, die erst mit der Zeit das Vertrauen und die Akzeptanz der Menschen gewonnen haben. Warum sollte also Bambus nicht auch in diese Liste aufgenommen werden?

Bambus hat einzigartige Eigenschaften. Daher sollte diese Pflanze unbedingt als strategisches Element für die konkrete Lösung von brennenden Problemen in Betracht gezogen werden, die auch Bereiche außerhalb der Architektur betreffen: die Abholzung der tropischen Regenwälder, die wirksame Förderung der Wirtschaft in den weltweit unterentwickeltsten Regionen und die Umsetzung kostengünstiger und umweltschonender Bauweisen. Bambusholz ist im Vergleich mit traditionellen Baumaterialien äußerst konkurrenzfähig: man denke nur daran, dass Bambus aufgrund seiner hohen Belastbarkeit und seines besonders geringen Gewichts als „pflanzlicher Stahl" bezeichnet wird.

Um als Baustoff dienen zu können, muss eine Tanne 12 bis 15 Jahre wachsen, eine Steineiche sogar mindestens 120 Jahre. Bambus ist bereits nach drei Jahren bereit für die Verwendung. Seine Form ist hervorragend, und was Vorzüge, Gewicht und Haltbarkeit anbelangt, ist Bambus mit Kohlenstofffasern vergleichbar, denn seine Stämme sind hohl und leicht und sie bestehen aus unglaublich belastbaren Fasern. Bambus gehört zu den Pflanzen, die während ihrer Lebensdauer am meisten CO_2 absorbieren; er setzt außerdem 35% mehr Sauerstoff als andere Bäume gleicher Größe frei, trägt zur Verhinderung der Bodenerosion bei und wächst vor allem in den ärmsten Regionen unserer Erde. Von besonderer Bedeutung ist auch die Tatsache, dass aus einem Bambusrohr Jahr für Jahr neue Halme wachsen, die nach drei bis fünf Jahren geerntet werden können, ohne dass dadurch die Ausdehnung des Bambuswalds beeinträchtigt würde. Niemand kann

also leugnen, dass es sich um eine erstklassige erneuerbare Ressource handelt. Es ist einfach unglaublich, dass Bambus in Europa und anderen Regionen noch nicht regelmäßig als Baustoff genutzt wird.

Der Import von Bambus aus den Ländern mit der höchsten Produktion, insbesondere aus Lateinamerika und Asien, fördert – sofern die regulären Handelswege und Routen des Seeverkehrs eingehalten werden – die lokale Wirtschaft jener Entwicklungsländer, insbesondere auch über die Vergabe von Mikrokrediten.

Die Notwendigkeit, Bauprojekte unter Berücksichtigung der Nachhaltigkeitsprinzipien für Umwelt, Wirtschaft und Gesellschaft zu entwickeln, hat mittlerweile Architekten und Bauingenieure aus aller Welt dazu gebracht, Energie und Arbeit in die Forschung und das Experimentieren mit diesem Naturmaterial zu investieren.

Die im vorliegenden Band vom Kunsthistoriker Àlex Sánchez Vidiella vorgestellten Projekte sind der Beweis dafür, dass es mit Intelligenz und einfacher Umsetzung durchaus möglich ist, neue Wege für die Architektur vorzuschlagen, die die Umwelt schützen und zur Lösung von gesellschaftlichen und wirtschaftlichen Schwierigkeiten wie auch von Umweltproblemen beitragen.

Dieses Buch ist ein Zeugnis der großen Vielfalt an Architektur- und Designprojekten, die auf dem Einsatz von Bambus basieren und sich von den traditionellen Ästhetik bis zur zeitgenössischen Avantgarde bewegen. Handwerker, Architekten, Ingenieure, Designer und Vertriebsunternehmen aus der ganzen Welt haben mit ihren überraschenden und beeindruckenden Kreationen zu dieser breit gefächerten Sammlung an Beispielen beigetragen. Insbesondere hervorzuheben ist das Kapitel über Design, das sowohl die bei der breiten Öffentlichkeit bekannteste Facette von Bambus als auch weniger alltägliche Anwendungen dieses erstklassigen Materials vorstellt.

Bambus, ein seit vielen Jahrhunderten genutztes Material, ist dank seiner vielseitigen Einsatzmöglichkeiten in den unterschiedlichsten Bereichen – von der Architektur über Industriedesign bis hin zum Bauingenieurwesen – derzeit weltweit im Gespräch.

Mauricio Cárdenas Laverde
Architekt aus Kolumbien, Gründer des Studios Cárdenas Conscious Design in Mailand (Italien), Verfasser zahlreicher Artikel und eines Buchs über Bambus als Baumaterial. Seine Projekte, bei denen Bambus Verwendung findet, wurden mit bedeutenden internationalen Preisen ausgezeichnet.

Nous vivons un tournant historique unique marqué par la convergence des problèmes environnementaux, sociaux et économiques. Le bambou apporte une réponse novatrice aux difficultés de la société contemporaine. Avec lui, on s'achemine vers des solutions reposant sur le développement de nouvelles technologies et la redécouverte de matériaux traditionnels, tant il est indispensable de s'engager dans un mode de développement durable fondé sur l'économie d'énergie et l'exploitation rationnelle des ressources naturelles.

L'utilisation du bambou, et de tout ce qu'offre la nature, ne va pas sans difficultés puisqu'elle exige de concilier la tradition et les exigences des normes de construction en vigueur.

Dans le contexte culturel, social, économique et industriel des pays développés, le bambou inspire la méfiance parce que ce n'est pas un matériau habituellement employé dans le bâtiment. C'est une réalité, mais n'est-ce pas le cas de la majorité des matériaux aujourd'hui couramment utilisés qui se sont faits accepter avec le temps ? Pourquoi le bambou ne viendrait-il pas rejoindre cette longue liste ?

Les caractéristiques du bambou sont si remarquables qu'il serait dommage de ne pas en faire un élément stratégique pour résoudre des problèmes actuels qui ne se limitent pas à l'architecture : l'inquiétante régression des forêts tropicales, le soutien des économies des régions du globe les moins développées et la mise en œuvre de procédés de construction à faible coût respectueuse de l'environnement. Face à la concurrence du bambou, les matériaux traditionnels n'ont qu'à bien se tenir. Il suffit de penser à ses propriétés physiques, sa résistance mécanique et sa remarquable légèreté. C'est pour toutes ces raisons qu'on le surnomme « acier végétal ».

Avant d'être employé dans la construction, un sapin doit avoir entre 12 et 15 ans, un chêne vert au moins 120 ans ; le bambou, seulement 3 ans. Sa forme est idéale. Sa légèreté et sa résistance sont comparables à celles de la fibre de carbone. C'est une tige creuse, légère, composée de fibres très résistantes. Non seulement c'est l'une des plantes qui absorbent le plus de CO_2 durant son cycle de vie, mais sa production d'oxygène est de 35 % supérieure à celle des arbres de dimension comparable. De surcroît, il permet de limiter l'érosion et pousse dans les régions les plus pauvres de la planète. Tous les ans, un pied de bambou produit des rejets qui pourront à leur tour être coupés dans les trois ou cinq prochaines années sans compromettre l'équilibre naturel de la bambouseraie. Force est de reconnaître qu'il

s'agit d'une ressource éminemment renouvelable. On s'étonne donc que l'Europe et tout le monde occidental n'aient pas encore adopté le bambou comme matériau de construction.

Les grands producteurs de bambou sont en Amérique latine et en Asie. Soumise aux lois régissant le commerce international et le transport maritime, son importation favorise d'autant plus le décollage économique de ces pays en voie de développement que, parallèlement, des systèmes de microcrédit sont mis en place.

L'obligation de concevoir des programmes respectant les normes du développement durable et s'inscrivant dans une économie à visage humain conduit architectes et ingénieurs du monde entier à investir leur énergie et leur intelligence dans la recherche et à expérimenter avec ce merveilleux matériau.

Réunis par l'historien de l'art Àlex Sánchez Vidiella, les plans présentés dans cet ouvrage démontrent qu'ingéniosité et simplicité de manipulation sont les meilleures alliées pour promouvoir une nouvelle pratique architecturale respectueuse de l'environnement, capable de contribuer à résoudre nos problèmes sociaux, économiques et écologiques.

Ce livre manifeste la grande diversité des constructions et réalisations en bambou qui vont de l'esthétique la plus traditionnelle aux lignes contemporaines les plus avant-gardistes. Artisans, architectes, ingénieurs et stylistes, avec les sociétés distributrices du monde entier, ont contribué à cette large sélection de constructions aussi surprenantes que spectaculaires. Nous avons également tenu à réserver une place aux objets en bambou, des plus connus du grand public à ceux dont l'usage est plus confidentiel.

Le bambou est un matériau de tradition séculaire qui fait aujourd'hui son grand retour sur la scène internationale où ses multiples qualités l'ont imposé dans plusieurs domaines dont l'architecture, le design industriel et l'ingénierie structurelle.

Mauricio Cárdenas Laverde
Architecte colombien, fondateur de Studio Cárdenas Conscious Design à Milan, il est l'auteur de nombreux articles et d'un livre sur l'usage du bambou dans le bâtiment. Les édifices dans lesquels il utilise le bambou ont reçu les plus grandes récompenses internationales.

Op dit bijzondere historische moment waarop milieu- en sociale thema's nauw in verband worden gebracht met economische onderwerpen, biedt bamboe een innovatieve oplossing voor de problematiek van hedendaagse bouwprojecten. In feite voorziet de huidige weg van het bewuste bouwproject de ontwikkeling van nieuwe technologieën en de herontdekking van traditionele materialen. Het is namelijk absoluut noodzakelijk om het duurzaamheidsprobleem niet alleen door middel van energiebesparing maar ook door het gebruik van natuurlijke materialen aan te pakken.

Het gebruik van dit materiaal, net als van andere producten uit de natuur, brengt afwisselende moeilijkheden met zich mee waaronder culturele problemen en bezwaren op het gebied van de geldige bouwvoorschriften.

In de culturele, sociale, economische en industriële context van ontwikkelde landen wordt bamboe met argwaan bekeken en gezien als een vreemd materiaal voor plaatselijke toepassingen in de bouw. Dat is inderdaad zo, net als de meeste alledaagse materialen die tegenwoordig gebruikt worden en die na verloop van tijd uiteindelijk zijn geaccepteerd. Dus waarom zouden we in deze lijst ook niet bamboe op kunnen nemen?

Bamboe is een plant met zulke speciale eigenschappen dat zij als een strategisch element kan worden beschouwd in de concrete oplossing van zeer actuele problemen die sectoren buiten de architectuur om bestrijken: de gevaarlijke vermindering van tropische bossen, de effectieve steun aan de economieën van de minder ontwikkelde regio's van de planeet en de toepassing van milieuvriendelijke lowcost bouwpraktijken. Bamboe heeft ten opzichte van traditionele materialen een hoog concurrentievermogen: het volstaat eraan te denken dat bamboe door zijn mechanische weerstand in combinatie met zijn ontzettend lichte gewicht tegenwoordig wordt beschouwd als het "plantaardige staal".

Om te kunnen worden gebruikt als bouwmateriaal heeft een spar 12 tot 15 jaar nodig om te groeien, een steeneik ten minste 120 jaar. Bamboe is in slechts drie jaar gebruiksklaar. Zijn vorm is voortreffelijk. Qua rendement, lichtheid en weerstand wordt bamboe vergeleken met koolstofvezel: het is leeg, licht en bestaat uit zeer sterke vezels. Bamboe is één van de planten die tijdens zijn levenscyclus de grootste hoeveelheid CO_2 absorbeert en produceert 35% meer zuurstof dan andere bomen van dezelfde afmetingen. Maar dat niet alleen, de plant verhindert bovendien erosie en groeit met name in de armste regio's van de wereld. Ook belangrijk is het feit dat uit een bamboestengel elk jaar negen halmen groeien die in drie à vijf jaar gekapt kunnen worden, zonder de afmetingen van het bos aan te tasten. Er is zonder enige twijfel sprake van een in hoge mate hernieuwbare hulpbron. Het is dan ook ongelooflijk dat bamboe nog niet in Europa en andere landen wordt gebruikt als alledaags bouwelement.

De invoer vanuit productielanden, in het bijzonder uit Latijns-Amerikaanse en Aziatische landen, langs de regelmatige commerciële verkeersroutes, bevordert de plaatselijke economieën van die ontwikkelingslanden, met name via het microkrediet.

Tegenwoordig zet de eis om conform de ecologische, economische en sociale duurzaamheidsprincipes te ontwerpen architecten en ingenieurs uit de hele wereld ertoe om hun energie en werk te investeren in het onderzoek van en het experimenteren met dit natuurlijke materiaal.

De in dit door de kunsthistoricus Àlex Sánchez Vidiella uitgegeven boek geïllustreerde projecten zijn, elk op een originele manier, het concrete bewijs van het feit dat het met intelligentie en een simpel beleid perfect haalbaar is om met nieuwe voorstellen voor milieuvriendelijke architectuur te komen en bij te dragen aan de oplossingen van sociale, economische en milieuproblemen.

Het boek is een voorbeeld van de keur van architectonische projecten en ontwerpen waarin bamboe is gebruikt en die uiterst traditioneel tot zeer modern kunnen zijn. Ambachtslieden, architecten, ingenieurs, designers en distributiebedrijven uit de hele wereld hebben bijgedragen aan deze uitgebreide selectie verrassende en spectaculaire creaties. Er moet bijzondere aandacht geschonken worden aan de paragraaf over design waarin het voor het grote publiek bekendste facet van bamboe en de niet-alledaagse toepassingen van dit magnifieke materiaal worden weerspiegeld.

Bamboe, een materiaal met een eeuwenoude traditie, keert vandaag de dag terug op het wereldtoneel en vindt, dankzij zijn veelzijdigheid, toepassingen in diverse sectoren, van de architectuur tot de industriële vormgeving en de structurele engineering.

Mauricio Cárdenas Laverde
Colombiaanse architect, oprichter van Studio Cárdenas Conscious Design in Milaan, Italië, schrijver van talrijke artikelen en een boek over bamboe als bouwmateriaal. Zijn projecten waarin bamboe wordt gebruikt hebben belangrijke internationale prijzen gewonnen.

In questo particolare momento storico in cui le tematiche ambientali e sociali sono strettamente legate a quelle economiche, il bambù offre una risposta innovativa ai problemi architettonici contemporanei. Infatti il percorso attuale della progettazione responsabile prevede lo sviluppo di nuove tecnologie e la riscoperta di materiali tradizionali dato che diventa imprescindibile affrontare il tema della sostenibilità, non solo attraverso il risparmio energetico, ma anche tramite l'impiego di materiali naturali.

L'utilizzo di questo materiale, così come di altri prodotti della natura, comporta varie difficoltà, tra queste quella culturale e delle normative vigenti in campo edilizio.

Nel contesto culturale, sociale, economico e industriale dei paesi sviluppati, il bambù è visto con sfiducia ed è considerato un materiale estraneo agli usi costruttivi locali. Effettivamente è così... come per la maggior parte dei materiali comuni attualmente utilizzati, che con il tempo sono stati accettati. Quindi perché non inserire in questo elenco anche il bambù?

Il bambù è una pianta dalle caratteristiche così speciali da essere considerata un elemento strategico nella risoluzione pratica di problemi di grande attualità che comprendono campi al di fuori dell'architettura: la pericolosa riduzione delle foreste tropicali, il sostegno efficace alle economie delle regioni meno sviluppate del pianeta e l'applicazione di pratiche costruttive a basso costo che diano priorità al rispetto dell'ambiente. Rispetto ai materiali tradizionali offre vantaggi molto competitivi: basti pensare che il bambù, grazie alle sue caratteristiche fisiche di resistenza meccanica cui si combina un'estrema leggerezza, è considerato attualmente una sorta di «acciaio vegetale».

Per poter essere utilizzato come materiale da costruzione, un abete deve crescere per 12-15 anni, una quercia almeno 120. Il bambù è pronto dopo soli tre anni. Ha una forma eccellente. In termini di prestazioni, leggerezza e resistenza è comparabile alla fibra di carbonio: è vuoto, leggero e composto da fibre molto resistenti. Non solo è una delle piante che assorbono maggiore quantità di CO_2 durante il proprio ciclo di vita e generano il 35% di ossigeno in più rispetto ad altri alberi delle stesse dimensioni, ma contribuisce anche a ridurre l'erosione e cresce soprattutto nelle zone più povere del pianeta. Importante è anche il fatto che da un palo di bambù nascano ogni anno nuovi germogli, pronti per essere tagliati dopo tre-cinque

anni senza alterare le dimensioni della foresta. Senza dubbio dobbiamo ammettere che ci troviamo davanti a una risorsa con un alto tasso di rinnovabilità. Sembra dunque incredibile che ancora in Europa e in altri paesi non venga utilizzato il bambù come comune elemento costruttivo.

La sua importazione dai principali paesi produttori – in particolare in America Latina e Asia – seguendo i normali canali di traffico commerciale e marittimo dà impulso alle economie locali dei paesi in via di sviluppo, soprattutto attraverso il microcredito.

Attualmente l'esigenza di progettare ispirandosi a principi di sostenibilità ambientale, economica e sociale, spinge architetti e ingegneri di tutto il mondo a investire energie e lavoro nella ricerca e nella sperimentazione con questo materiale naturale.

I progetti presentati in questo libro realizzato dallo storico dell'arte Àlex Sánchez Vidiella, ciascuno in modo originale, sono la prova concreta del fatto che con l'intelligenza e una gestione semplice è assolutamente possibile proporre nuovi modi di fare architettura nel rispetto dell'ambiente contribuendo a risolvere problemi sociali, economici e ambientali.

Il libro raccoglie una grande varietà di progetti architettonici e disegni che prevedono l'impiego del bambù e si muovono tra l'estetica più tradizionale e l'avanguardia più contemporanea. Artigiani, architetti, ingegneri, progettisti e distributori di tutto il mondo hanno contribuito a quest'ampia selezione con creazioni sorprendenti e spettacolari. Particolarmente degna di nota è la sezione dedicata ai progetti in cui troviamo sia gli aspetti del bambù più conosciuti dal grande pubblico, sia gli usi meno quotidiani di questo magnifico materiale.

Il bambù, materiale di tradizione secolare, torna oggi sulla scena mondiale trovando applicazione, grazie alla sua versatilità, in molteplici ambiti dall'architettura fino al design industriale e l'ingegneria strutturale.

Mauricio Cárdenas Laverde
Architetto colombiano, fondatore dello Studio Cárdenas Conscious Design di Milano (Italia), è autore di numerosi articoli e di un libro sul bambù come materiale da costruzione. I suoi progetti che vedono l'impiego del bambù hanno ricevuto importanti riconoscimenti internazionali.

En este momento histórico particular en el que las cuestiones ambientales y sociales se relacionan fuertemente con las económicas, el bambú ofrece una respuesta innovadora a los problemas del proyecto contemporáneo. De hecho, el camino actual del proyecto consciente prevé el desarrollo de nuevas tecnologías y el redescubrimiento de materiales tradicionales, pues se hace indispensable afrontar la sostenibilidad no solo a través del ahorro energético, sino también a través de la utilización de materiales naturales.

La utilización del bambú, como la de otros productos de la naturaleza, comporta variadas dificultades, entre ellas la cultural y la de las normativas de construcción vigentes.

En el contexto cultural, social, económico e industrial de los países desarrollados, el bambú es visto con desconfianza y como un material extraño a los usos locales de la construcción. Y, efectivamente, lo es, como la mayor parte de los materiales comunes y utilizados actualmente, que con el tiempo han ido siendo aceptados. Entonces, ¿por qué no incluir en esta lista también al bambú?

El bambú es una planta con características tan especiales que lo convierten en un elemento estratégico en la solución concreta de problemas de gran actualidad que abarcan campos fuera de la arquitectura: la peligrosa disminución de los bosques tropicales, el apoyo a las economías de las regiones menos desarrolladas del planeta y la aplicación de prácticas de construcción de bajo costo que dan prioridad al medio ambiente. Presenta una alta competitividad frente a materiales tradicionales: por su característica física de resistencia mecánica, unida a su extrema ligereza, es considerado actualmente el «acero vegetal».

Para poder ser utilizado como material de construcción, un abeto necesita crecer de 12 a 15 años; una encina, al menos 120. El bambú está listo en solo tres años. Su forma es excelente. En términos de prestación, ligereza y resistencia, se compara con la fibra de carbono: Está hueco, es ligero y está compuesto por fibras muy resistentes. No solo es una de las plantas que absorben mayor cantidad de CO_2 durante su ciclo de vida, sino que genera un 35% más de oxígeno que otros árboles de las mismas dimensiones, evita la erosión y crece especialmente en las regiones más pobres del planeta. Importante es también el hecho de que de un palo de bambú crecen cada año nuevos culmos, que están listos para ser cortados en un periodo de entre tres y cinco años, sin comprometer las dimensiones del bosque. Sin duda, debemos admitir que nos encontramos frente a recursos altamente renovables. Es increíble, entonces, que el bambú no sea utilizado todavía en Europa y otros países como elemento constructivo común.

Su importación desde los países con mayor producción, en particular los de América Latina y Asia, siguiendo los canales regulares de tráfico comercial y marítimo, fomenta las economías locales de aquellos países en vía de desarrollo, especialmente a través del microcrédito.

Actualmente, la exigencia de proyectar de acuerdo con principios de sostenibilidad ambiental, económica y social lleva a arquitectos e ingenieros de todo el mundo a invertir tiempo y esfuerzo en la investigación y la experimentación de este material natural.

Los proyectos recogidos en este libro, editado por el historiador de arte Àlex Sánchez Vidiella, cada uno de manera original, son una prueba concreta de que, con inteligencia y un manejo simple, es perfectamente viable proponer nuevas maneras de hacer arquitectura respetando el medio ambiente y contribuyendo a resolver problemas sociales, económicos y ambientales.

Estas páginas constituyen una muestra de la gran variedad de proyectos arquitectónicos y diseños creados en bambú que se mueven entre la estética más tradicional y la vanguardia más contemporánea. Artesanos, arquitectos, ingenieros, diseñadores y compañías distribuidoras de todo el mundo han contribuido a esta amplia selección con creaciones sorprendentes y espectaculares. Cabe destacar el apartado de diseño, en el que se reflejan la faceta del bambú más conocida por el gran público y los usos no cotidianos de este magnífico material.

El bambú, un material de tradición secular en algunas culturas, regresa hoy a la escena mundial, encontrando, gracias a su versatilidad, aplicaciones en varios ámbitos, desde la arquitectura hasta el diseño industrial y la ingeniería estructural.

Mauricio Cárdenas Laverde
Arquitecto colombiano, fundador de Studio Cárdenas Conscious Design en Milán (Italia) y autor de numerosos artículos y un libro sobre el bambú como material de construcción. Sus proyectos que utilizan el bambú han recibido importantes premios internacionales.

ARCHITECTURE

Soe Ker Tie House

The architecture firm received a commission to design and build homes for refugee children from the Karen ethnic group in this settlement. The architects offered a private space, a residence, and a neighborhood where the children could interact, play, and socialize. Owing to their appearance, the buildings are known as the "butterfly houses." The predominant material is woven bamboo, employing a craft technique that is a feature of houses in this area.

Das Architektenbüro hatte den Auftrag erhalten, Häuser für Flüchtlingskinder dieser Siedlung aus dem Volksstamm der Karen zu entwerfen und zu bauen. Die Architekten schufen einen Privatraum, ein Haus zum Leben und ein Viertel, in dem die Kinder spielen und sich austauschen können. Aufgrund ihres Aussehens sind die Gebäude unter dem Namen „Schmetterlingshäuser" bekannt. Das Hauptmaterial ist geflochtener Bambus, eine handwerkliche Technik, die in den einheimischen Häusern der Umgebung zum Einsatz kommt.

Le bureau d'études avait été chargé de concevoir et de construire des maisons pour les enfants réfugiés de l'ethnie karen, une population persécutée. Les architectes ont proposé un ensemble comprenant un espace privé, un lieu de vie collectif et un espace de socialisation où les enfants pourraient jouer entre eux. Leurs pans évoquant des ailes, les constructions ont été surnommées « les maisons du papillon ». Murs et cloisons sont en bambou tissé, une technique de vannerie artisanale utilisée dans la construction.

Het architectenbureau ontving de opdracht om opvanghuizen voor kindvluchtelingen van de etnische minderheidsgroep de Karen, te ontwerpen. De architecten ontwierpen een privé-vertrek, een woonhuis en een plaats waar de kinderen met elkaar konden spelen en zich op sociaal vlak konden ontwikkelen. De gebouwen zijn vanwege hun uiterlijk bekend als "vlinderhuizen". Het belangrijkste materiaal is gevlochten bamboe, een ambachtelijke techniek die in de huizen van de streek wordt gebruikt.

Lo studio di architetti ha ricevuto l'incarico di progettare e realizzare delle abitazioni per i bambini rifugiati di questa popolazione, di etnia karen. Gli architetti hanno proposto uno spazio privato, una casa dove vivere e un quartiere dove i bambini potessero interagire, giocare e socializzare. Per il loro aspetto, gli edifici sono noti come "le case della farfalla". Il principale materiale utilizzato è il bambù intrecciato, una tecnica artigianale utilizzata nelle case locali della zona.

El estudio de arquitectura recibió el encargo de diseñar y construir casas para los niños refugiados de esta población, de etnia karen. Los arquitectos ofrecieron un espacio privado, una casa para vivir y un barrio donde los niños pudieran interactuar, jugar y socializar. Debido a su apariencia, los edificios se conocen como «las casas de la mariposa». El principal material es el bambú tejido, una técnica artesanal utilizada en las casas locales de la zona.

Pasi Aalto, Andreas Grøntvedt Gjertsen, Yashar Hanstad, Magnus Henriksen, Line Ramstad, Erlend Bauck Sole/TYIN tegnestue
Noh Bo, Thailand, 2009
© Pasi Aalto

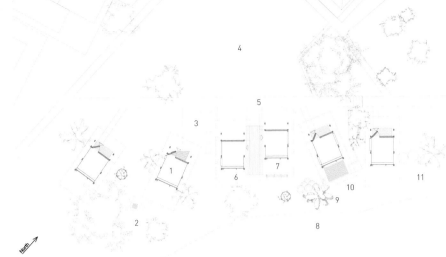

Site plan / Plan du site

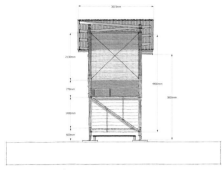

Back elevation / Élévation arrière

1. Quite bench / Banc de repos
2. Chesstable in the shade of a big tree / Table d'échecs à l'ombre d'un grand arbre
3. Yard with BBQ and benches / Jardin avec barbecue et bancs
4. Open courtyard / Cour à ciel ouvert
5. Path made of local brick / Chemin en briques locales
6. Common entrance for two units / Entrée commune pour les deux unités
7. Swing / Balançoire
8. Riverbed / Lit de la rivière
9. Stair of old tyres / Escalier
10. Secluded porch / Porche isolé
11. Elevated water storage / Citerne d'eau

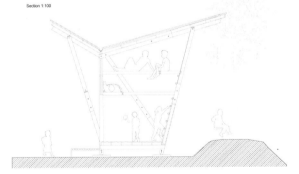

Section 1:100

Section / Coupe

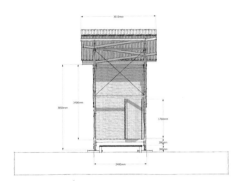

Front elevation / Élévation frontale

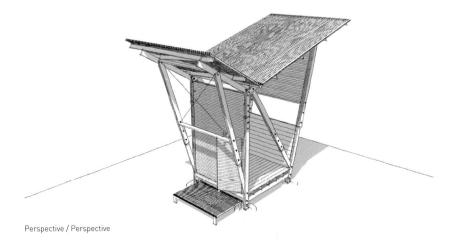

Perspective / Perspective

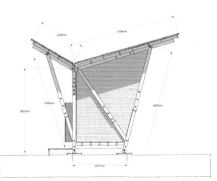

Side elevation / Élévation latérale

The special roof shape provides natural ventilation and collects rainwater. Bamboo was used on façades and the sides of the houses, perfectly combined with steel and wood.

Die besondere Form des Dachs ermöglicht eine natürliche Belüftung und fängt Regenwasser auf. Bambus wurde an den Fassaden und Seiten in perfektem Einklang mit Eisen und Holz eingesetzt.

La forme particulière du toit permet une ventilation naturelle et la récupération des eaux de pluie. Le bambou, utilisé pour les façades et les murs latéraux, est en parfaite symbiose avec le fer et le bois.

De opmerkelijke vorm van het dak maakt natuurlijke ventilatie en het opvangen van regenwater mogelijk. Het bamboe is gebruikt op de gevels en de zijwanden en is perfect gecombineerd met ijzer en hout.

La particolare forma del soffitto consente una ventilazione naturale e la raccolta dell'acqua piovana. Il bambù è stato utilizzato sulle facciate e sulle pareti laterali, combinandosi perfettamente con il ferro e il legno.

La particular forma del techo permite una ventilación natural y recoge el agua de lluvia. El bambú fue utilizado en las fachadas y en los laterales, en perfecta comunión con el hierro y la madera.

Mason Lane Farm

For their design of this new complex housing an agricultural machinery workshop, filling station, and grain and hay barn, the architects adopted a sustainable, passive approach and economical, low-maintenance criteria. Barn B stands out from the two main buildings because of its bamboo latticework grid cladding. The material was sourced from a nearby field. Features include natural daylight and the views from the inside.

Für den Entwurf dieses neuen Komplexes, der aus einer Werkstatt landwirtschaftlicher Geräte, Tankstelle und einem Getreide- und Heuspeicher besteht, haben die Architekten nachhaltigen passiven Ansätzen und wirtschaftlichen Kriterien leichter Wartung den Vorzug gegeben. Von den beiden Hauptgebäuden ragt der Getreidespeicher B besonders hervor, der mit einem Gitternetz aus in der Umgebung gesammeltem Bambus verkleidet ist. Das natürliche Licht und die Belüftung sowie die Ausblicke, die die Innenräume bieten, sind dessen Markenzeichen.

Les architectes chargés de la conception de cet ensemble de hangars qui comprend un atelier pour machines agricoles, une pompe à gas-oil et des greniers à grain et foin ont imaginé une construction passive, économique et facile d'entretien. Le grenier B, revêtu d'une cloison réticulaire fabriquée avec des bambous coupés sur une parcelle proche, éclipse l'autre bâtiment. La lumière et la ventilation naturelles, ainsi que la vue depuis les espaces intérieurs, sont d'autres particularités remarquables de ce complexe agricole.

Voor het ontwerp van dit nieuwe complex, dat dienst doet als werkplaats voor landbouwmachines, tankstation en opslagplaats voor graan en hooi, hebben de architecten gekozen voor een passieve, duurzame aanpak met economische, onderhoudsvriendelijke criteria. Van de twee hoofdgebouwen valt de graanschuur B op, die bekleed is met een maaswerk van bamboe afkomstig uit een nabijgelegen veld. Daglicht en natuurlijke ventilatie zijn andere belangrijke punten, evenals het uitzicht dat men van binnenuit heeft.

Per il progetto di questo nuovo complesso che serve da officina per i macchinari agricoli, da pompa di benzina e magazzino per stoccare grano e fieno, gli architetti hanno optato per soluzioni sostenibili, passive e criteri di economicità e facile manutenzione. Tra i due edifici principali si impone il granaio B, rivestito da una maglia reticolare in bambù raccolto in un campo vicino. La luce e la ventilazione naturale, oltre al panorama di cui si gode dagli spazi interni, sono altri elementi degni di nota.

Para el diseño de este nuevo complejo que sirve de taller de maquinaria agrícola, de gasolinera y de almacé de granos y heno, los arquitectos adoptaron enfoques sostenibles pasivos y criterios económicos de fácil mantenimiento. De los dos edificios principales destaca el granero B, revestido por una malla reticular de bambú recogido de un campo cercano. La luz y ventilación naturales, así como las vistas que se obtienen desde los espacios interiores, son otros elementos destacables.

De Leon & Primmer Architecture Workshop
Goshen, KY, United States, 2009
© Roberto de Leon, Jr./De Leon & Primmer Architecture Workshop

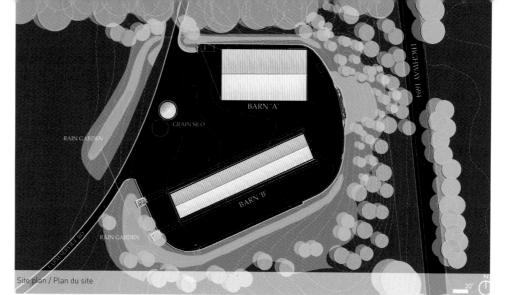

Site plan / Plan du site

BARN 'A'

GRAIN SILO

RAIN GARDEN

RAIN GARDEN

HIGHWAY 1694

BARN 'B'

FARM SERVICE RD

20' N

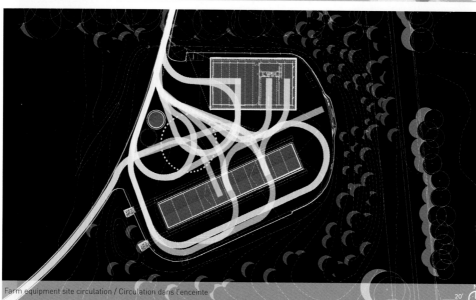

Farm equipment site circulation / Circulation dans l'enceinte

20' N

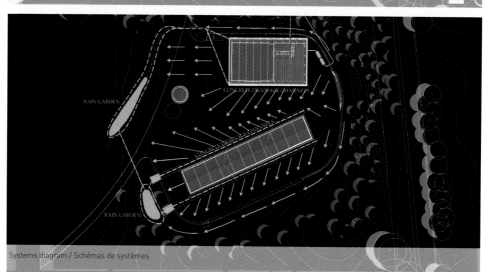

Systems diagram / Schémas de systèmes

RAIN GARDEN

CONCRETE DRAINAGE CHANNELS

CONCRETE DRAINAGE CHANNELS

RAIN GARDEN

The use of bamboo is a take on the square hay bales stored inside and this material also forms a breathable skin that enables the hay to air dry naturally.

Der Einsatz von Bambus ist eine Anspielung auf die quadratischen Heuballen, die dort gelagert werden, und der Werkstoff bietet zudem eine atmungsfähige Haut, die das Trocknen des Heus durch die natürliche Ventilation fördert.

La cloison ajourée en bambou rappelle les balles de foin carrées stockées à l'intérieur. C'est une véritable peau qui respire et qui assure une ventilation naturelle facilitant le séchage des herbes.

De toepassing van bamboe is een knipoog naar de vierhoekige hooibalen die daar opgeslagen liggen. Bovendien vormt het een ademende "huid" waardoor de installatie is voorzien van natuurlijke ventilatie en droog blijft.

L'uso del bambù si adatta bene alle balle squadrate di fieno che qui vengono stoccate, oltre a offrire un rivestimento traspirante che consente l'asciugatura della pianta tramite la ventilazione naturale.

La utilización del bambú es un guiño a las balas cuadradas del heno que allí se almacenan y, además, proporciona una piel transpirable que permite el secado de la planta por medio de la ventilación natural.

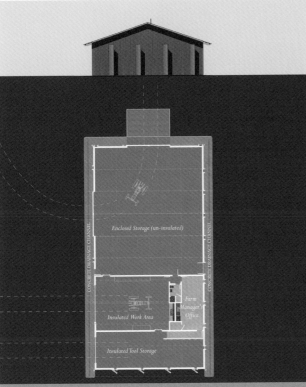

Elevation and plan / Élévation et plan

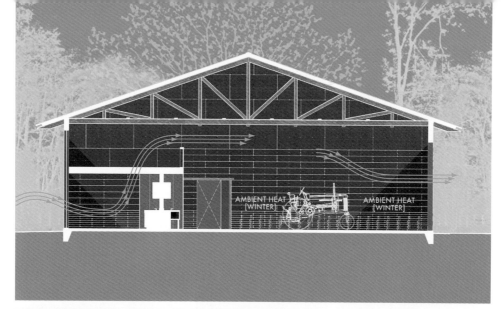

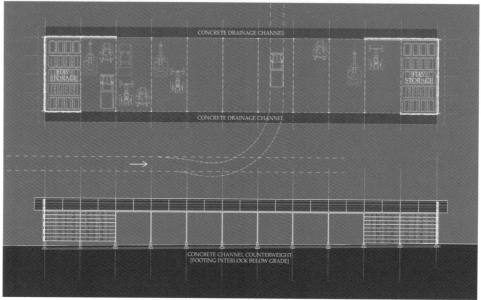

CONCRETE DRAINAGE CHANNEL

HAY STORAGE

CONCRETE DRAINAGE CHANNEL

HAY STORAGE

CONCRETE CHANNEL COUNTERWEIGHT
[FOOTING INTERLOCK BELOW GRADE]

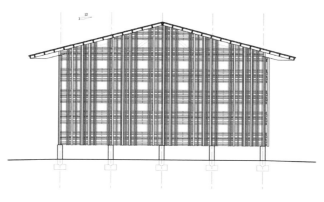

Section, plan and elevation / Coupe, plan et élévation

Bamboo Forest House

Located in a densely built-up area, this home stands out from the others by its exterior screen made of bamboo. The canes envelop the building, creating a barrier that separates it from the street to protect privacy. The impression given from the inside is one of being surrounded by a forest. The bamboo posts are supported by a single structure that is hidden from view, letting them appear to float in the air. The design is the result of research combining high-tech procedures, low-tech manufacturing, and environmentalism.

ROEWU architecture
Luo-dong, Taiwan, 2008
© ROEWU architecture

Mitten in einem dicht besiedelten Stadtgebiet gelegen, fällt dieses Haus unter allen anderen durch seinen Außenschirm aus Bambus auf. Die Bambusstäbe umgeben das Bauwerk und bilden eine Barriere zwischen der Straße und der Privatsphäre. Im Inneren hat man sofort das Gefühl, von einem organischen Wald umgeben zu sein. Die Bambuspfetten scheinen in der Luft zu schweben, da sie nur durch eine einzige, verdeckte Struktur befestigt sind. Das Design ist das Resultat einer Forschung, die *High-tech*, *Low-tech*-Fabrikation und Ökologie miteinander verbindet.

Située dans une zone urbaine dense, cette maison doit sa singularité à son habillage extérieur en bambou. Les tiges qui l'enveloppent protègent l'intimité des habitants des intrusions de la rue. De l'intérieur, on a l'impression d'être au beau milieu d'un bois. Les bambous, maintenus par une unique structure invisible, semblent flotter dans l'air. Cette solution est l'aboutissement d'une recherche visant à associer technologies de pointe, fabrication artisanale et écologie.

Dit huis, gelegen in een dichtbevolkt stedelijk gebied, valt op tussen de andere vanwege zijn bamboe buitenscherm. Het gebouw is omhuld door bamboestengels die de straat en het privé-leven van elkaar afscheiden. Binnen heeft men het gevoel omringd te zijn door een organisch bos. De bamboe staanders lijken in de lucht te zweven doordat ze zijn vastgemaakt aan een onzichtbare structuur. Het ontwerp was het resultaat van een onderzoek waarin verschillende *high-tech* technieken, *low-tech*-vervaardiging en milieutheorieën worden gecombineerd.

Ubicata in una densa area urbana, questa casa si impone per la struttura esterna realizzata in bambù. Le canne avvolgono la costruzione per creare una barriera tra strada e dimensione privata. Dall'interno, la sensazione che si percepisce è quella di trovarsi circondati da un bosco organico. Gli steli di bambù sembrano essere sospesi in aria dato che sono fissati a un'unica struttura nascosta. Il progetto è frutto di una ricerca che ha combinato tecniche *high-tech*, produzione *low-tech* e attenzione all'ambiente.

Situada en una densa área urbana, esta casa destaca entre las demás por su pantalla exterior construida en bambú. Las cañas envuelven la construcción para crear una barrera entre la calle y la vida privada. Desde el interior, la sensación que se percibe es la de estar rodeado de un bosque orgánico. Los postes de bambú parecen flotar en el aire, ya que están fijados por una única estructura que queda oculta. El diseño fue el resultado de una investigación que combinaba técnicas *high-tech*, fabricación *low-tech* y ecologismo.

Site plan / Plan du site

The daylight falling on the bamboo screen create patterns of light and shade that are projected inside the house and onto the façade.

Tagsüber nimmt der Bambusschirm das Sonnenlicht auf und bildet Licht- und Schattenspiele, die sich sowohl im Inneren des Hauses als auch an der Außenfassade widerspiegeln.

De jour, l'habillage de bambou capte la lumière du soleil créant des jeux d'ombres et de lumières qui se projettent autant à l'intérieur de la maison que sur sa façade.

Overdag wordt het zonlicht opgevangen door het bamboe, waardoor er een licht- en schaduwspel ontstaan dat zowel binnenshuis als op de buitengevel wordt geprojecteerd.

Durante il giorno la schermatura in bambù capta la luce solare per creare giochi di luci e ombre che si proiettano sia all'interno della casa che sulla facciata esterna.

Durante el día, la pantalla de bambú capta la luz del sol para crear juegos de luces y sombras que se proyectan tanto en el interior de la casa como en la fachada exterior.

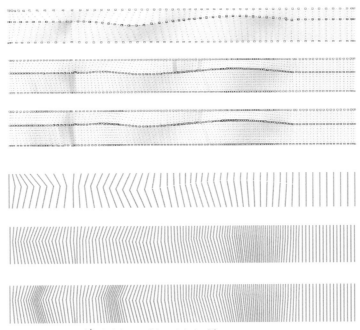

Surface and density study / Étude de la superficie et de la densité

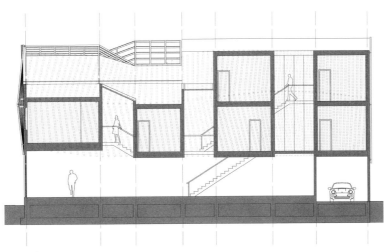

Section / Coupe

Casa Cohuatichan

This country house features a bamboo structural system that rises tree-like from the ground to support the roof. The architects rejected the use of this material for merely decorative purposes. In addition to guadua bamboo, the building makes use of natural materials, including three different kinds of stone. The intention is to offer a new way of understanding architecture and Mexican craft skills.

In diesem Haus auf dem Land wurde Bambus als Tragwerksystem eingesetzt; wie ein Baum scheint es vom Boden emporzuragen, um die Decke zu tragen. Die Architekten wollten dieses Material nicht einfach nur als Dekorationselement nutzen. Neben Guadua-Bambus ist das Bauwerk durch den Gebrauch natürlicher Materialien wie drei Arten von Steinen gekennzeichnet. Absicht war es, eine neue Art des Verständnisses von Architektur sowie die handwerkliche Kunst des mexikanischen Volks zu zeigen.

Pour cette maison de campagne, le bambou forme la structure qui, à l'instar d'un arbre, semble sortir du sol pour soutenir la couverture. Toutefois, pour la réalisation des éléments décoratifs, les architectes préférèrent utiliser d'autres matériaux naturels, dont trois différents types de pierres. Leur volonté était de montrer une nouvelle manière de comprendre l'architecture et le génie artisanal du peuple mexicain.

In deze plattelandswoning wordt bamboe gebruikt in een structuur die, net als een boom, uit de grond lijkt te komen om het dak te ondersteunen. De architecten zagen af van het gebruik van dit materiaal als decoratief element. Naast het gebruik van gradua bamboe kenmerkt het bouwwerk zich door de toepassing van natuurlijke materialen zoals drie verschillende steensoorten. Het streven was om de architectuur en de ambachtelijke bekwaamheid van het Mexicaanse volk op een nieuwe manier te laten zien.

In questa casa di campagna il bambù viene utilizzato come sistema strutturale che, come un albero, sembra emergere dal terreno per sostenere il tetto. Gli architetti hanno rifiutato l'uso di questo materiale come elemento decorativo. Oltre al bambù guadua, la struttura si caratterizza per l'uso di materiali naturali come tre tipi diversi di pietra. L'obiettivo è proporre un nuovo modo di intendere l'architettura e mostrare le competenze artigianali del popolo messicano.

En esta casa de campo, el bambú se utiliza como un sistema estructural que, como un árbol, parece emerger del suelo para sostener la cubierta. Los arquitectos rechazaron el uso de este material como elemento decorativo. Además del bambú guadua, la construcción se caracteriza por el empleo de materiales naturales, como tres tipos de piedra diferentes. La voluntad es mostrar una nueva forma de entender la arquitectura y la capacidad artesanal del pueblo mexicano.

Ricardo Leyva Cervantes/Ojtat
Cuetzalan, Mexico, 2008
© Ojtat

Bamboo is used in two different ways: large canes are used in the structure supporting the house, and laminated bamboo is used for flooring.

Bambus wird auf zwei verschiedene Weisen eingesetzt: großformatige Abmessungen für die Schaffung der Struktur, die das Haus trägt, und in Lamellen zum Verlegen des Innenbodens.

Le bambou s'utilise sous deux formes différentes : dans la structure et pour la décoration. Les éléments de grande portée servent à créer l'armature du bâtiment tandis que les lattes dessinent la disposition des planchers.

Bamboe wordt op twee verschillende manieren gebruikt: in grote afmetingen voor de draagstructuur van de woning en in laminaat voor de vloeren.

Il bambù viene impiegato in due modi diversi: di grandi dimensioni per la creazione della struttura che supporta l'abitazione e laminato per il pavimento interno.

El bambú se emplea de dos formas distintas: de grandes dimensiones, para la creación de la estructura que sustenta la vivienda, y laminado, para la disposición del suelo interior.

Passive House in Bessancourt

The main feature of this house is its external façade structure, made from wood and covered in a second skin of untreated bamboo. Light penetrating the interior is filtered by the bamboo canes, creating patterns of light and shade that are reflected onto the floor and walls. This home was built to sustainability and energy efficiency criteria; among others, it features untreated natural materials, low-energy lighting, and photovoltaic panels.

Dieses Haus besticht besonders durch die externe Struktur der Fassade aus Holz, die durch eine zweite Haut aus unbehandeltem Bambus verkleidet ist. Das Licht, das ins Innere eindringt, wird durch die Anordnung der Bambusstämme unterbrochen, wodurch Licht-/Schattenspiele geschaffen werden, die sich auf dem Boden und an den Wänden widerspiegeln. Die Wohnstätte wurde nach Maßgabe nachhaltiger Kriterien und der Energieeffizienz gebaut, wie etwa mit unbehandelten Naturmaterialien, Sparbeleuchtung und Photovoltaikpaneelen.

C'est surtout la structure de sa façade à ossature de bois habillée d'une deuxième peau en bambou non traité qui fait la particularité de cette maison. La disposition horizontale des tiges fragmente le flux lumineux qui pénètre à l'intérieur, générant un jeu d'ombres et de lumières sur les sols et les murs. Le logement a été construit pour répondre aux exigences du développement durable en matière d'efficacité énergétique. Il est en matériaux naturels non traités, l'éclairage est à basse consommation et l'énergie est fournie par les panneaux photovoltaïques.

Dit huis valt vooral op door de externe structuur van de houten gevel met een bekleding van onbehandeld bamboe. Het licht dat naar binnen doordringt wordt getemperd door de opstelling van bamboestengels, waardoor een clair-obscur spel op de vloer en de muren ontstaat. De woning is gebouwd met criteria van duurzaamheid en energiezuinigheid, bijvoorbeeld met natuurlijke, onbehandelde materialen, verlichting met spaarlampen en zonnepanelen.

Questa casa si impone principalmente per la struttura esterna della facciata, in legno e rivestita da un secondo strato di bambù non trattato. La luce che penetra all'interno è interrotta dalla disposizione delle canne di bambù, producendo così dei giochi di chiaro-scuro che si riflettono sul pavimento e sulle pareti. L'abitazione è stata realizzata applicando criteri di sostenibilità e di efficienza energetica, ad esempio con l'impiego di materiali naturali non trattati, illuminazione a basso consumo e pannelli fotovoltaici.

Esta casa destaca principalmente por la estructura externa de la fachada, de madera y cubierta con una segunda piel de bambú no tratado. La luz que penetra en el interior se interrumpe por la disposición de las cañas de bambú, lo que genera juegos de claroscuros que se reflejan en el suelo y en las paredes. La vivienda ha sido construida bajo criterios sostenibles y de eficiencia energética; por ejemplo, con materiales naturales sin tratar, iluminación de bajo consumo y paneles fotovoltaicos.

Karawitz Architecture
Bessancourt, France, 2008
© Karawitz Architecture

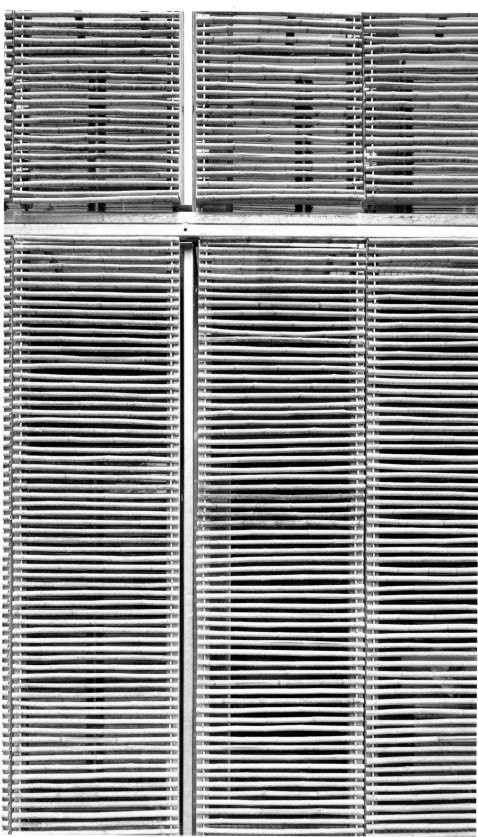

The traditional design conceals the sustainable energy features of a passive house: closed on the north face to limit heat loss and open to the south to make good use of sunlight.

Traditionell entworfen, wurde dieses Haus nach den eigenen nachhaltigen Energiekriterien eines passiven Hauses konzipiert: gen Norden abgeschottet, um den Wärmeverlust einzudämmen, und gen Süden geöffnet, um sich das Sonnenlicht zu Nutze zu machen.

De plan traditionnel, cette réalisation a été conçue selon les critères propres à une maison passive : elle est fermée au nord pour limiter la perte de chaleur et ouverte au sud pour bénéficier de la lumière du soleil.

Voor deze woning met een traditioneel ontwerp is rekening gehouden met de criteria van duurzame energie die eigen zijn aan die van een passief huis: gesloten op het noorden om warmteverlies tegen te gaan en open op het zuiden om het zonlicht zo goed mogelijk te benutten.

Con un impianto tradizionale, la struttura è stata pensata con i criteri energetici sostenibili propri di una casa passiva: chiusa a nord per limitare la dispersione di calore e aperta a sud per sfruttare al massimo la luce solare.

De diseño tradicional, esta casa fue concebida con los criterios energéticos sostenibles propios de una casa pasiva: cerrada hacia el norte para limitar la pérdida del calor y abierta al sur para aprovechar la luz solar.

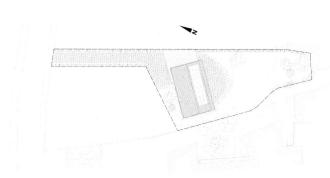

Site plan / Plan du site

Cross section / Coupe transversale

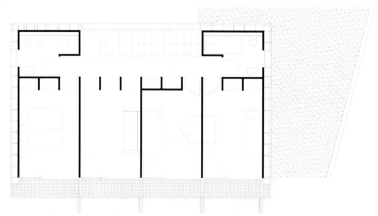

Upper level / Plan du niveau supérieur

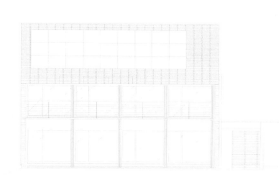

Elevation 1 / Élévation 1

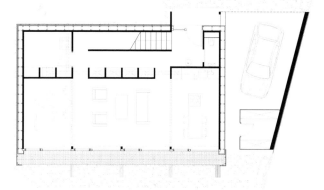

Lower level / Plan du niveau inférieur

0   1   5   10 m

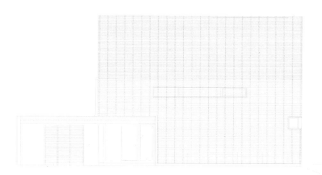

Elevation 2 / Élévation 2

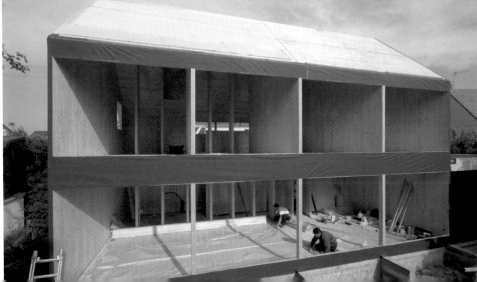

Chinauta House

The architects of this house in Las Pirámides development decided to use guadua bamboo as a building material. The bamboo is present in many forms: as canes when used in columns, roof frames, wall panels, furnishings, lamps, accessories, railings, windows, and doors; split bamboo for flat ceilings, finishings, and partition walls; and in fine strips for the shutters that allow the breeze to enter.

Beim Bau des in der Siedlung Las Pirámides gelegenen Hauses haben die Architekten sich für Guadua-Bambus als Baustoff entschieden. Bambus wird hier in seinen vielfältigen Formen präsentiert: massiv für die Säulen, die Dachstrukturen, Bohlen, Möbel, Lampen, Accessoires, Geländer, Fenster und Türen; als Matten für die abgehängten Decken, Abschlüsse und Trennwände; sowie als Lamellen für die Lüftungsjalousien.

Pour construire cette villa, dans le lotissement Las Pirámides, les architectes ont opté pour l'utilisation de la guadua (variété de bambou surnommée « acier végétal ») comme matériel de construction. Omniprésent, le bambou se décline sous toutes les formes : massif pour les colonnes et les poutres des toitures ; en plaquages pour les meubles, lampes, accessoires, balustrades, fenêtres et portes ; en panneaux tissés pour les faux plafonds, les couronnements et les cloisons ; et en lamellé-collé pour les ouvertures assurant la ventilation.

Bij de bouw van het huis, gelegen in de urbanisatie Las Pirámides besloten de architecten om guadua als bouwmateriaal te gebruiken. Het bamboe komt hier in vele vormen terug: massief in de zuilen, dakstructuren, platen, meubels, lampen, accessoires, hekwerk, ramen en deuren; gevlochten in plafonds, afwerkingen en de scheidsmuren; en als latwerk in de ventilatieluiken.

Nella realizzazione della casa, ubicata all'interno del complesso residenziale Las Pirámides, gli architetti hanno deciso di utilizzare il bambù guadua come materiale costruttivo. Il bambù si presenta qui nelle sue molteplici forme: nella versione massiccia quando è utilizzato per le colonne, la struttura dei soffitti/tetti, i lastre, i mobili, le lampade, gli accessori, le ringhiere, le finestre e le porte; sotto forma di vimini per la realizzazione di soffitti piatti, ribattiture e pareti divisorie; come listoni per le persiane che servono alla ventilazione.

En la construcción de la casa, ubicada dentro de la urbanización Las Pirámides, los arquitectos decidieron utilizar la guadua como material constructivo. El bambú se presenta aquí en sus múltiples formas: maciza para las columnas, las estructura de las cubiertas, las placas, los muebles, las lámparas, los accesorios, las barandas, las ventanas y las puertas; en esterilla para los cielos rasos, los remates y los muros divisorios; y en lata para las persianas de ventilación.

ZUARQ Arquitectos
Fusugasugá, Colombia, 2006
© Jessica Cohen, Mario Negrett, Carolina Zuluaga

Guadua bamboo played a starring role in the construction of this house, which contains four bedrooms over two floors, plus a lounge with floor-to-ceiling windows, dining room, kitchen, and deep balconies.

Guadua-Bambus spielt die Hauptrolle beim Bau dieses Wohnhauses, das vier Schlafzimmer auf zwei Etagen neben einem Panoramasalon, Esszimmer, Küche und Terrassen umfasst.

La guadua joue un rôle majeur dans la construction de ce logement, qui comprend quatre chambres sur deux étages, un salon panoramique, une salle à manger, une cuisine et des terrasses.

Guadua was een belangrijke element voor de bouw van deze woning met vier slaapkamers, verdeeld over twee verdiepingen, een zitkamer en erker, eetkamer, keuken en terrassen.

La guadua ha avuto un ruolo molto importante nella realizzazione dell'abitazione, composta da quattro camere distribuite su due piani, oltre a un salone con vista, una sala da pranzo, una cucina e le terrazze.

La guadua adquirió un gran protagonismo en la construcción de la vivienda, que alberga cuatro dormitorios distribuidos en dos pisos, además de un salón mirador, comedor, cocina y terrazas.

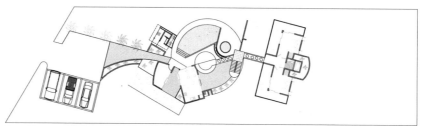

Ground floor plan / Plan du premier niveau

Second floor plan / Plan du second niveau

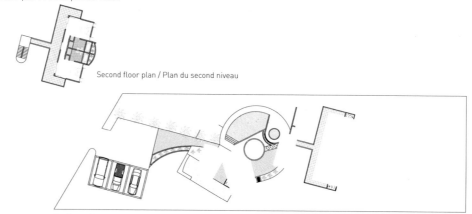

Roof plan / Plan du toit

Sanitary facilities on the ground floor / Installations sanitaires du premier niveau

Sanitary facilities on the second floor / Installations sanitaires du second niveau

Water facilities on the ground floor / Installations hydrauliques du premier niveau

Water facilities on the second floor / Installations hydrauliques du second niveau

Right side façade / Façade du côté droit

Left side façade / Façade du côté gauche

Rear façade / Façade arrière

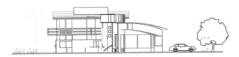

Main façade / Façade principale

De Hann TreeHouse

This treehouse was designed as a space for lounging and relaxing while admiring the landscape. The project consisted of a main cabin from which suspended bridges provide access to two platforms. The structure can be reached in two ways: by a broad spiral staircase or by two ladders. The architects chose different types of wood for the building: fir, briar root, South African reed, redwood, and, predominantly, bamboo.

Das Baumhaus wurde als Raum zum Sitzen und Erholen beim Betrachten der Landschaft konzipiert. Das Konzept besteht aus einer Hauptkabine, von der Hängebrücken ausgehen, die Zugang zu zwei Plattformen bieten. Der Zugang zum Bauwerk kann auf zwei Weisen erfolgen: über eine breite Wendeltreppe oder über zwei senkrechte Leitern. Die Architekten haben für ihren Bau verschiedene Holztypen ausgewählt: Tanne, Heidekraut, südafrikanisches Rohr, rotes Holz und vor allem aber Bambus.

La maison arbre fut conçue comme un espace où venir s'asseoir et se relaxer en contemplant le paysage. L'ensemble réunit l'habitacle central d'où partent deux ponts sur pilotis qui conduisent à deux plateformes. On accède à la construction en empruntant soit un large escalier incurvé, soit deux échelles verticales. Les architectes ont eu recours à plusieurs types de bois pour la construction : sapin, bruyère, roseau d'Afrique du Sud, bois rouge sont associés au bambou, qui est majoritaire.

Het boomhuis is bedacht als zit- en ontspanningsruimte en biedt uitzicht over het landschap. Het project bestaat uit een hoofdcabine die met hangbruggen is verbonden met twee platforms. Men heeft op twee manieren toegang tot het bouwwerk: via een wenteltrap of via twee verticale trappen. De architecten selecteerden verschillende materialen voor de bouw: sparren, heide, Zuid-Afrikaans riet, rood hout en bovenal bamboe.

La casa-albero è stata concepita come uno spazio dove sedersi e rilassarsi mentre si contempla il paesaggio. Il progetto consiste in una cabina principale da cui si dipartono dei ponti sospesi che consentono di accedere a due piattaforme. L'accesso alla struttura può avvenire in due modi: attraverso un'ampia scala a chiocciola o due scale verticali. Gli architetti hanno scelto vari tipi di legno per la costruzione: abete, erica, canna sudafricana, legno rosso e, soprattutto, bambù.

Esta casa árbol fue concebida como un espacio destinado para sentarse y relajarse mientras se contempla el paisaje. El proyecto consiste en una cabina principal de la que parten puentes colgantes que dan acceso a dos plataformas. El acceso a la construcción se puede efectuar de dos maneras: por una amplia escalera de caracol o por dos escaleras verticales. Los arquitectos seleccionaron varios tipos de madera para la construcción: abeto, brezo, caña sudafricana, madera roja y, sobre todo, bambú.

TreeHouse Company
Kent, United Kingdom, 2005
© TreeHouse Company

The bamboo was used to build beams, columns, the roof structure, stairs, and handrails. The large poles provide the structure with great stability.

Bambus wurde zum Bau der Querbalken, Säulen, Dachstruktur, Leitern und Handgeländer eingesetzt. Die breiten Stämme verleihen dem Tragwerk große Stabilität.

Poutres, colonnes, charpente, escaliers et rampes sont ici en bambou. Des tiges de large diamètre garantissent la stabilité de la structure.

Bamboe werd gebruikt voor het maken van de balken, zuilen, dakstructuur, trappen en trapleuningen. Dankzij de lange stokken is de structuur zeer stabiel.

Il bambù è stato utilizzato per travi, colonne, la struttura del soffitto, scale e corrimano. I pali di grandi dimensioni conferiscono molta stabilità alla struttura.

El bambú se empleó para construir las vigas, las columnas, la estructura del techo, las escaleras y los pasamanos. Los palos de grandes dimensiones proporcionan gran estabilidad a la estructura.

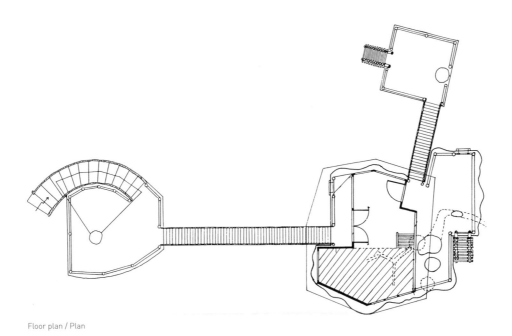

Floor plan / Plan

Pacific Tahitian

The client's brief was for a fully sustainable vacation home. Consequently, an expert in this kind of construction, David Sands, was commissioned with the project, to be located on the exotic island of Maui. Bamboo Living is one of the few companies in the world devoted to building prefabricated homes entirely from bamboo. Prefabrication meant that the rich ecosystem of the site would not be altered with the assembly process.

David Sands/Bamboo Living
Maui, HI, United States, 2009
© Carrie Branovan

Der Kunde wollte ein vollkommen nachhaltiges Ferienhaus. Hierfür hat er das Projekt einem Fachmann für diese Art von Bauwerken anvertraut, David Sands, der dieses neue Grundeigentum auf der exotischen Insel Maui angesiedelt hat. Die Firma Bamboo Living ist eine der wenigen Unternehmen weltweit, die sich dem Bau von rein aus Bambus hergestellten Fertighäusern widmet. Und da es sich um ein Fertighaus handelt, wurde auch das artenreiche Ökosystem, in das die Konstruktion eingesetzt wurde, nicht durch seinen Aufbau in Mitleidenschaft gezogen.

Le client voulait une résidence secondaire entièrement passive. Il en a confié la réalisation à David Sands, expert dans ce domaine. La nouvelle propriété se trouve sur l'île de Maui (Hawaï). La société Bamboo Living est une des rares entreprises au monde à se consacrer à la construction de maisons préfabriquées entièrement en bambou. L'usage de préfabriqué permet de limiter l'impact du montage sur cet écosystème riche.

De klant wenste een verblijf om te ontspannen, dat bovendien helemaal duurzaam moest zijn. Daartoe droeg hij dit project op aan een expert in dergelijke constructies, David Sands, die het nieuwe eigendom neerzette op het exotische eiland Maui. Het bedrijf Bamboo Living is een van de weinige bedrijven ter wereld dat toegespitst is op de bouw van helemaal in bamboe geprefabriceerde woningen. Doordat het geprefabriceerd is wordt het rijke ecosysteem waarop het bouwwerk komt te staan niet aangetast door de montage.

Il cliente desiderava un'abitazione per i periodi di vacanza e svago che fosse totalmente sostenibile. A tal fine ha incaricato del progetto un esperto in costruzioni di questo tipo, David Sands, che ha ubicato la nuova proprietà nell'esotica isola di Maui. La società Bamboo Living è una delle poche aziende a livello mondiale che si dedicano alla realizzazione di case prefabbricate interamente in bambù. Essendo prefabbricata, il ricco ecosistema sul quale è stata posizionata la struttura non ha subito alcuna alterazione.

El cliente quería una vivienda de recreo que fuera enteramente sostenible. Para tal fin encargó este proyecto a un experto en construcciones de este tipo, David Sands, que ubicó la nueva propiedad en la exótica isla de Maui. Bamboo Living es una de las pocas compañías mundiales que se dedican a la construcción de casas prefabricadas íntegramente con bambú. Al ser prefabricada, el rico ecosistema sobre el que situó la construcción no se vio alterado por el montaje.

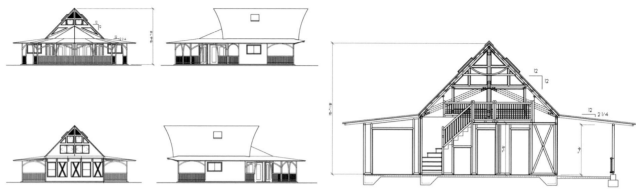

Front elevation, rear elevation, side elevations and section / Élévation frontale, élévation arrière, élévations latérales et coupe

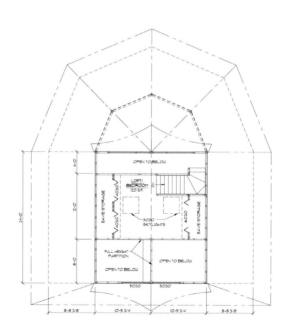

Second floor plan and ground floor plan / Premier étage et rez-de-chaussée

This house is both markedly traditional and as exotic as its location. The design features and the structure were built entirely out of thick bamboo canes.

Im auffallend traditionellen Stil, aber gleichzeitig exotisch, wie dies für seine Lage nicht anders sein könnte, wurde dieses Haus vollständig aus langröhrigem Bambus gebaut, sowohl die Designelemente als auch das Tragwerk.

Alliant les valeurs traditionnelles et l'exotisme propre au lieu où elle fut édifiée, cette maison fut entièrement construite en grandes tiges de bambou, autant pour les éléments décoratifs que pour l'ossature.

Het huis, met zijn markante traditionele en tegelijkertijd exotische stijl, kenmerkend voor de streek waar het kwam te staan, is voor zowel de design-elementen als de structuur helemaal opgebouwd uit grote bamboestengels,.

In stile marcatamente tradizionale ed esotico, tipico della zona in cui è ubicata, la casa è stata costruita interamente in bambù a canna grande, sia per quanto riguarda gli arredi che la struttura.

De marcado estilo tradicional y a la vez tan exótico como la zona donde se ubicó, la casa fue construida íntegramente con bambú de caña grande, tanto los elementos de diseño como la estructura.

Cottage

This project consisted of remodeling an old ruined house as a small guest residence. The owners' brief was for a quiet refuge that was accessible, environmentally friendly, and close to the main residence. To comply with these requirements, the architects incorporated sources of renewable energy and materials with low environmental impact. Treated bamboo was the most widely used material for roofing, floors, and windows.

Die Intervention bestand daraus, ein altes Haus in schlechtem Zustand zu renovieren und es in eine kleine Gästeherberge zu verwandeln. Die Eigentümer hatten ein ruhiges Refugium im Sinne, das leicht zugänglich und ökologisch in der Nähe zum Haupthaus gebaut werden sollte. Um diese Ziele zu verwirklichen, haben die Architekten auf erneuerbare Energien und umweltfreundliche Materialien gesetzt. Behandelter Bambus wurde dabei im Inneren am häufigsten zum Bau der Dächer, Böden und Fenster eingesetzt.

Une vieille bicoque en mauvais état s'est muée en un gîte accueillant pour les invités. Les propriétaires voulaient un refuge paisible, facile d'accès et de construction écologique, à deux pas de leur maison. Pour répondre à leur demande, les architectes ont prévu l'utilisation d'énergie renouvelable et de matériaux respectueux de l'environnement. Le bambou traité est le plus employé pour l'intérieur, la toiture, les sols et les fenêtres.

De aanpak bestond uit het restaureren van een oud huis in slechte staat tot een klein gastenverblijf. De eigenaren wilden een rustig, goed toegankelijk onderkomen met een ecologische constructie, in de buurt van de hoofdwoning. Om deze doelstellingen te kunnen verwezenlijken hebben de architecten hernieuwbare energiebronnen en milieuvriendelijke materialen gebruikt. Behandeld bamboe is het materiaal dat het meest gebruikt wordt in het interieur voor daken, vloeren en ramen.

L'intervento ha previsto la ristrutturazione di un'antica casa in pessime condizioni per trasformarla in una piccola abitazione per gli ospiti. I proprietari desideravano un rifugio tranquillo, facilmente accessibile ed ecologicamente compatibile, vicino all'abitazione principale. Per ottenere questi obiettivi, gli architetti hanno inserito delle fonti di energia rinnovabile e materiali rispettosi dell'ambiente. Il bambù trattato è stato il materiale più utilizzato negli ambienti interni per la realizzazione di soffitti, pavimenti e finestre.

La intervención consistió en remodelar una antigua casa en mal estado para convertirla en una pequeña vivienda para huéspedes. Los propietarios querían un refugio tranquilo, de fácil acceso y de construcción ecológica, cercano a la vivienda principal. Para conseguir estos objetivos, los arquitectos incorporaron fuentes de energía renovables y materiales que respetan el medio ambiente. El bambú tratado fue el más utilizado en el interior para construir techos, suelos y ventanas.

Gray Organschi Architecture
Guilford, CT, United States, 2008
© Gray Organschi Architecture

The design features a living area with kitchen, two bedrooms, and one bathroom. Bamboo was chosen as the most suitable material according to sustainability criteria.

Dieses Vorhaben umfasste ein Wohnzimmer mit Küche, ein Schlafzimmer, ein Bad sowie ein zweites Zimmer. Im Hinblick auf seine Nachhaltigkeit wurde Bambus als angemessenstes Material gewählt.

La redistribution a permis la création d'un séjour avec cuisine américaine, de deux pièces et d'une salle de bains. Le bambou s'est imposé pour ce projet pensé dans la perspective du développement durable.

In het project is voorzien in een zitkamer met keuken, een slaapkamer, badkamer en een extra slaapkamer. In overeenstemming met de duurzaamheidscriteria is bamboe uitgekozen als het meest geschikte materiaal.

Nel progetto sono stati inseriti un salotto con cucina, una camera da letto, un bagno e una seconda camera. Seguendo i criteri di sostenibilità, è stato scelto il bambù come il materiale più adatto.

En el proyecto se ubicaron una sala de estar con cocina, un dormitorio, un baño y una segunda habitación. Siguiendo criterios de sostenibilidad, se eligió el bambú como el material más adecuado.

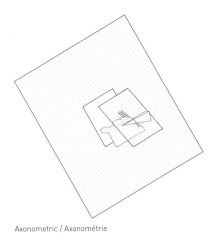

Axonometric / Axonométrie

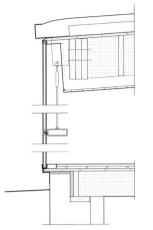

Construction details / Détails de construction

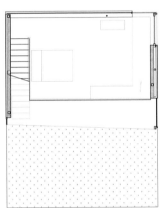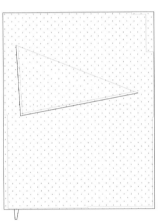

Roof plans / Plans du toit

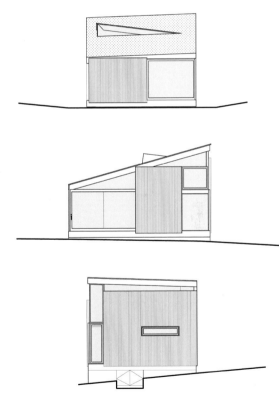

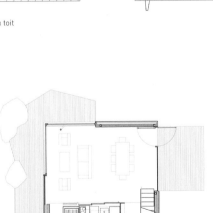

Floor plan / Plan

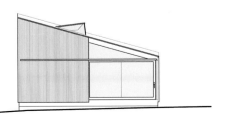

Elevations / Élévations

Artist's Studio

The architectural firm received a commission to remodel a small apartment for an artist. The project involved a complete refurbishment, including the kitchen, bathroom, furnishings, and finishes. Bamboo is a feature of most of the furniture and the floor, which is harmoniously combined with other materials: glass, stone, and ceramic. The treated bamboo floor defines spaces and brings visual warmth to the the design.

Das Architektenbüro erhielt den Auftrag, das kleine Apartment eines Künstlers neu zu gestalten. Das Projekt sah eine komplette Renovierung vor, die auch die Küche, das Bad, das Mobiliar und die Endbearbeitungen miteinschloss. Hervorzuheben ist der Einsatz von Bambus für die meisten Möbel und auf dem Boden. Bambus harmoniert hier stilvoll mit den anderen benutzten Materialien: Glas, Stein und Keramik. Der Boden aus behandeltem Bambus definiert die Räume und umgibt das Ganze mit visueller Wärme.

En réponse à une demande de rénover un petit appartement destiné à un artiste, le bureau d'études a entièrement redistribué l'espace, aménageant cuisine et salle de bains, et a aussi bien imaginé le mobilier que les finitions. La plupart des meubles et les sols sont en bambou. Celui-ci s'associe harmonieusement aux autres matériaux comme le verre, la pierre et la céramique. Le parquet en bambou traité définit les espaces et apporte une chaleur visuelle à l'ensemble.

Het architectenbureau kreeg de opdracht om een klein appartement voor een kunstenaar te verbouwen. Het project bestaat uit een volledige restauratie die de keuken, badkamer, het meubilair en de afwerkingen omvat. Opvallend is het gebruik van bamboe voor de meeste meubels en in de vloer, waar het harmonieus combineert met de andere gebruikte materialen: glas, steen en keramiek. Met de bamboevloer wordt getracht om de ruimtes te definiëren en om het geheel visuele warmte te geven.

Lo studio di architetti ha ricevuto l'incarico di ristrutturare un piccolo appartamento per un artista. Il progetto consiste in un intervento di ammodernamento completo che comprende la cucina, il bagno, gli arredi e le finiture. Degno di nota è l'utilizzo del bambù per la maggior parte dei mobili e per il pavimento, che si combina armonicamente con gli altri materiali impiegati: vetro, ceramica e pietra. Il pavimento in bambù trattato definisce gli spazi e apporta calore visivo all'insieme.

El estudio de arquitectura recibió el encargo de remodelar un pequeño apartamento para un artista. El proyecto consistió en una remodelación completa, que incluía la cocina, el cuarto de baño, el mobiliario y los acabados. Destaca la utilización del bambú en la mayoría de los muebles y en el suelo, que combina de manera armoniosa con los otros materiales utilizados: vidrio, piedra y cerámica. El suelo de bambú tratado define los espacios y aporta calidez visual al conjunto.

BUILD LLC
Seattle, WA, United States, 2009
© BUILD LLC

One current use for bamboo, owing to its low cost and maintenance, is interior design. Bamboo was used in this project for the furniture and flooring.

Eine der aktuellsten Nutzungen von Bambus ist die Innenausstattung, dank seiner geringen Kosten und wenig intensiven Wartung. Bei diesem Projekt wurde das Naturmaterial für Möbel und als Bodenbelag eingesetzt.

Aujourd'hui, son faible coût et de sa facilité d'entretien recommande le bambou pour les aménagements intérieurs. Il fournit le mobilier et les sols de cet appartement.

Een van de huidige toepassingen van bamboe is in de binnenhuisarchitectuur, vanwege de lage kosten en het weinige onderhoud. In dit project is het materiaal gebruikt in het meubilair en in de vloer.

Uno degli usi attuali del bambù, grazie al costo ridotto e alla scarsa manutenzione richiesta, è quello del design di interni. In questo progetto il materiale è stato utilizzato negli arredi e nel pavimento.

Uno de los usos actuales del bambú, por su reducido coste y bajo mantenimiento, es el interiorismo. En este proyecto, el material ha sido utilizado en el mobiliario y en el suelo.

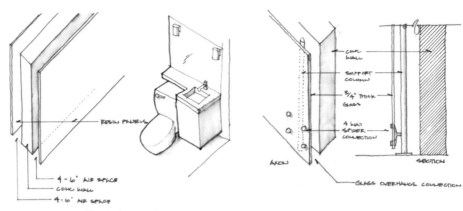

Conceptual drawings / Dessins de conception

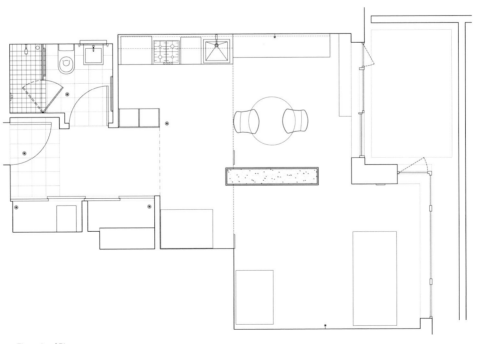

Floor plan / Plan

Great (Bamboo) Wall

Kengo Kuma was chosen together with ten other architects to design residences for a forest next to the Great Wall of China. The only common requisite for the design of the homes was that of causing the least possible impact on the terrain. The Japanese architect chose bamboo as the main material for his project because it is the symbol of cultural exchange between China and Japan. The bamboo was used to build a curtain wall that acts as a filter for light and wind.

Kengo Kuma & Associates
Beijing, China, 2002
© Satoshi Asakawa

Kengo Kuma wurde zusammen mit weiteren zehn asiatischen Architekten ausgewählt, um Wohngebäude in einem Wald an der Chinesischen Mauer zu entwerfen. Die einzige gemeinsame Auflage bei der Planung der hundert Wohneinheiten war, so geringe Umweltauswirkungen wie nur möglich in der Umgebung zu verursachen. Der japanische Architekt hat sich für Bambus als Hauptmaterial zur Umsetzung seines Projekts entschieden, ist dieser Baustoff doch ein Sinnbild des kulturellen Austauschs zwischen China und Japan. Mit Bambus wurde eine Wand/Vorhang gebaut, der als Licht- und Windschutzfilter fungiert.

Kengo Kuma et dix autres architectes asiatiques ont été retenus pour concevoir le village expérimental dans la zone boisée proche de la Grande Muraille de Chine. Le cahier des charges leur imposait à tous de minimiser au maximum l'impact de la centaine de villas sur le milieu. L'architecte japonais a choisi le bambou comme principal matériau de construction pour son projet parce qu'il symbolise les échanges culturels entre la Chine et le Japon. Le mur-rideau en bambou filtre à la fois la lumière et le vent.

Kengo Kuma is samen met nog tien andere Aziatische architecten uitgekozen voor het ontwerpen van een aantal woningen in het bos vlakbij de Grote Muur van China. Het enige gemeenschappelijke vereiste bij het plannen van de honderd huizen was dat ze zo weinig mogelijk impact op de geografie mochten veroorzaken. De Japanse architect koos bamboe als belangrijkste materiaal voor zijn project, omdat dat symbool staat voor de culturele uitwisseling tussen China en Japan. Met bamboe werd een soort gordijnmuur gemaakt die dienst doet als lucht- en windfilter.

Kengo Kuma è stato scelto insieme a dieci architetti asiatici per progettare alcune abitazioni in una zona boschiva nei pressi della Grande Muraglia cinese. L'unico requisito comune del progetto delle cento abitazioni era avere il minimo impatto ambientale possibile sull'ambiente circostante. L'architetto giapponese ha scelto il bambù come materiale principale per realizzare il suo progetto dato che è simbolo dello scambio culturale tra Cina e Giappone. Con il bambù è stato realizzato un muro-tenda che filtra la luce e il vento.

Kengo Kuma fue seleccionado junto a diez arquitectos asiáticos para diseñar residencias situadas en el bosque junto a la Gran Muralla china. El único requisito común a la hora de planificar el centenar de viviendas fue el de causar el menor impacto posible en el entorno. El arquitecto japonés eligió el bambú como material principal para crear su proyecto porque es un símbolo del intercambio cultural entre China y Japón. Con el bambú se construyó un muro-cortina que funciona como filtro de la luz y del viento.

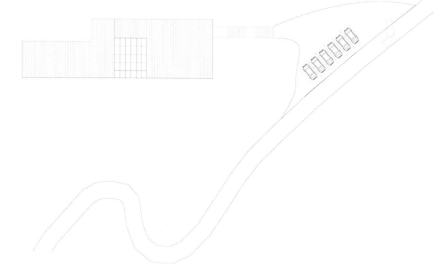

Roof plan / Plan du toit

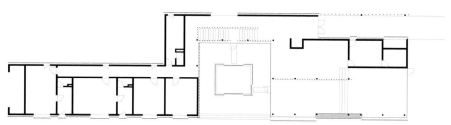

Second floor plan / Plan du niveau supérieur

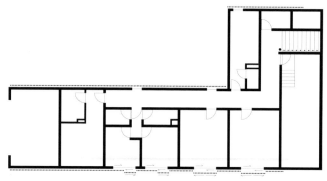

Ground floor plan / Plan du niveau inférieur

Bamboo was also used in the interior for partitions to divide spaces and to create a warm and rhythmic atmosphere.

Bambus wird auch im Inneren für die Raumtrennungen der Wohnung eingesetzt, nicht zuletzt, weil er ein warmes und wohltemperiertes Ambiente schafft.

Également utilisé à l'intérieur pour matérialiser les divisions spatiales du logement, le bambou rythme l'espace et crée une ambiance chaleureuse.

Bamboe wordt ook binnenshuis gebruikt voor de indelingen van de ruimtes en schept bovendien een warme en ritmische sfeer.

Il bambù viene utilizzato anche all'interno per definire le divisioni spaziali della casa, oltre a creare un ambiente accogliente e ritmico.

El bambú se utiliza también en el interior para proyectar las divisiones espaciales de la vivienda, y además crea un ambiente cálido y rítmico.

Sketch / Croquis

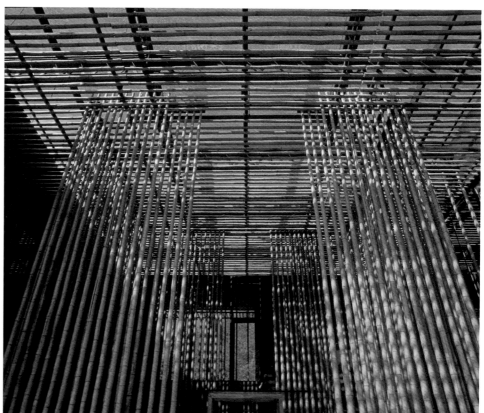

Sketch / Croquis

South elevation / Élévation sud

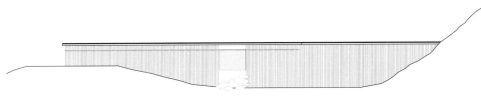

North elevation / Élévation nord

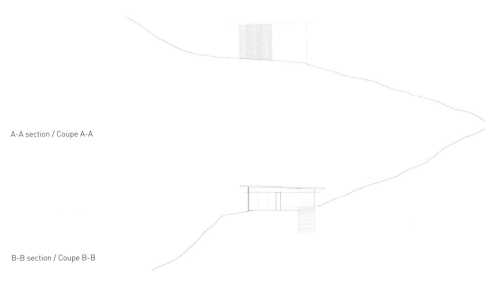

A-A section / Coupe A-A

B-B section / Coupe B-B

Carabanchel Social Housing

This project consists of a parallelogram measuring 100 × 45 m (328 × 148 ft) with a double orientation. Features include the 1.5 m (5 ft) wide terraces running the length of the façade, forming a semi-exterior space that can be used at different times of the year. Louvered bamboo shutters provide necessary protection from sunlight coming from the east and west and serve as a security feature for the homes. They can be also be opened completely when required to offer full enjoyment of the private gardens.

Das Projekt besteht aus einem Parallelogramm von 100 × 45 m, das eine doppelte Ausrichtung bietet. Am Bauwerk ragen die 1,5 m breiten Terrassen entlang der Fassade hervor, die einen Halbinnenraum bilden, der in den verschiedenen Jahreszeiten unterschiedlich genutzt werden kann. Da diese mit Jalousien aus Bambuslamellen abgeschlossen sind, bieten sie den notwenigen Schutz gegen Sonnenstrahlen aus dem Osten und Westen und fungieren gleichzeitig als Schirmelement der Wohnungen. Falls gewünscht, lassen diese sich komplett öffnen, damit man sich der Privatgärten erfreuen kann.

Ce projet est un parallélogramme de 100 × 45 m qui bénéficie d'une double orientation. Larges de 1,50 m, les terrasses en saillie, qui courent le long de la façade, offrent un espace semi-extérieur appréciable à la belle saison. Fermées par des persiennes en lames de bambou, elles protègent contre un excès de lumière solaire au levant comme au couchant. Elles assurent aussi la sécurité des logements. Quand on le souhaite, il suffit de les ouvrir pour profiter des jardins privés.

Het project bestaat uit een parallellogram van 100 × 45 m dat naar twee richtingen georiënteerd is. Opvallend zijn de terrassen van 1,5 m breed langs de hele gevel, die een halfoverdekte ruimte doen ontstaan die in bepaalde seizoenen kan worden gebruikt. Doordat ze zijn afgesloten met bamboe zonneblinden bieden ze de nodige bescherming tegen zonlicht uit het oosten en westen en dragen ze bij aan de beveiliging van de woningen. Ze kunnen desgewenst ook helemaal worden geopend, zodat men kan genieten van de privé-tuinen.

Il progetto è costituito da un parallelogramma di 100 × 45 m con un doppio orientamento. Nella struttura si impongono le terrazze di 1,5 m di larghezza, situate lungo la facciata, che danno vita a uno spazio semi-esterno utilizzabile in alcuni periodi dell'anno. Essendo chiuse tramite persiane realizzate con lastre di bambù, offrono la protezione necessaria dalla luce solare da est a ovest oltre a garantire la sicurezza dell'abitazione. Se lo si desidera, possono essere aperte completamente per godere della vista sui giardini privati.

El proyecto consiste en un paralelogramo de 100 × 45 m que ofrece una doble orientación. De la construcción destacan las terrazas de 1,5 m de ancho situadas a lo largo de la fachada y que conforman un espacio semiexterior utilizable en ciertas épocas del año. Al estar cerradas con persianas construidas con láminas de bambú, proporcionan la protección necesaria de la luz solar del este y del oeste, y funcionan como elemento de seguridad para las viviendas. Cuando se desee, también se pueden abrir por completo para disfrutar de los jardines privados.

Foreign Office Architects (FOA)
Carabanchel, Spain, 2007
© Francisco Andeyro García, Alejandro García González, Hugh Pearman

This rectangular volume contains 88 homes and is enveloped by a bamboo skin built using traditional methods. Folding shutters were installed at random on the façade.

Dieses rechteckige Volumen umfasst 88 Wohnungen und ist mit einer handwerklich geschaffenen Bambushaut überzogen. Die abnehmbaren Fensterläden an der Fassade wurden nach dem Zufallsprinzip angebracht.

Ce volume rectangulaire, qui abrite 88 logements, est enveloppé d'une peau de bambou fabriquée artisanalement. Les contrevents orientables sont disposés de manière aléatoire sur la façade.

Dit rechthoekige blok omvat 88 woningen en is voorzien van een ambachtelijk vervaardigde bamboebekleding. Op de gevel zijn op willekeurig plaatsen neerklapbare luiken geïnstalleerd.

Questo volume rettangolare contiene 88 abitazioni ed è avvolto da una «pelle» di bambù realizzata artigianalmente. Qua e là sono state inserite sulla facciata delle controfinestre apribili.

Este volumen rectangular contiene 88 viviendas y está envuelto por una piel de bambú construida de forma artesanal. Se han instalado aleatoriamente contraventanas abatibles en la fachada.

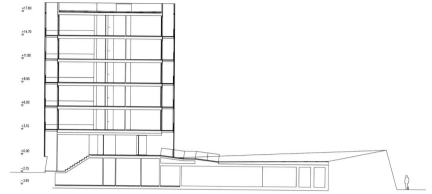

Cross section / Coupe transversale

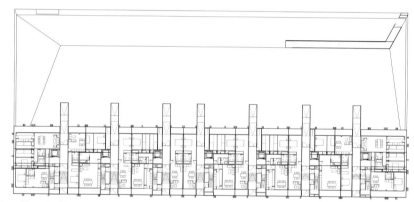

Ground floor plan / Plan du niveau principal

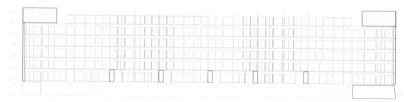

Longitudinal section / Coupe longitudinale

Madrid-Barajas Airport

212,000 m² (2,281,950 sq ft) of bamboo clad the internal face of the roof of the new T4 terminal of Madrid-Barajas international airport. This project is considered to be the world's largest made from bamboo. This material was chosen as a natural and sustainable alternative to wood. The fireproofed bamboo enabled warm interior spaces to be created. A special technique was employed to make the panels flexible for bending and adapting to the undulating metal structure.

212.000 m² Bambus bedecken das Dach des neuen Terminals T4 des internationalen Flughafens Madrid-Barajas. Es gilt als größtes Bauvorhaben der Welt aus Bambus. Dieses Material wurde als natürliche Lösung und nachhaltige Alternative zu Holz gewählt. Die Bambuslamellen wurden brandsicher behandelt und schaffen warme Innenräume. Dank einer besonderen Technik, konnten die Paneele flexibel gemacht werden, um sie zu biegen, damit sie sich in die gewellte Metallstruktur einfügen können.

212 000 m² de bambou couvrent le toit du nouveau terminal T4 de l'aéroport international de Madrid-Barajas. C'est la plus vaste surface réalisée en bambou au monde. Ce matériau a été choisi parce qu'il offrait une alternative naturelle et durable au bois. Les plaques de bambou ignifugées concourent à la création d'espaces intérieurs chaleureux. Grâce à leur structure particulière, les panneaux remarquablement flexibles épousent les courbes de la structure métallique ondulée.

Een oppervlak van 212.000 m² bamboe vormt het plafond van de nieuwe terminal T4 van de internationale luchthaven Madrid-Barajas. Dit wordt beschouwd als het grootste in bamboe vervaardigde project ter wereld. Dit materiaal werd gekozen als een natuurlijk en duurzaam alternatief voor hout. De bamboeplaten zijn behandeld met een brandwerende oplossing en dragen bij aan een warme entourage van het interieur. Dankzij een speciale techniek zijn de panelen flexibel gemaakt zodat ze konden worden gebogen en aangepast aan de golvende metaalstructuur.

212.000 m² di bambù coprono il soffitto del nuovo terminal T4 dell'aeroporto internazionale di Madrid-Barajas. Si tratta del progetto più grande al mondo realizzato in bambù. Questo materiale è stato scelto come una soluzione naturale e sostenibile alternativa al legno. Le lastre di bambù sono state trattate per diventare ignifughe e consentono di creare accoglienti spazi interni. Grazie a una speciale tecnica, i pannelli sono stati resi flessibili affinché potessero essere curvati e adattati alla struttura metallica ondulata.

Un total de 212.000 m² de bambú cubren el techo de la nueva terminal T4 del aeropuerto internacional de Madrid-Barajas. Está considerado como el proyecto más grande del mundo realizado con bambú. Este material fue seleccionado como una solución natural y sostenible alternativa a la madera. Las láminas de bambú fueron tratadas para ser ignífugas y permiten la creación de espacios interiores cálidos. Gracias a una técnica especial, los paneles se hicieron flexibles para que se pudieran curvar y se ajustaran a la estructura metálica ondulada.

Estudio Lamela Arquitectos, Richard Rogers Partnership
Barajas, Spain, 2004
© Manuel Renau

Elevation / Élévation

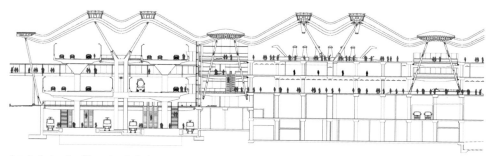

Longitudinal section / Coupe longitudinale

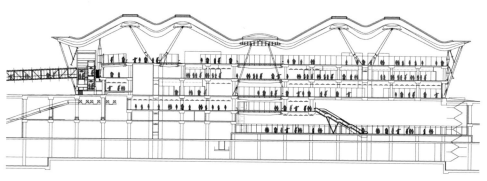

Cross section / Coupe transversale

Featuring among the many aspects of sustainable architecture present in Madrid-Barajas Airport is the monumental undulating roof lined with bamboo strips that is inspired by the silhouette of a bird in flight.

Unter den zahlreichen Aspekten der nachhaltigen Architektur des Airports Madrid-Barajas besticht die monumentale, gewellte Dachabdeckung, die mit Bambuslamellen ausgekleidet ist, und an die Silhouette eines Vogels im Flug erinnern.

L'aéroport de Madrid-Barajas se caractérise par son architecture inscrite dans le développement durable. Sa monumentale toiture ondulée, formée de lames de bambou cintrées qui évoque la silhouette d'un oiseau en plein vol, en est l'élément le plus remarquable.

Onder de vele aspecten van duurzame architectuur van de luchthaven Madrid-Barajas, valt het monumentale golvende dak, bedekt met bamboepanelen op, die doet denken aan het silhouet van een vogel in volle vlucht.

Tra i molteplici aspetti dell'architettura sostenibile dell'aeroporto di Madrid-Barajas emerge il monumentale soffitto ondulato in lastre di bambù che ricorda la forma di un uccello in volo.

De entre los muchos aspectos de arquitectura sostenible del aeropuerto de Madrid-Barajas, destaca la monumental cubierta ondulada forrada de lamas de bambú, que remite a la silueta de un ave en pleno vuelo.

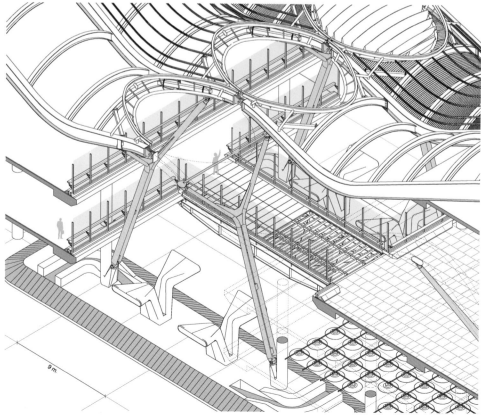

9 m

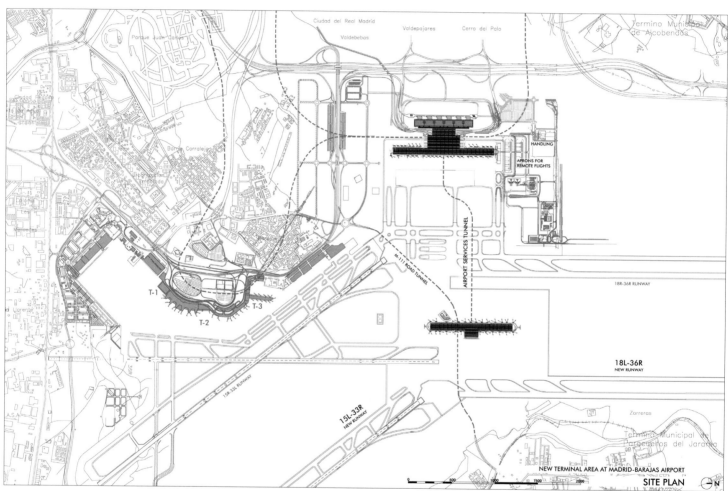

Site plan / Plan du site

Park Albatros Camping

This project consists of two large separate areas with ample greenery, spaces for tents and cabins, and for meetings, services, and recreation. The architects were inspired in their design by single-celled circular marine organisms. The spaces are grouped by different associations as a series of exteriors and interiors that seem to have been sculpted by the wind and sand. Bamboo canes were used to make the roof and curved walls.

Das Projekt umfasst weite, voneinander mit großzügigen Grünzonen getrennte Flächen, Parzellen für Läden und Bungalows, Versammlungssäle, Service- und Freizeitbereiche. Zum Entwurf haben sich die Architekten an einzelligen Meereslebewesen in Kreisform inspiriert. Die Räume werden nach unterschiedlichen Assoziationen zusammen gruppiert. Inneres und Äußeres scheint von Wind und Sand geformt zu sein. Die Bambusstämme wurden eingesetzt, um das Dach und die geneigten Wände zu schaffen.

Le complexe occupe deux vastes zones séparées comprenant de grands espaces verts, des parcelles pour les boutiques et les bungalows, des salles de réunion, des zones de services et des aires de loisirs. Des organismes marins unicellulaires circulaires ont inspiré aux architectes l'implantation des constructions. Les espaces sont réunis selon divers modes d'associations suivant un système où extérieurs et intérieurs semblent avoir été modelés par le vent et le sable. Les tiges de bambou forment le toit, la palissade et les murs courbes.

Het project beslaat twee van elkaar afgescheiden zones, met een groot oppervlak en ruime groenstroken, percelen voor tenten en bungalows, vergaderzalen en diensten- en recreatieruimtes. Bij het bedenken van het ontwerp hebben de architecten zich laten inspireren door eencellige zee-organismen met ronde vormen. De ruimtes zijn gegroepeerd op basis van verschillende associaties, waarbij een systeem voor exteriors en interieurs is gevolgd dat door de wind en het zand lijkt te zijn vormgegeven. De bamboestengels zijn gebruikt voor het dak en de ronde muren.

Il progetto copre due aree separate di grandi dimensioni con ampie zone verdi, lotti per negozi e bungalow, zone comuni, aree dedicate ai servizi e al divertimento. Per il progetto, gli architetti si sono ispirati agli organismi unicellulari marini di forma circolare. Gli spazi sono raggruppati per associazioni seguendo un sistema di ambienti esterni e interni che sembrano essere stati modellati dal vento e dalla sabbia. Le canne di bambù sono state impiegate per il soffitto e le pareti curve.

El proyecto cubre dos áreas separadas de gran tamaño con amplias zonas verdes, parcelas para tiendas y bungalós, y espacios de reunión, servicios y ocio. Para plantear el diseño, los arquitectos se inspiraron en los organismos unicelulares marinos de formas circulares. Los espacios se agrupan por asociaciones diferentes siguiendo un sistema de exteriores e interiores que parecen haber sido moldeados por el viento y la arena. Las cañas de bambú se emplearon para crear el techo y las paredes curvas.

Studio Archea
Rimigliano, Italy, 2007
© A & B Photodesign, Pietro Savorelli

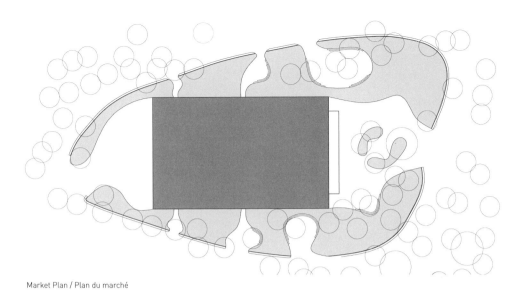

Market Plan / Plan du marché

Market detailed section / Coupe détaillée du marché

Planimetry / Planimétrie

Service area detailed section / Coupe détaillée de l'aire de service

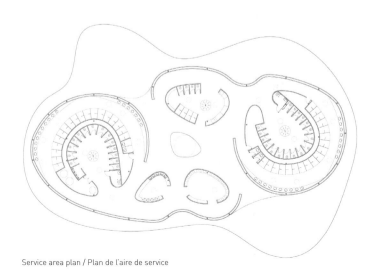

Service area plan / Plan de l'aire de service

Bamboo was the material that best enabled the architects to design a project where the forms and colors were taken from the natural setting. The almost primitive architecture was easily assembled.

Bambus war das Material, das es den Architekten am besten gestattet hat, ein Projekt zu entwerfen, dessen Formen und Farben aus der natürlichen Umgebung stammen. Die Konstruktion ist beinah primitiv und leicht aufzubauen.

Le bambou est le matériau qui offrait le plus d'options aux architectes pour concevoir un projet dont les formes et les couleurs sont empruntées au milieu naturel. Cette architecture caractérisée par la simplicité des assemblages, nous ramène aux arts premiers.

Bamboe was het materiaal dat de architecten het best in staat stelde om een project te ontwikkelen met vormen en kleuren die uit de natuurlijke omgeving zijn overgenomen. De architectuur is bijna primitief en de montage eenvoudig.

Il bambù è il materiale che meglio ha consentito agli architetti di realizzare un progetto le cui forme e colori riprendano l'ambiente naturale. L'architettura è quasi primitiva e la struttura risulta facilmente montabile.

El bambú fue el material que mejor permitió a los arquitectos diseñar el proyecto ,cuyas formas y colores se tomaron del entorno natural. La arquitectura es casi primitiva y de fácil montaje.

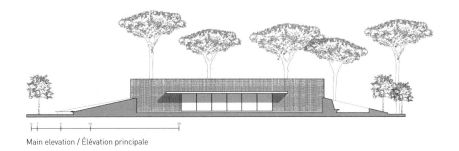

Main elevation / Élévation principale

Longitudinal section / Coupe longitudinale

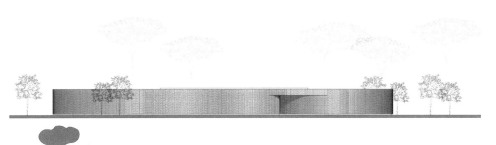

South elevation / Élévation sud

Showroom in Cross

This sales office for development projects is located at the intersection of two main streets. The interior space is divided into five small rooms, three of which are built from glass bricks, a fourth from stone, and the last all in wood. The three main glass rooms serve as sales offices, while the stone room is for displays, and the room in wood houses the restrooms. The façade features bamboo strips.

Zhang Lei/AZL architects
Shanghai, China, 2005
© Zhang Lei/AZL architects

Dieses Verkaufsbüro für Projektentwicklung befindet sich an der Kreuzung zweier Hauptstraßen. Im Inneren unterteilt sich der Raum in fünf kleine Zimmer, drei davon sind aus Glasbaustein, ein viertes aus Stein und das letzte ganz aus Holz. Die drei Hauptglassäle fungieren als Verkaufsbüros, während der aus Stein der Showroom ist und in dem aus Holz die Toiletten untergebracht sind. Besonders hervorhebenswert sind die an der Außenfassade installierten Bambusstäbe.

Ce bureau de ventes pour le développement de projets en construction se situe à l'intersection de deux rues importantes. À l'intérieur, l'espace se divise en cinq petites pièces, dont trois sont en briques de verre, la quatrième est en pierre et la dernière tout en bois. Les trois pièces vitrées sont les bureaux de vente, celle en pierre est la salle d'exposition et celle en bois abrite les sanitaires. On remarque les tiges de bambou qui rythment la façade.

Dit verkoopkantoor voor projectontwikkeling bevindt zich op een kruising tussen twee hoofdstraten. Het interieur is ingedeeld in vijf kleine kamers, waarvan er drie zijn uitgevoerd in glazen bouwstenen, een vierde in steen en de laatste helemaal in hout. De drie glazen hoofdzalen worden gebruikt als verkoopkantoor, terwijl de stenen zaal een expositieruimte is en in het houten vertrek de toiletten zijn ondergebracht. Opvallend zijn de bamboe latten die op de buitengevel zijn geïnstalleerd.

Questo ufficio vendite per lo sviluppo di progetti si trova all'incrocio di due strade principali. All'interno lo spazio è distribuito in cinque piccole stanze, tre delle quali sono realizzate in pavé, una quarta in pietra e l'ultima interamente in legno. I tre saloni principali in vetro servono da ufficio vendite, mentre quella in pietra ospita l'esposizione e quella in legno i bagni. Interessanti sono i listoni di bambù applicati sulla facciata esterna.

Esta oficina de ventas para el desarrollo de proyectos se encuentra ubicada en el cruce entre dos calles principales. En el interior, el espacio se distribuye en cinco pequeñas habitaciones, tres de las cuales están fabricadas con pavés, una cuarta con piedra y la última es toda en madera. Las tres salas principales de vidrio funcionan como oficina de ventas, mientras que la de piedra es el expositor y la de madera contiene los baños. Destacan los listones de bambú instalados en la fachada exterior.

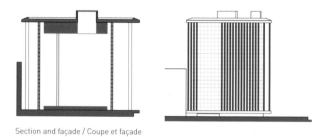

Section and façade / Coupe et façade

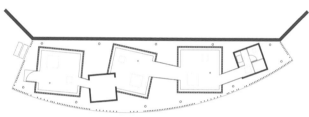

Floor plan / Plan

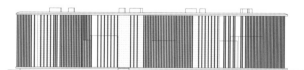

Main façade / Façade principale

The wall separating the sales office from the exterior walkway is made from glass bricks, inside which treated bamboo canes were placed to emphasize the building's transparency.

Die Trennung zwischen dem Verkaufsbüro und der Fußgängerzone erfolgt durch einen Glasbausteinwand, an deren Außenseite behandelte Bambusstämme angebracht sind, die den Transparenzwillen des Gebäudes unterstreichen.

La séparation entre les bureaux de ventes et la salle d'exposition est une cloison de briques de verre. Sur la face extérieure, la disposition des tiges de bambou traitées souligne la volonté de transparence du bâtiment.

De scheiding tussen het verkoopkantoor en de voetgangerszone is verkregen door middel van een muur van glazen stenen, die van buiten bekleed is met behandelde bamboestengels die de transparantie van het gebouw onderstrepen.

La separazione tra l'ufficio vendite e la zona di visita è realizzata tramite una parete di pavé nella cui parte esterna sono disposte delle canne di bambù trattate che sottolineano il desiderio di trasparenza dell'edificio.

La separación entre la oficina de ventas y la zona peatonal se realiza con una pared de pavés, en cuyo exterior se disponen cañas de bambú tratadas que enfatizan la voluntad de transparencia del edificio.

Education Center
at Soneva Kiri Resort

The architects of the Soneva Kiri Resort used organic design to create a series of ecological icons. The most striking building is the learning center that allows children to gain environmental awareness through fun activities. Among others, the interior houses a movie theater/auditorium, a library, art room, and music room. The structure and roof are made of Thai bamboo, while the interior features wood and rattan sourced from local plantations.

Im Soneva Kiri Resort haben die Architekten eine Reihe ökologischer Ikonen des organischen Designs geschaffen. Das am meisten hervorstechende Gebäude ist das Bildungs- und Lernzentrum, das es Ki ndern ermöglicht, ihr Umweltbewusstsein durch spielerische Aktivitäten zu schärfen. Im Inneren befinden sich u.a. ein Kino-Hörsaal, eine Bücherei, ein Kunstsaal und eine Musikaula. Tragwerk und Dach sind aus thailändischem Bambus gefertigt und für das Innere kam Holz und Rattan aus lokalem Anbau zum Einsatz.

Les architectes qui ont collaboré au village de vacances, Soneva Kiri Resort, ont créé une série d'icônes écologiques aux motifs organiques. Le bâtiment le plus remarquable est le centre éducatif qui sensibilise les enfants à l'écologie à travers des activités ludiques. Le complexe comprend également une salle de cinéma-auditorium, une bibliothèque, une salle consacrée aux arts plastiques et une autre à la musique. La structure et le toit sont construits en bambou thaïlandais. Les aménagements intérieurs sont en bois et rotin provenant de plantations locales.

In het Soneva Kiri Resort maakten de architecten een aantal ecologische iconen met organisch ontwerp. Het opvallendste gebouw is het educatiecentrum waar kinderen door middel van ludieke activiteiten bewust worden gemaakt van het milieu. In het centrum zijn onder andere een filmzaal-auditorium, kunstruimte en muziekzaal ingericht. De structuur en het dak zijn opgebouwd uit Thais bamboe en in het interieur is gebruik gemaakt van hout en ratan, afkomstig van plaatselijke plantages.

Nel Soneva Kiri Resort, gli architetti hanno creato una serie di icone ecologiche dal design organico. L'edificio più particolare è il centro educativo e di apprendimento che consente ai bambini di acquisire la coscienza ecologica tramite attività di intrattenimento. All'interno si trovano, tra gli altri, un cine-auditorium, una biblioteca, una sala artistica e un'aula di musica. La struttura e il soffitto sono realizzati in bambù tailandese e all'interno è stato utilizzato del rattan proveniente dalle piantagioni locali.

En el Soneva Kiri Resort, los arquitectos crearon una serie de iconos ecológicos de diseños orgánicos. El edificio más destacado es el centro educativo y de aprendizaje, que permite a los niños tomar conciencia ecológica mediante actividades de entretenimiento. En el interior se ubican, entre otros, un cine-auditorio, una biblioteca, una sala de arte y un aula de música. La estructura y el techo están construidos con bambú tailandés y en el interior se han utilizado madera y ratán de plantaciones locales.

24H › Architecture
Koh Kut, Thailand, 2009
© Boris Zeisser/24H › Architecture,
  Kiattipong Panchee, 24H › Architecture

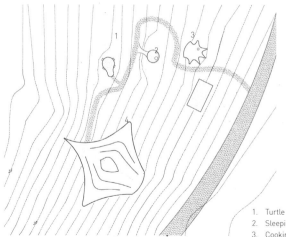

Site plan / Plan du site

1. Turtle toilet / Sanitaires
2. Sleeping pod / Chambres
3. Cooking cave / Cuisine
4. The den / Bâtiment principal

Floor plan / Plan

1. Music room / Salle de musique
2. Art room / Salle d'art
3. Chill balcony / Balcon
4. Auditorium / Auditorium
5. Library / Bibliothèque
6. Glide / Balançoire
7. Fashion room / Salle de mode

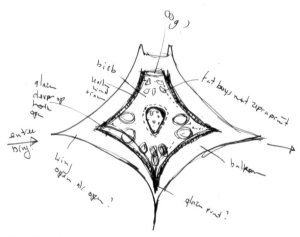

Sketch / Croquis

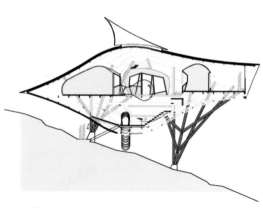

Section / Coupe

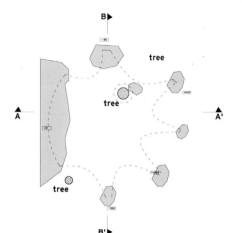

Site plan / Plan du site

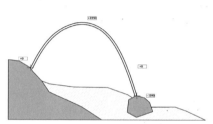

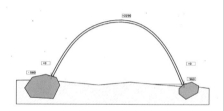

Section A-A' and section B-B' / Coupe A-A' et coupe B-B'

This project was an opportunity to show that bamboo is one of the most suitable materials for modern architecture. The length of the bamboo enabled a spectacular structure to be created.

Mit diesem Projekt haben die Architekten bewiesen, dass Bambus eines der geeignetsten Materialien für die moderne Architektur sein kann. Die Länge der Bambushalme hat es ermöglich, eine eindrucksvolle Struktur zu schaffen.

Avec ce projet, les architectes ont fait la démonstration que le bambou est l'un des matériaux les plus adaptés à l'architecture moderne. La longueur des tiges permet de créer une structure spectaculaire.

Met dit project hebben de architecten bewezen dat bamboe een van de meest geschikte materialen is voor de moderne architectuur. Dankzij de lengte van de bamboestengels hebben zij een spectaculaire structuur kunnen maken.

Con questo progetto gli architetti hanno dimostrato che il bambù è uno dei materiali più adatti all'architettura moderna. La lunghezza del bambù ha consentito di creare una struttura spettacolare.

Con este proyecto los arquitectos demostraron que el bambú es uno de los materiales más idóneos para la arquitectura moderna. La longitud del bambú permitió crear una espectacular estructura.

Ground floor plan / Niveau inférieur

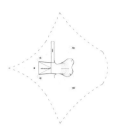

Entrance floor plan / Plan de l'entrée

Second floor plan / Premier niveau

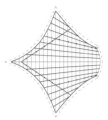

Roof structure plan / Plan des structures du toit

Floor plan / Plan

Front elevation / Élévation frontale

Back elevation / Élévation posterieure

Side elevation / Élévation latérale

Longitudinal section / Coupe longitudinale

Cross section / Coupe transversale

Footing detail of small column / Détail de construction des petites colonnes

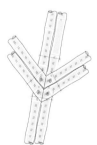

Column detail / Détail des colonnes

Roof edge detail / Détail de construction des bords du plafond

Garita

This two-story lodge is designed to be cooled by the air currents that are prevalent in the area. The lower level contains the reception area, bathroom, garden and spiral staircase leading to the observation deck located on the upper level. The qualities of guadua bamboo enabled the architects to design the building in this material, and to create its curving roof with broad eaves at different heights. The bamboo was protected from moisture in the soil by means of large pedestals.

Das Pförtnerhaus besteht aus zwei Etagen, die so konzipiert wurden, dass sie Luftzüge durchlassen, die dem Ort ständige Kühle verschaffen. Im ersten Stock befinden sich die Rezeption, das Bad, der Garten und die Wendeltreppe, die zur Ausblicksplattform auf der zweiten Etage führt. Guadua hat den Architekten den Gesamtbau des Volumens ermöglicht sowie die Ausführung der gewölbten Decken mit großen Dachtraufen auf verschiedenen Höhen. Der Bambus wurde gegen die allfällige Feuchtigkeit des Bodens mittels großer Sockel isoliert.

Cette loge sur deux niveaux est conçue pour faciliter la circulation de l'air qui en permanence rafraîchit le lieu. Au rez-de-chaussée : la réception et les sanitaires, le jardin ; l'escalier en colimaçon conduit à la terrasse panoramique. L'utilisation de guadua a permis aux architectes de construire l'intégralité de ce volume, et d'exploiter le potentiel des courbes pour la toiture et les grands avant-toits latéraux. De plus, le bambou est protégé de l'humidité qui pourrait monter du sol grâce aux grands socles.

De portiersloge bestaat uit twee verdiepingen, waardoor ventilatie mogelijk is en de ruimte voortdurend gekoeld wordt. Op de begane grond bevinden zich de receptie, de badkamer en de tuin en een wenteltrap die naar het uitkijkpunt op de tweede verdieping leidt. De architecten konden met de guadua het hele volume opbouwen, alsmede de golvende daken met grote luifeldaken op verschillende hoogtes. Het bamboe werd verder tegen mogelijke vocht van de vloer afgeschermd door enkele grote sokkels.

La portineria si sviluppa su due piani progettati per consentire il passaggio di correnti d'aria che rinfrescano costantemente il luogo. Al primo piano troviamo la reception, il bagno, il giardino e la scala a chiocciola che porta al punto panoramico, situato al secondo piano. La guadua è stata utilizzata per realizzare l'intero volume, oltre che per gestire i tetti curvi con grandi gronde a varie altezze. Inoltre il bambù è stato isolato dalla potenziale umidità del terreno tramite dei grandi piedistalli.

La portería consta de dos plantas diseñadas para permitir el paso de corrientes de aire que refrescan permanentemente el lugar. En la primera planta se ubican el área de recepción, el baño, el jardín y la escalera de caracol que conduce al mirador, situado en la segunda planta. La guadua permitió a los arquitectos la construcción total del volumen, así como el manejo de cubiertas curvas con grandes aleros a diferente altura. Además, el bambú se aisló de la posible humedad del suelo mediante unos grandes pedestales.

ZUARQ Arquitectos
Carmen de Apicalá, Colombia, 2006
© Jessica Cohen, Mario Negrett, Carolina Zuluaga

Section / Coupe

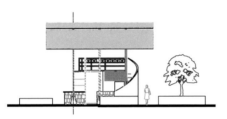

Right side façade / Façade du côté droit

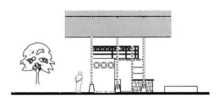

Left side façade / Façade du côté gauche

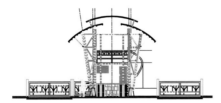

Main façade / Façade principale

Rear façade / Façade arrière

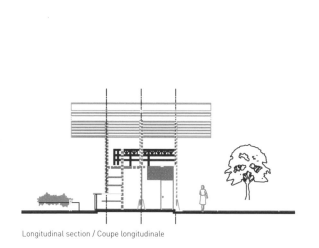

Longitudinal section / Coupe longitudinale

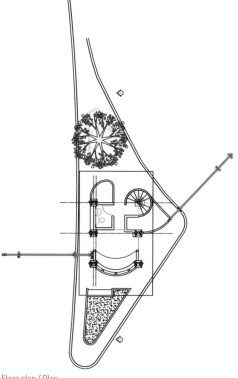

Floor plan / Plan

Guadua angustifolia Kunth bamboo was chosen as it is the most outstanding variety available in the Americas, in addition to it being the most common type used in traditional structures and the variety offering the best architectural results.

Es wurde Guadua angustifolia Kunth gewählt, weil dies die exzellenteste Bambusart Amerikas ist, die am meisten in traditionellen Bauwerken eingesetzt wird und das beste architektonische Ergebnis bietet.

La Guadua angustifolia Kunth s'est imposée pour ce projet car c'est la variété de bambou la plus remarquable du continent américain. C'est la plus employée dans les constructions traditionnelles et la plus polyvalente en architecture.

Gekozen is voor Guadua angustifolia Kunth omdat dat de beste bamboesoort van Amerika is, die veelvuldig gebruikt wordt in traditionele constructies en de beste bouwresultaten geeft.

È stata scelta la Guadua angustifolia Kunth poiché è il tipo di bambù più importante in America, quello più usato nelle costruzioni tradizionali e che offre i migliori risultati architettonici.

Se seleccionó la Guadua angustifolia Kunth por ser el tipo de bambú más sobresaliente de América, el más utilizado en las construcciones tradicionales y el que mejor resultado arquitectónico ofrece.

Chapel

Owing to the climate of the location with its high temperatures, the design was for a volume with large openings that let in light and sea breezes, and opened out to the landscape. The architects decided to combine different natural lightweight materials, among which bamboo played a predominant role. The guadua variety of bamboo was chosen as the best for integrating nature into a place of worship. Bamboo also achieved cost savings and made the chapel low maintenance.

Aufgrund der besonderen Witterungsverhältnisse dieses Orts, der durch hohe Temperaturen gekennzeichnet ist, entschied man sich für den Bau eines Volumens mit großen Öffnungen, die das Licht, die Meeresbrise und Landschaft hereinlassen. Die Architekten wollten verschiedene natürliche und leichte Materialien miteinander verbinden, unter denen besonders Bambus hervorsticht. Es wurde Guadua als die Bambusart gewählt, die sich besser in die Natur des Andachtsortes einfügt. Der Bambus hat auch dazu beigetragen, die Kosten und die Wartungsanfälligkeit der Kapelle zu verringern.

Le climat très chaud explique la conception de ce volume composé de larges ouvertures qui laissent entrer la lumière, les brises marines et permettent une immersion dans le paysage. Les architectes ont misé sur l'association de plusieurs matériaux naturels légers, privilégiant le bambou. La guadua s'est imposée parce qu'avec elle, la nature s'intègre harmonieusement dans ce lieu de prière. De plus, son emploi permet de diminuer les coûts de construction et d'entretien de la chapelle.

Vanwege de bijzondere plaatselijke klimaatomstandigheden, die gekenmerkt worden door hoge temperaturen, werd besloten om het bouwwerk te voorzien van openingen die licht en wind uit zee doorlaten en uitzicht over het landschap mogelijk maken. De architecten besloten om diverse natuurlijke en lichte materialen te combineren, waaronder met name bamboe. Guadua werd uitgekozen als bamboesoort die de natuur het beste laat integreren in deze gebedsruimte. Bovendien konden de uitgaven en de onderhoudskosten van de kapel dankzij het gebruik van bamboe laag blijven.

Dato il particolare clima del luogo, caratterizzato da alte temperature, è stato deciso di realizzare un volume con grandi aperture che consentono il passaggio di luce, brezza marina e il contatto con il paesaggio. Gli architetti hanno deciso di combinare diversi materiali naturali e leggeri, tra questi in modo particolare il bambù. La guadua è stata scelta come il tipo di bambù che meglio integra la natura con il luogo per la preghiera. Inoltre il bambù ha consentito di ridurre i costi e la manutenzione della cappella.

Debido al particular clima del lugar, caracterizado por altas temperaturas, se decidió construir un volumen compuesto por grandes aberturas que dan paso a la luz, a las brisas marinas y al paisaje. Los arquitectos decidieron combinar diversos materiales naturales y ligeros, entre los cuales destaca especialmente el bambú. Se seleccionó la guadua como el tipo de bambú que mejor integra la naturaleza con el lugar para la oración. Además, el bambú ayudó a abaratar el coste y el mantenimiento de la capilla.

ZUARQ Arquitectos
Carmen de Apicalá, Colombia, 2006
© Jessica Cohen, Mario Negrett,
 Carolina Zuluaga

The large columns, railings, and roof structure were made out of bamboo. The guadua was used strategically in joists and roof beams.

Große Säulen, Brüstungen, Geländer und die Struktur der Abdeckungen wurden alle aus Bambus gebaut. Guadua wurde strategisch auf den Stützsäulen und der Verteilung der Balken angebracht.

Hautes colonnes, balustrades, rampes et charpentes sont en bambou. La guadua a été stratégiquement placée en renfort dans les colonnes sur lesquelles repose l'édifice et dans la distribution des poutres.

Grote zuilen, balustrades, leuningen en de dakstructuur zijn in bamboe vervaardigd. De guadua is strategisch geplaatst op de steunzuilen en in de balkenstructuur.

Grandi colonne, ringhiere, corrimano e la struttura del tetto sono stati realizzati in bambù. La guadua è stata sistemata strategicamente nelle colonne di supporto e nella distribuzione delle travi.

Grandes columnas, barandas, pasamanos y la estructura de las cubiertas fueron construidas con bambú. La guadua se colocó estratégicamente en las columnas de apoyo y en la distribución de las vigas.

Bamboo Bridge
at Soneva Kiri Resort

This bridge, designed to be a large-scale sculpture made entirely from bamboo, leads visitors to the main resort installations. Measuring 30 m/98 ft in length, its structure comprises two inclined shields forming asymmetric horn-like slopes at each end. These horns are connected by a central beam with a gradient reminiscent of the naturally ventilated roofs that are a feature of the vernacular architecture of tropical areas in Asia.

Jorg Stamm (architect), Bambooroo, Mark Emery (general contractor)
Koh Kut, Thailand, 2009
© Mark Emery

Die Bambusbrücke wurde als großformatige Skulptur angelegt, die vollkommen aus diesem Material gefertigt wurde. Sie führt den Besucher zu den Haupteinrichtungen dieser Ferienanlage. Mit seinen 30 m Länge besteht die Struktur aus geneigten Schildern, die durch asymmetrische Hörner an den Enden verlängert. Diese Hörner sind durch einen Zentralbalken verbunden, der durch seine Neigung an die natürlichen Ventilationsdächer der einheimischen Architektur im tropischen Asien erinnert.

Ce pont couvert, exclusivement construit en bambou, a été conçu comme une sculpture géante. Il conduit les visiteurs aux principales installations de ce complexe touristique. D'une longueur de 30 m, la toiture consiste en deux pans incurvés et inclinés reliés par une poutre faîtière qui va d'une extrémité à l'autre. Ils se terminent en pointes asymétriques. Leur inclinaison rappelle celle des toits qui assurent une ventilation naturelle dans l'architecture vernaculaire de l'Asie tropicale.

Deze helemaal van bamboe gemaakte brug is bedacht als een beeldhouwwerk van grote afmetingen en leidt de bezoekers tot aan de belangrijkste voorzieningen van het toeristische complex. De 30 m lange structuur bestaat uit twee schuine "schilden" die hellingen vormen die in de uiteinden uitlopen in de vorm van asymmetrische hoorns Deze hoorns zijn onderling verbonden door een centrale balk die vanwege zijn inclinatie doet denken aan de daken met natuurlijke ventilatie van de inheemse architectuur van tropisch Azië.

Il ponte di bambù è stato concepito come una scultura di grandi dimensioni, realizzata interamente con questo materiale, che conduce gli utenti alle strutture principali del complesso turistico. Lungo 30 m, la sua struttura è composta da due scudi inclinati che danno vita a delle corna asimmetriche poste su ciascuna estremità. Queste corna sono collegate da una trave centrale che ricorda, per la sua inclinazione, i soffitti a ventilazione naturale dell'architettura tipica dell'Asia tropicale.

El puente que conduce a los usuarios hasta las instalaciones principales del complejo turístico fue concebido como una escultura de grandes dimensiones construida íntegramente con bambú. De 30 m de longitud, su estructura se compone de dos escudos inclinados que crean pendientes en forma de cuernos asimétricos en cada extremo. Estos cuernos están conectados por una viga central que recuerda por su inclinación a los techos de ventilación natural de la arquitectura vernácula del Asia tropical.

This bridge is a example of engineering that gives broad scope to bamboo as a material, challenging our perception and breaking new ground for all types of construction.

Die Bambusbrücke ist ein Paradebeispiel wie vielfältig das Material auch im Ingenieurwesen eingesetzt werden kann. Hier ist unsere Auffassungsgabe herausgefordert, ein neuer Präzedenzfall ist für alle künftigen Konstruktionstypologien geschaffen.

Véritable prouesse du génie civil, ce pont en bambou, qui démontre la grande capacité de portée du matériau, défie les sens. Il établit un nouveau précédent pour toutes les typologies de constructions.

De bamboe brug is een voorbeeld van vérreikende techniek van het materiaal dat onze waarneming uitdaagt en een precedent schept voor alle constructieve indelingen.

Il ponte di bambù è un simbolo di ingegno per il risultato che si è riusciti a ottenere con questo materiale, che sfida la nostra percezione e definisce un nuovo punto di riferimento per tutte le tipologie costruttive.

El puente de bambú es una obra de ingeniería que muestra el gran alcance del material, que desafía nuestra percepción y establece un nuevo precedente para todas las tipologías constructivas que se realizan.

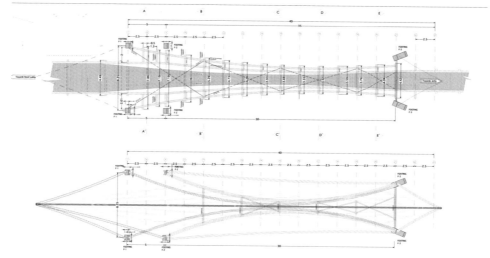

Floor plan and general plan / Plan et plan général

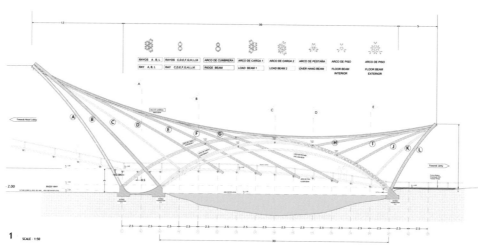

Longitudinal section / Coupe longitudinale

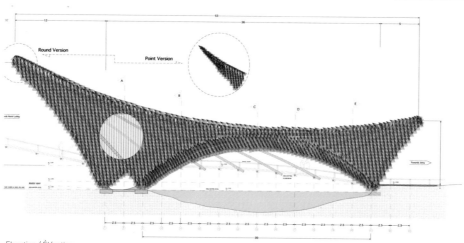

Elevation / Élévation

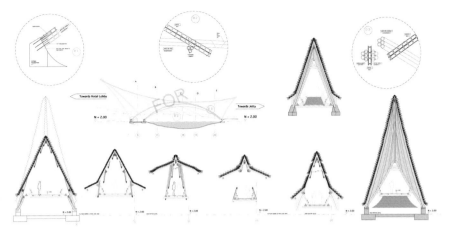

Construction details and sections / Coupes et détails de construction

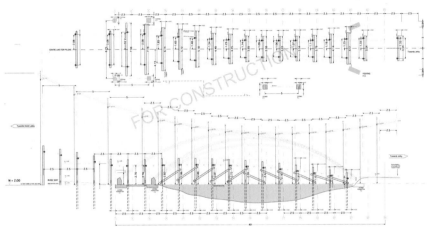

Footing and scaffolding setout / Plan et élévation préparatifs des échafaudages

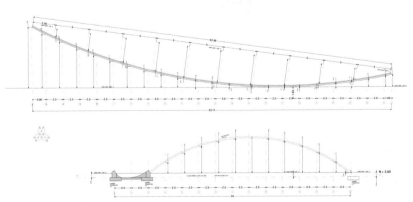

Arc setout plans / Plans préparatifs des arcs

wNw Café

The beauty of bamboo was incorporated into the building of this restaurant as a structural and decorative feature. The architects used the principles of aerodynamic design for the spaces, such as computer-generated simulation, which served to study air flow and the capacity for cooling water. The entire building was made with 7,000 bamboo members that were treated employing traditional Vietnamese methods. The structure does away with the need for concrete columns.

Die Schönheit des Bambus floss in den Bau dieses Restaurants als Tragwerk- und Dekorationselement ein. Die Architekten nutzten die Grundsätze der aerodynamischen Raumgestaltung, wie etwa computererzeugte Simulierungen, die dazu gedient haben, die Luftströme und Kühlfähigkeit des Wassers zu eruieren. Das gesamte Gebäude wurde aus 7.000 Bambuselemente gebaut, die mit traditionellen vietnamesischen Methoden behandelt wurden. Die Struktur verzichtet bewusst auf Betonsäulen.

Dans la réalisation de ce restaurant, le bambou s'est imposé autant pour sa beauté comme élément décoratif que pour sa résistance comme élément structurel. Les architectes ont exploité les principes de l'aérodynamisme et étudié les flux d'air et la capacité de refroidissement de l'eau en faisant des simulations sur ordinateur. L'édifice ne comprend pas moins de 7 000 éléments de bambou préalablement traité selon les méthodes traditionnelles vietnamiennes. Cette structure ouverte se passe de colonnes de béton.

De schoonheid van bamboe heeft in de constructie van dit restaurant een plaatsje verworven als structureel en decoratief element. De architecten zijn uitgegaan van de principes van aërodynamische ontwerp en hebben computersimulaties uitgevoerd voor het bestuderen van de luchtstroom en de koelcapaciteit van het water. Het gebouw is opgebouwd uit 7.000 bamboe-elementen die behandeld zijn volgens traditionele Vietnamese methodes. In de structuur zijn geen betonnen zuilen nodig.

La bellezza del bambù si integra nel progetto di questo ristorante come elemento strutturale e decorativo. Gli architetti hanno utilizzato i principi dell'aerodinamicità, come le simulazioni prodotte tramite computer, per gli spazi serviti per studiare il flusso d'aria e la capacità di raffreddamento dell'acqua. L'intero edificio è costruito con 7.000 elementi di bambù, trattati con i metodi tradizionali vietnamiti. La struttura non ha bisogno di colonne di cemento.

La belleza del bambú se ha incorporado en la construcción de este restaurante como elemento estructural y decorativo. Los arquitectos utilizaron para los espacios los principios del diseño aerodinámico, como las simulaciones generadas por ordenador, que sirvieron para estudiar el flujo de aire y la capacidad de enfriamiento del agua. Todo el edificio está construido con 7.000 elementos de bambú que han sido tratados con los métodos tradicionales vietnamitas. La estructura prescinde de columnas de hormigón.

**Vo Trong Nghia (main architect),
Nguyen Hoa Hiep, Sakata Minoru,
Ohara Hisanori**
Thu Dau Mot, Vietnam, 2006
© Dinh Thu Thuy

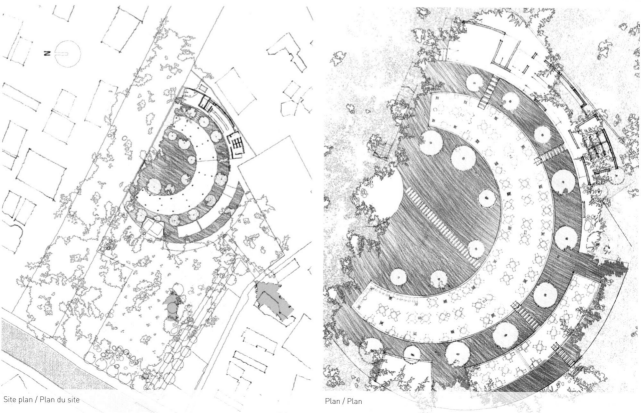

Site plan / Plan du site

Plan / Plan

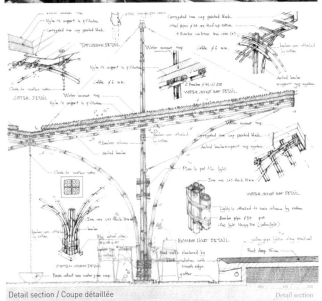

Detail section / Coupe détaillée

Detail section

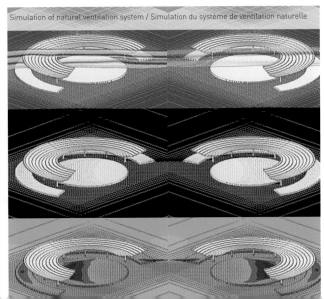

Simulation of natural ventilation system / Simulation du système de ventilation naturelle

A striking feature is the plant-inspired V-shaped roof. It respects the surrounding trees while leaving an open space that offers amazing views.

Es besticht das Dach pflanzlicher Inspiration, das in V-Form entworfen wurde, und zum einen die umgebenden Bäume achtet und zum anderen Raum offen lässt, für imponierende Ausblicke.

On admire le toit d'inspiration naturaliste dont la forme en V respecte les arbres environnants et dont la vaste ouverture laisse admirer un impressionnant panorama.

Opvallend is het op de vegetatie geïnspireerde dak dat in V-vorm is ontworpen en dat enerzijds de bomen van de omgeving respecteert en anderzijds een ruimte met een indrukwekkend uitzicht biedt.

Si impone il soffitto di ispirazione vegetale a V che da un lato rispetta gli alberi circostanti e dall'altro lascia uno spazio aperto con un panorama mozzafiato.

Destaca el techo de inspiración vegetal diseñado en forma de V que, por un lado, respeta los árboles circundantes y, por el otro, deja un espacio abierto con impresionantes vistas.

Green School

This project is a giant laboratory located on a sustainable campus on both sides of the Ayung River. The campus was designed to operate with alternative energy sources, such as hydraulic and solar power. It contains classrooms, a gymnasium, meeting rooms, student housing, offices, cafeterias, and restrooms. The buildings were made from local bamboo, grown utilizing sustainable methods and employed innovatively and experimentally.

Das Projekt ist ein gigantisches Labor innerhalb eines nachhaltigen Campus zu beiden Ufern des Flusses Ayung. Der Campus ist so konzipiert, dass er allein mit erneuerbaren Energien, wie Wasser- und Solarenergie auskommt. Auf dem Campus befinden sich die Hörsäle, eine Turnhalle, Konferenzsäle, ein Studentenwohnheim, Büros, Cafeterien und Toiletten. Die Gebäude wurden mit lokalem Bambus gebaut, der aus nachhaltigem Anbau stammt, und hier innovativ und experimentell eingesetzt wurde.

Ce projet est un gigantesque laboratoire situé sur un campus durable établi sur les berges de l'Ayung. L'université a été conçue pour n'être alimentée que par des énergies renouvelables comme le solaire et l'hydro-électricité. Le site comprend des salles de cours, un gymnase, des salles de réunion, des résidences universitaires, des bureaux, des cafétérias et des sanitaires. Les bâtiments sont construits dans une variété de bambou locale, cultivée dans le respect de l'environnement, et utilisée d'une manière novatrice et expérimentale.

Het project bestaat uit een gigantisch laboratorium in een duurzame campus die aan weerszijden van de rivier de Ayung ligt. De campus is ontwikkeld om te werken op alternatieve energieën, zoals hydraulische en zonne-energie. Binnenin bevinden zich collegezalen, een fitnessruimte, vergaderzalen, studentenwoningen, kantoren, coffeeshops en toiletten. De gebouwen zijn opgebouwd met plaatselijk bamboe dat met duurzame methodes verbouwd wordt en op innoverende en experimentele wijze is toegepast.

Il progetto è un gigantesco laboratorio all'interno di un campus sostenibile, situato lungo le due rive del fiume Ayung. Il campus è stato concepito per funzionare con energie alternative, come quella idraulica e quella solare. All'interno troviamo delle aule, una palestra, alcune sale riunioni, residenze per gli studenti, uffici, bar e bagni. Gli edifici sono stati realizzati con il bambù locale, coltivato con metodi sostenibili e utilizzato in modo innovativo e sperimentale.

El proyecto es un gigantesco laboratorio ubicado dentro de un campus sostenible situado a ambos lados del río Ayung. El campus fue concebido para funcionar con energías alternativas, como la hidráulica y la solar. En el interior se encuentran aulas, un gimnasio, salas de reunión, residencias estudiantiles, oficinas, cafeterías y baños. Los edificios han sido construidos con bambú local, cultivado con métodos sostenibles, y utilizado de forma innovadora y experimental.

John and Cynthia Hardy/PT Bambu, Aga Khan Development Network
Badung, Indonesia, 2007
© Aga Khan Development Network, Ahkamul Hakim, PT Bambu

The most striking of the buildings has a spiral design. The use of bamboo as the main material for innovative construction has given rise to experimental architecture.

Das auffälligste Gebäude ist das in Spiralform. Der Einsatz von Bambus als neuartiger Hauptbaustoff macht dieses zu experimenteller Baukunst.

L'immeuble en spirale est celui qui se fait le plus remarquer. L'utilisation du bambou comme principal matériau de construction permet une architecture pionnière audacieuse.

Het opvallendste is het spiraalvormige gebouw. Het gebruik van bamboe als belangrijkste innoverende bouwmateriaal maakt de weg vrij voor experimentele architectuur.

Tra gli edifici, il più particolare è quello a forma di spirale. L'uso del bambù come materiale principale da costruzione, altamente innovativo, dà vita a un'architettura sperimentale.

De entre los edificios, el más destacado es el construido en forma de espiral. El uso del bambú como principal material de construcción innovador da lugar a una arquitectura experimental.

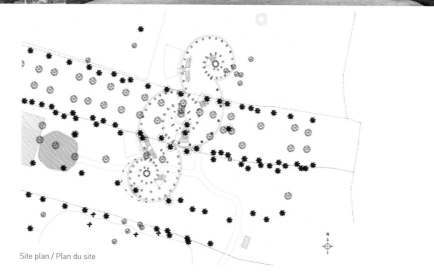

Site plan / Plan du site

Aula de Capacitación Flor del Bosque

Flor del Bosque is a space devoted to environmental education located in the park of the same name. The architects were inspired by the surrounding mountain landscape and reproduced it in the final design. The structure is based on the repetition of planes with variations in column height and tie beam length to achieve curvilinear forms in both floor plan and elevation. The materials employed are guadua bamboo and ferrocement, which are combined in the inclined angles of the outer walls.

Flor del Bosque ist ein Raum zur Umwelterziehung im Park des gleichen Namens. Die Architekten haben sich für ihr finales Design von den Gebirgsformationen, die ihm umgeben, inspirieren lassen. Die Struktur basiert auf der Wiederholung von Ebenen mit variierender Säulenhöhe und Balkenbreite, um gewölbte Formen sowohl in der Länge als auch in der Höhe zu erreichen. Die benutzten Materialien sind Guadua- Bambus und Eisenzement, die mit den geneigten Winkeln der Wände kombiniert werden.

Flor del Bosque est un espace consacré à l'éducation écologique situé dans le parc du même nom. Les architectes se sont inspiré des reliefs montagneux qui l'entourent pour aboutir à leur projet final. La structure s'appuie sur la répétition des plans à différents niveaux reposant sur des colonnes de différentes hauteurs pour obtenir les arrondis à tous les niveaux. Les matériaux utilisés sont la guadua et le ferrociment, dont l'association a permis la construction des murs aux pans inclinés.

Flor del Bosque is een ruimte die bestemd is voor milieu-educatie en is gelegen in het gelijknamige park. De architecten hebben zich voor het uiteindelijke ontwerp laten inspireren door de bergformatie waardoor het park omringd is. De structuur is gebaseerd op de herhaling van vlakken, met zuilen van verschillende hoogte en balken van verschillende lengtes om de gebogen vormen te verkrijgen, zowel horizontaal als verticaal. De materialen die gebruikt zijn, zijn guadua bamboe en ferrocement, die zijn samengevoegd in de schuine hoeken van de muren.

Flor del Bosque è uno spazio destinato all'educazione ambientale, ubicato all'interno del parco omonimo. Gli architetti si sono ispirati alla formazione montuosa che lo circonda per creare il progetto finale. La struttura si basa sulla ripetizione di piani con varianti nell'altezza della colonna e nella lunghezza delle travi per ottenere le forme curvilinee sia sulla pianta che al livello superiore. I materiali utilizzati sono il bambù guadua e il ferrocemento, che si incontrano negli angoli inclinati delle pareti.

Flor del Bosque es un espacio destinado a la educación ambiental ubicado en el parque del mismo nombre. Los arquitectos se inspiraron en la formación montañosa que lo rodea para crear el diseño final. La estructura está basada en la repetición de planos con variante en altura de columna y largo de trabe para conseguir las formas curvilíneas tanto en planta como en alzado. Los materiales utilizados son el bambú guadua y el ferrocemento, que se conjugan en los ángulos inclinados de los muros.

Ricardo Leyva Cervantes/Ojtat
Puebla, Mexico, 2005
© Ojtat, Sófocles Hernández

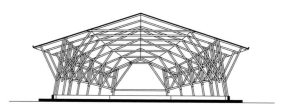

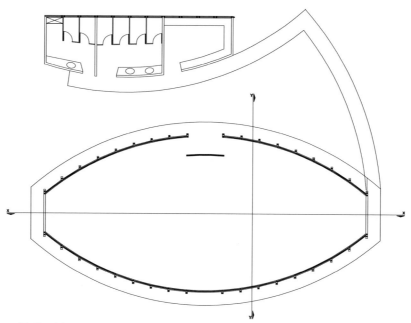

Sections, elevation and plan / Coupes, élévation et plan

The spectacular effect of this classroom lies in the use of bamboo as a main structural feature. This material is found in beams, pillars, and windows.

Die Auffälligkeit dieses Hörsaals liegt im Gebrauch von Bambus als Hauptelement für den Bau des Tragwerks. Dieses Material wird auch zur Erzeugung von Balken, Säulen und Fenster eingesetzt.

C'est l'utilisation du bambou comme principal élément de construction de la structure qui rend cet amphithéâtre spectaculaire. Poutres, piliers et fenêtres sont en acier végétal.

Het spectaculaire van deze aula zit hem in het gebruik van bamboe als hoofdelement voor de bouw van de structuur. Het materiaal wordt gebruikt om balken, pilaren en ramen te maken.

La spettacolarità di quest'aula risiede nell'utilizzo del bambù come elemento principale per la realizzazione della struttura. Questo materiale viene utilizzato per creare travi, pilastri e finestre.

La espectacularidad de esta aula reside en la utilización del bambú como elemento principal para la construcción de la estructura. El material se usa para crear vigas, pilares y ventanas.

La Vong Restaurant

This spectacular structure is found on the outskirts of Hanoi, approximately 30 km (19 miles) from the center of the city. Located near a river, the La Vong restaurant features a spectacular circular roof with simple forms in the local architectural tradition. This circular building was made from 38 prefabricated bamboo units. This material enabled very long and high roof structures to be built. Large bamboo poles projected from the center provide the building with additional space.

In der Umgebung von Hanoi, etwa 30 km westlich der Stadtmitte, befindet sich dieses Aufsehen erregende Bauwerk. Das Restaurant La Vong in der Nähe eines Flusses besticht vor allem durch sein spektakuläres Runddach mit einfachen Formen und durch seine lokale architektonische Tradition. Das Gebäude mit rundem Grundriss ist aus 38 vorgefertigten Bambus-Einheiten zusammengesetzt. Dieses Material hat es gestattet, hohe und sehr lange Dächer zu schaffen. Von der Mitte aus strahlen lange Bambusstäbe aus, die das Gebäude größer aussehen lassen.

Cet édifice spectaculaire se situe dans les faubourgs de Hanoï, quelque 30 km à l'ouest du centre-ville. Proche des berges d'un cours d'eau, le restaurant *La Vong* se fait d'abord remarquer par la simplicité de sa toiture circulaire dans la tradition architecturale locale. La salle ronde de ce restaurant se compose de 38 unités préfabriquées en bambou. Ce matériau a permis de faire des poutres très hautes et d'une grande longueur. Les grandes tiges qui partent du centre participent à l'époustouflant esthétisme de l'édifice.

Dit spectaculaire bouwwerk staat in een buitenwijk van Hanoi, op ongeveer 30 km ten westen van de binnenstad. Het vlakbij een rivier gelegen restaurant La Vong valt vooral op door zijn indrukwekkende ronde dak met eenvoudige vormen, waarmee de plaatselijke architectonische traditie wordt voortgezet. Het gebouw, met een cirkelvormig grondvlak, is opgebouwd uit 38 geprefabriceerde bamboe-eenheden. Met dit materiaal heeft men hoge plafonds verkregen. Vanuit het midden komen grote bamboe latten naar boven, die het gebouw een extra dimensie geven.

Nei pressi di Hanói, circa 30 km a ovest del centro della città, troviamo questo edificio spettacolare. Situato vicino a un fiume, il ristorante La Vong si impone soprattutto per lo spettacolare soffitto circolare dalle forme semplici, ispirato alla tradizione architettonica locale. L'edificio a pianta circolare è realizzato impiegando 38 unità prefabbricate in bambù. Questo materiale ha consentito di creare soffitti alti e sfruttare una grande lunghezza. Dal centro si dipartono grandi listoni di bambù che ampliano ulteriormente l'edificio.

En las afueras de Hanói, unos 30 km aproximadamente hacia el oeste del centro de la ciudad, está localizada esta espectacular construcción. Situado cercano a un río, el restaurante La Vong destaca sobre todo por su espectacular techo circular de formas sencillas y de tradición arquitectónica local. El edificio, de planta circular, está construido con 38 unidades prefabricadas de bambú. Este material permitió crear techos altos y una gran longitud. Del centro parten grandes listones de bambú que proporcionan una extensión extra al edificio.

Vo Trong Nghia
Hanoi, Vietnam, 2011
© Nguyen Quang Phuc,
Vo Trong Nghia Co.,Ltd

Natural light can penetrate the bamboo frame to create interesting light and shade effects in the interior. Use was made of the natural conditions to create a comfortable and relaxing place.

Das Bambusschild lässt natürliches Licht ins Innere hinein, wodurch ein interessantes Zusammenspiel aus Licht und Schatten kreiert wird. Durch Nutzung der natürlichen Bedingungen wurde ein gemütlicher und bequemer Raum geschaffen.

L'ossature en bambou laisse le jour pénétrer à l'intérieur pour créer un intéressant jeu d'ombres et de lumières. Ce lieu confortable propice à la détente a été créé simplement en profitant des conditions naturelles.

Dankzij de bamboe draagconstructie kan het daglicht naar binnen doordringen, zodat een interessant licht- en schaduwspel ontstaat. Doordat profijt is getrokken uit de natuurlijke omstandigheden is een comfortabele ontspanningsruimte gecreëerd.

Lo scheletro di bambù fa sì che la luce naturale penetri all'interno per creare un interessante gioco di luci e ombre. Sfruttando le condizioni naturali del luogo, è stato creato un ambiente confortevole e rilassato.

El armazón de bambú permite que la luz natural penetre en el interior para crear un interesante juego de luces y sombras. Gracias al aprovechamiento de las condiciones naturales, se ha creado un lugar relajado y confortable.

wNw Bar

Located on an artificial lake, this project was designed as a multi-purpose closed space for events such as concerts, shows, and ceremonies. The spectacular dome measuring 10 m (33 ft) in height and 15 m (49 ft) in diameter was made with an arched bamboo structural system formed from 48 prefabricated units. Each of them consisted of several bamboo members joined together. The building uses natural energy from the wind and the cold water of the lake to generate natural ventilation in the interior.

Das auf einem künstlichen See gelegene Bauprojekt wurde als geschlossener Raum für verschiedene Nutzungen wie Konzerte, Aufführungen, Zeremonien, usw. konzipiert. Um die spektakuläre 10 m hohe Kuppel mit 15 m Durchmesser zu bauen, wurde ein Struktursystem aus Bambusbögen erzeugt, die aus 48 vorgefertigten Einheiten besteht. Eine jede von ihnen besteht wiederum aus verschiedenen untereinander verbundenen Bambuselementen. Das Gebäude nutzt die naturgegebene Energie von Wind und das kalte Seewasser, um das Innere auf natürliche Weise zu belüften.

Cette salle, située sur un lac artificiel, fut conçue comme un espace clos à usage polyvalent : concerts, spectacles, cérémonies... La création de la spectaculaire coupole de 10 m de haut et 15 m de diamètre a été possible grâce à un système structurel en arcs de bambou formé de 48 unités préfabriquées consistant chacune en plusieurs éléments de bambou reliés entre eux. La ventilation intérieure du bâtiment utilise l'énergie naturelle éolienne et l'eau froide du lac.

Het project, dat gelegen is in een kunstmatig aangelegd meer, is ontworpen als gesloten ruimte voor diverse evenementen, zoals muziekconcerten, uitvoeringen, ceremonies, etc. Om de indrukwekkende koepel van 10 m hoog en met een diameter van 15 m te creëren werd een boogvormige bamboestructuur vervaardigd, bestaande uit 48 geprefabriceerde eenheden. Elk daarvan is opgebouwd uit diverse onderling verbonden bamboe-elementen. Het gebouw gebruikt natuurlijke windenergie en het koude water van het meer voor natuurlijke ventilatie binnen.

Il progetto, ubicato su un lago artificiale, è stato pensato come uno spazio chiuso per usi diversi come concerti di musica, spettacoli, cerimonie, ecc. Per realizzare la spettacolare cupola di 10 m di altezza e 15 m di diametro, è stato costruito un sistema strutturale ad arco in bambù formato da 48 elementi prefabbricati. Ognuno è composto da vari elementi in bambù uniti tra loro. L'edificio sfrutta l'energia naturale del vento e l'acqua fredda del lago per produrre ventilazione naturale interna.

El proyecto, ubicado en un lago artificial, fue diseñado como un espacio cerrado para usos diversos, tales como conciertos, espectáculos, ceremonias, etc. Para la espectacular cúpula de 10 m de alto y 15 m de diámetro, se creó un sistema estructural en arco de bambú formado por 48 unidades prefabricadas. Cada una de ellas está constituida de varios elementos de bambú unidos entre sí. El edificio utiliza la energía natural del viento y el agua fría del lago para generar ventilación natural en el interior.

Vo Trong Nghia
Thu Dau Mot, Vietnam, 2008
© Phan Quang

The design of the bar blends
seamlessly with the surroundings
and represents both modernity and
tradition. A striking feature is the
opening in the roof, with a diameter
of 1.5 m (5 ft), which serves as an
outlet for warm air.

Das Design der Bar passt sich perfekt
an die Umgebung an und stellt
gleichzeitig Modernität und Tradition
dar. Auffällig ist die Öffnung im Dach
mit einem Durchmesser von 1,5 m
zum Abzug der warmen Luft.

Synthèse de la modernité et de
la tradition, le bar, par son dessin,
s'harmonise à la perfection avec
tout ce qui l'entoure. On remarque
l'ouverture pratiquée dans le toit,
d'un diamètre de 1,5 m, par où
s'évacue l'air chaud.

Het ontwerp voor de bar is perfect
in harmonie met de omgeving en
vertegenwoordigt moderniteit en
traditie. Opvallend is de opening
in het dak, met een diameter van
1,5 m, waardoor warme lucht wordt
afgevoerd.

Il progetto del bar si armonizza
perfettamente con l'ambiente
circostante e rappresenta modernità
e tradizione. Degna di nota è l'apertura
del soffitto, con un diametro di 1,5 m,
che consente la fuoriuscita di aria
calda.

El diseño del bar armoniza a la
perfección con el entorno que lo rodea
y representa modernidad y tradición.
Destaca la abertura en el techo, con un
diámetro de 1,5 m, para la evacuación
de aire caliente.

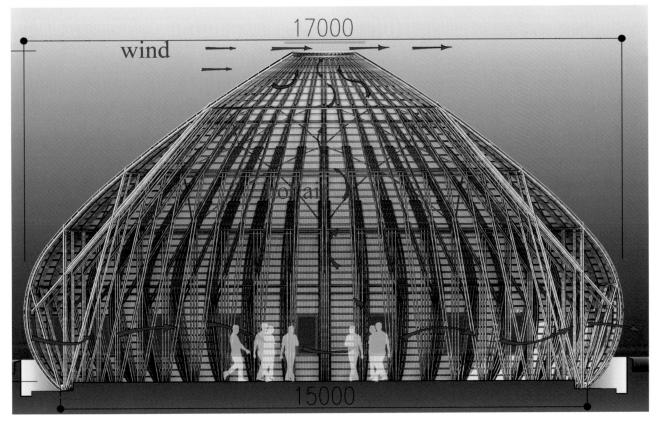

wind

17000

15000

Parque Arboledas Rementería

The architects' work involved remodeling an existing park and turning it into an information, documentation, and environmental recreation center while maintaining its use as an urban green space. The space will contain a library, daycare center, adult exercise area, and cafeteria. The main volume was built using natural and recycled materials to reduce the need for industrial materials that cause deforestation and pollution. The structure is made from the bamboo variety *Guadua aculeata*.

Die Intervention der Architekten betraf die Neugestaltung eines bereits existierenden Parks, um als einen Informations-, Dokumentations- und Umwelterholungspark mit Stadtparkcharakter aufzuwerten. Der Komplex wird aus einer Bibliothek, einem Kindergarten und Trimm-Dich-Bereich für Erwachsene sowie einer Cafeteria bestehen. Beim Bau des Hauptgebäudes wurden natürliche oder recycelte Materialien eingesetzt, um industrielle Werkstoffe zu vermeiden, die zum Baumsterben und zur Umweltverschmutzung beitragen. Die Struktur wurde aus *Guadua aculeata*-Bambus gebaut.

L'intervention des architectes a consisté à transformer un parc existant pour en faire un site d'informations, de documentation et de régénération du milieu à vocation de parc urbain. On y trouve une bibliothèque, une garderie, une aire de sport destinée aux adultes et une cafétéria. Le bâtiment principal est construit en matériaux naturels ou recyclés afin de limiter l'emploi de produits industriels polluants qui participent à la déforestation. La structure est en bambou du genre *Guadua* et de l'espèce *aculeata*.

Het werk van de architecten bestond uit het ombouwen van een bestaand park tot een informatie-, documentatie en recreatiezone en stadspark. Het park heeft een bibliotheek, crèche, een sportzone voor volwassenen en een koffiehuis. Bij de bouw van het hoofdgebouw werd gebruik gemaakt van natuurlijke of gerecyclede materialen, om het gebruik van vervuilende geïndustrialiseerde materialen die ontbossing in de hand werken te vermijden. De structuur is opgebouwd uit *Guadua aculeata* bamboe.

L'intervento degli architetti ha previsto il recupero di un parco esistente per trasformarlo in un centro informazioni, di documentazione e ricreativo ambientale con vocazione di parco urbano. Lo spazio comprende una biblioteca, un asilo, un'area di pratica per gli adulti e un bar. Nella realizzazione dell'edificio principale sono stati utilizzati materiali naturali o riciclati per ridurre l'uso di prodotti industriali che causano deforestazione e inquinamento. La struttura è realizzata con il bambù *Guadua aculeata*.

La intervención de los arquitectos fue la recuperación de un parque existente para convertirlo en un centro de información, documentación y recreación ambiental con vocación de parque urbano. El espacio cuenta con una biblioteca, una guardería, un área de ejercicio para adultos y una cafetería. En la construcción del edificio principal se utilizaron materiales naturales o reciclados para reducir el uso de materiales industrializados que deforestan y contaminan. La estructura está resuelta con bambú *Guadua aculeata*.

Ricardo Leyva Cervantes/Ojtat
Puebla, Mexico, 2010
© Ojtat

A sustainable bamboo structure of 800 m² (8,610 sq ft) was designed to support the roof and walls. Indigenous artisans from the Puebla Mountains were commissioned to build it.

Es wurde eine nachhaltige Bambuskonstruktion von 800 m² konzipiert, um die Dächer und Mauern zu tragen. Die indigenen Handwerker der Sierra de Puebla wurden mit ihrer Ausführung beauftragt.

Les artisans indigènes de la forêt de Puebla furent chargés de la réalisation de cette construction de 800 m² tout en bambou relevant d'une architecture compatible avec le développement durable.

Er werd een ontwerp gemaakt voor een duurzame bamboeconstructie van 800 m² om plafonds en muren te dragen. De inheemse ambachtslieden van de Sierra de Puebla waren belast met het vervaardigen ervan.

È stata realizzata una costruzione sostenibile in bambù di 800 m² per sostenere soffitti e pareti. Gli artigiani indigeni della campagna di Puebla hanno avuto l'incarico di portarla a termine.

Se diseñó una construcción sostenible de bambú de 800 m² para soportar techos y muros. Los artesanos indígenas de la sierra de Puebla fueron los encargados de realizarla.

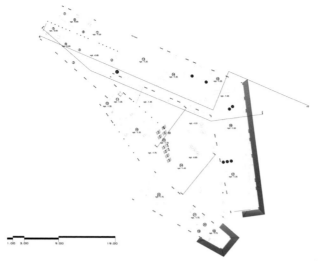

Site plan / Plan du site

Section A-A' / Coupe A-A'

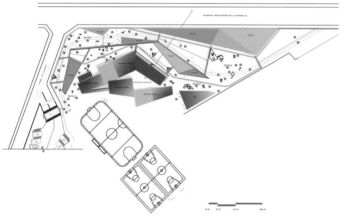
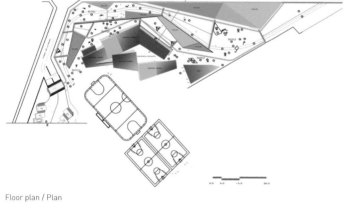

Floor plan / Plan

Section B-B' / Coupe B-B'

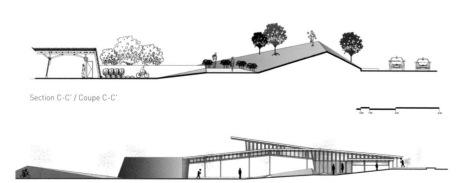

Section C-C' / Coupe C-C'

Section D-D' / Coupe D-D'

Interior façade – axes AD-T / Façade intérieure – axes AD-T

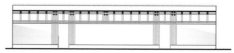

Interior façade – axes Q-AC / Façade intérieure – axes Q-AC

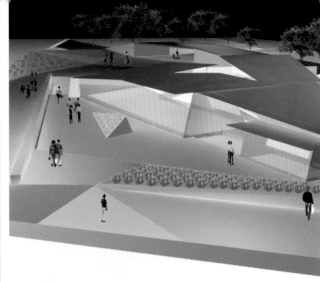

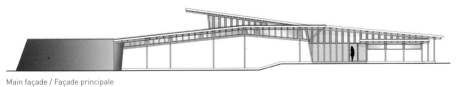

Main façade / Façade principale

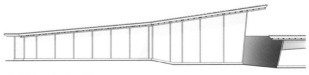

South façade / Façade sud

Hand-Made School

This school is the result of the shared experience of different groups of European artisans, architects, and students. The aim of the project was to improve current building and maintenance techniques through sustainability, and to reinforce regional identity in the creation of modern architecture. In addition to earth, mud and straw, bamboo was used in the roof and walls of the second floor, forming a frame of members to support walls, windows, and doors.

Die Schule ist das Ergebnis der Gemeinschaftsarbeit verschiedener Teams aus europäischen Handwerkern, Architekten und Studenten. Ziel des Projekts ist die Verbesserung der derzeitigen Bau- und Wartungstechniken durch Nachhaltigkeit sowie eine Stärkung der regionalen Identität. Beides zusammen macht diese moderne Architektur aus. Neben Erde, Ton und Stroh kam auch Bambus beim Bau des Dachs und der Wände des ersten Stocks zum Einsatz, womit ein Tragwerk für Wände, Fenster und Türen geschaffen wurde.

Cette école est le fruit des efforts conjoints de plusieurs équipes réunissant artisans, architectes et étudiants européens. Le projet visait à améliorer les structures de construction employées aujourd'hui. Il s'agissait aussi de faciliter leur entretien en faisant appel à des procédés durables tout en renforçant l'identité régionale de manière à faire naître une architecture moderne. Outre la terre, l'adobe et la paille, le bambou entre dans la construction du toit et des murs du premier étage, formant une structure de poutres entre lesquelles viennent se loger murs, fenêtres et portes.

De school is het resultaat van een samenwerkingsverband tussen Europese ambachtslieden, architecten en studenten. Het project heeft als doel het verbeteren van de huidige bouw- en onderhoudstechnieken door middel van duurzaamheid, alsmede het versterken van de regionale identiteit voor het genereren van moderne architectuur. Naast aarde, klei en stro is bij de bouw van het dak en de muren van de benedenverdieping gebruik gemaakt van bamboe, waarbij een draagconstructie van balken is gevormd voor muren, ramen en deuren.

La scuola è il risultato del lavoro congiunto di diverse squadre di artigiani, architetti e studenti europei. L'obiettivo del progetto era quello di migliorare le attuali tecniche costruttive e manutentive tramite la sostenibilità, oltre a rafforzare l'identità regionale per dare vita a un'architettura moderna. Oltre a terra, fango e paglia, è stato utilizzato il bambù nella realizzazione del soffitto e delle pareti del primo piano, costituendo così un telaio di travi in grado di sostenere pareti, finestre e porte.

Esta escuela es el resultado de una comunión de diferentes equipos, formados por artesanos, arquitectos y estudiantes europeos. El objetivo del proyecto era mejorar las actuales técnicas de construcción y mantenimiento mediante la sostenibilidad, así como reforzar la identidad regional para generar una arquitectura moderna. Además de tierra, barro y paja, se ha utilizado el bambú en la construcción del techo y de las paredes del primer piso, formando un armazón de vigas para paredes, ventanas y puertas.

Anna Heringer, Eike Roswag/ Ziegert|Roswag|Seiler Architekten Ingenieure, Aga Khan Development Network
Rudrapur, Bangladesh, 2005
© Aga Khan Development Network, Anna Heringer, Eike Roswag/ Ziegert|Roswag|Seiler Architekten Ingenieure

The use of bamboo for the second story walls and ceiling provide the building with natural ventilation and resistance to strong local winds, while enabling daylight to penetrate the open interior space.

Der Gebrauch von Bambus auf der ersten Etage, den Wänden und dem Dach ermöglicht eine natürliche Belüftung des Gebäudes, Widerstand gegen die örtlich vorherrschenden starken Winde und dass das Licht hell ins Innere vordringt.

L'utilisation du bambou pour le premier étage, dans les murs et le toit, permet une ventilation naturelle du bâtiment. Elle assure sa résistance à la force des vents locaux et laisse une lumière diaphane pénétrer à l'intérieur.

Het gebruik van bamboe in de eerste verdieping, de muren en het dak maakt natuurlijke ventilatie van het gebouw mogelijk en zorgt verder voor bestendigheid tegen de sterke plaatselijke winden en maakt dat het licht naar binnen kan schijnen.

L'uso del bambù al primo piano, sulle pareti e sul soffitto consente la ventilazione naturale, la resistenza ai forti venti che soffiano in questa zona e l'ingresso della luce all'interno della struttura.

El uso del bambú en el primer piso, las paredes y el techo permite la ventilación natural, la resistencia a los fuertes vientos locales y que la luz penetre diáfana en el interior.

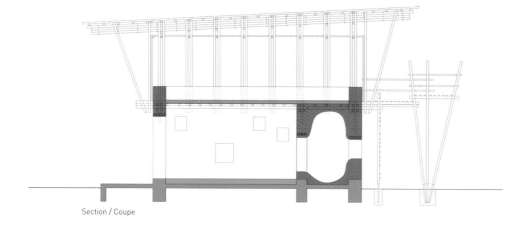

Section / Coupe

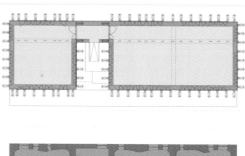
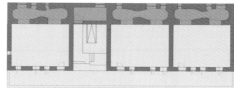

Plans / Plans

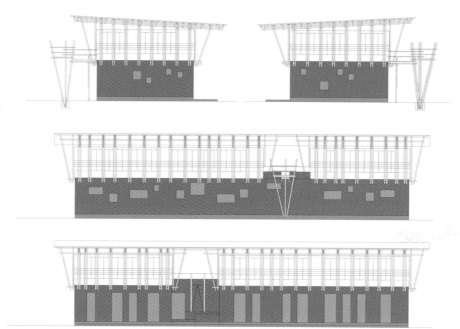

Elevations / Élévations

Ethiopia-Japanese Millennium Pavilion

The Ethiopian government invited their Japanese counterparts to build a monument commemorating the 2000th year of the Julian calendar. The architects decided to create two traditional structures that would integrate the two cultures architecturally. The Japanese pavilion serves as a socio-cultural exchange center for exhibitions and the performing arts, while the Ethiopian pavilion houses a gallery space and a rainwater purication system.

Die äthiopische Regierung hat die japanische gebeten, ein Denkmal zu Ehren des Jahres 2000 des julianischen Kalenders zu bauen. Die Architekten entscheiden sich, zwei traditionelle Strukturen zu schaffen, um die beiden architektonischen Kulturen zu vereinen. Der japanische Pavillon fungiert als Zentrum des soziokulturellen Austauschs für Ausstellungen und Bühnenvorführungen, während der äthiopische Pavillon als Galerieraum und großer Regenwasserkläranlage dient.

Le gouvernement éthiopien s'est tourné vers le Japon pour faire construire un monument commémoratif de l'an 2000 de notre calendrier. Les architectes décidèrent de créer deux structures traditionnelles pour réunir les deux traditions architecturales. Le pavillon japonais est un centre d'échanges culturels où sont présentés des expositions et des spectacles vivants. Le pavillon éthiopien comprend une galerie et uns station de filtrage de l'eau.

De Ethiopische regering nodigde de Japanner uit om een monument op te richten ter ere van het jaar 2000 van de Juliaanse kalender. De architecten besloten om twee traditionele structuren op te richten om de twee architectonische culturen te integreren. Het Japanse paviljoen fungeert als een sociaal-economisch uitwisselingscentrum voor tentoonstellingen en podiumkunsten, terwijl het paviljoen van Ethiopië dienst doet als galerie en als zuiveringssysteem voor regenwater.

Il governo etiope ha invitato il giapponese per realizzare un monumento commemorativo per l'anno 2000 del calendario giuliano. Gli architetti hanno deciso di creare due strutture tradizionali per integrare le due culture architettoniche. Il padiglione giapponese funziona come un centro di scambio socio-culturale per esposizioni ed eventi teatrali, mentre il padiglione etiope è una sorta di spazio-galleria e magazzino per l'acqua depurata.

El Gobierno etíope invitó al japonés para construir un monumento conmemorativo del año 2000 del calendario juliano. Los arquitectos decidieron crear dos estructuras tradicionales para integrar las dos culturas arquitectónicas. El pabellón japonés funciona como un centro de intercambio sociocultural para exposiciones y artes escénicas, mientras que el pabellón de Etiopía funciona como un espacio de galería y como almacén de agua depurada.

Atelier Tekuto, Fasil Giorgis
Gondar, Ethiopia, 2009
© Atelier Tekuto, Fasil Giorgis

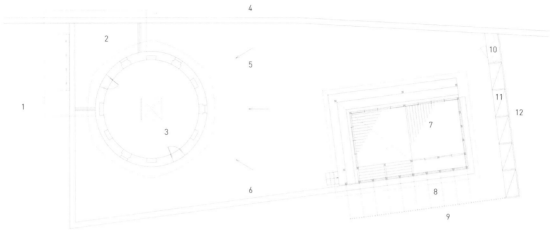

Plan / Plan

1. Water station / Stockage de l'eau
2. Gallery / Galerie
3. Nature purifier / Purificateur naturel
4. Existing stone wall / Murs de pierre existants
5. Catchment floor / Collecte de l'eau
6. Stone wall / Mur de pierre

7. Exhibition space / Espace d'expositions
8. Ceremony space / Espacio de cérémonie
9. Eucalyptus / Eucaliptus
10. Toilet / Toilettes
11. Bamboo wall / Paroi de bambou
12. Storage / Magasin

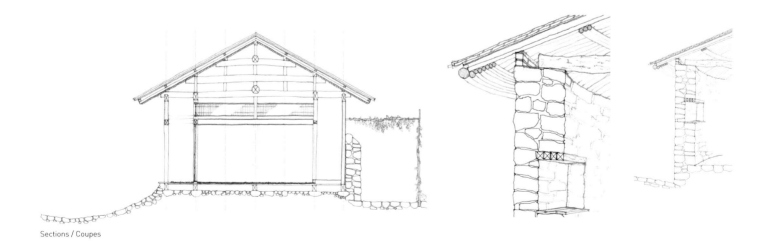

Sections / Coupes

Bamboo was combined with other locally-sourced materials for the roofs of both spaces. The striking feature of the Ethiopian pavilion is its traditional circular structure.

Bambus kombiniert mit anderen lokalen Materialien kam in beiden Räumen für den Bau der Dächer zum Einsatz. Der äthiopische Pavillon besticht durch seine traditionelle Rundstruktur.

Associé à d'autres matériaux, le bambou a été utilisé pour la toiture des deux pavillons. Celui de l'Éthiopie se reconnaît à sa forme circulaire traditionnelle.

In beide ruimtes is gebruik gemaakt van bamboe, dat voor de daken gecombineerd is met andere materialen uit de streek. Het Ethiopische paviljoen valt op door zijn traditionele ronde structuur.

Il bambù, combinato con altri materiali locali, è stato utilizzato in entrambi gli spazi per la realizzazione dei soffitti. Degno di nota è quello del padiglione etiope dalla tradizionale struttura circolare.

El bambú, combinado con otros materiales locales, fue utilizado en ambos espacios para crear los techos. Destaca el del pabellón etíope por su estructura circular tradicional.

Bamboo Pavilion in Berlin

This space was built to house open-air performances during the Festival of Vision, held in the German capital. The building symbolized the bilateral exchange between the Hong Kong Institute of Contemporary Culture and Muffathalle/Goethe-Forum. The bamboo pavilion was raised over the pond facing the House of World Cultures to represent two different cultural traditions. The triangular structure was built using a framework of transversal bamboo members.

Dieser Raum wurde für Open Air-Events im Rahmen des Festival of Vision geschaffen, das in der deutschen Hauptstadt veranstaltet wurde. Das Gebäude war Symbol des bilateral Austauschs zwischen dem Hong Kong Institute of Contemporary Culture und der Muffathalle/Goethe-Forum. Der Bambuspavillon wurde auf dem Teich gegenüber dem Haus der Kulturen der Welt errichtet und versinnbildlichte zwei ganz unterschiedliche Kulturtraditionen. Das Dreieckstragwerk wurde durch ein Geflecht aus Bambusstäben, die transversal angebracht wurden, geschaffen.

Cet espace fut construit pour accueillir les productions du théâtre en plein air pendant le Festival de la vision à Berlin. Cet édifice symbolise les échanges bilatéraux entre le Hongkong Institute of Contemporary Culture et le Muffathalle/Goethe-Forum. Élevé sur le bassin situé devant la Maison des cultures du monde, le pavillon de bambou incarnait deux traditions culturelles différentes. La structure triangulaire au premier plan est un entrelacs de tiges de bambou disposées transversalement.

Deze locatie is ingericht voor openluchtvoorstellingen tijdens het Festival of Vision dat in de Duitse hoofdstad werd gehouden. Het gebouw stond symbool voor de bilaterale uitwisseling tussen het Hong Kong Institute of Contemporary Culture en het Muffathalle/Goethe-Forum. Het bamboe paviljoen werd gebouwd in de vijver die voor het Haus der Kulturen der Welt ligt en vertegenwoordigt twee verschillende traditionele culturen. De driehoekige structuur is verkregen door een structuur van bamboelatten die de schuin op elkaar zijn gelegd.

Questo spazio è stato realizzato per ospitare performance all'aperto durante il Festival of Vision che si tiene nella capitale tedesca. L'edificio è divenuto simbolo dello scambio tra l'Hong Kong Institute of Contemporary Culture e il Muffathalle/Goethe-Forum. Il padiglione di bambù è stato realizzato sullo stagno davanti alla Casa delle Culture del Mondo in rappresentanza di due tradizioni culturali diverse. La struttura triangolare è stata realizzata tramite una rete di listoni di bambù disposti trasversalmente.

Este espacio fue construido para albergar actuaciones al aire libre en el Festival of Vision, celebrado en la capital alemana. El edificio fue símbolo del intercambio bilateral entre el Hong Kong Institute of Contemporary Culture y el Muffathalle/Goethe-Forum. El pabellón de bambú se erigió en el estanque que hay frente a la Casa de las Culturas del Mundo y representaba dos tradiciones culturales diferentes. La estructura triangular se creó mediante un entramado de listones de bambú dispuestos de manera transversal.

Rocco Yim, William Tam, Martin Fung/
Rocco Design Architects
Berlin, Germany, 2000
© Rocco Design Architects

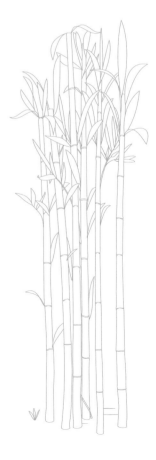

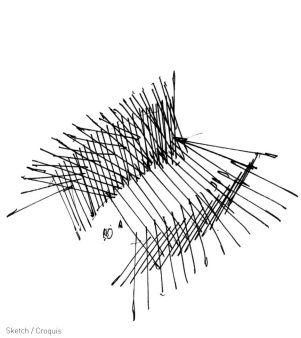

Sketch / Croquis

Built with traditional methods, the bamboo structure is harmoniously integrated with its contemporary visual aspect. The bamboo serves to enclose the space and as its stuctural support.

Die handwerkliche Ausführung des Bambustragwerks passt perfekt zu dem daraus entstehenden zeitgenössischen Aussehen des Pavillons. Bambus dient hier als äußere Brüstung und strukturelle Stütze.

La facture artisanale de la structure en bambou est en parfaite symbiose avec son apparence. Le bambou est autant une fermeture, qui tient l'extérieur à distance, qu'un appui structurel.

De ambachtelijke vervaardiging van de bamboestructuur combineert perfect met het eigentijdse visuele aspect dat daaruit voortvloeit. Het bamboe doet dienst als gevel en als draagstructuur.

La fattura artigianale della struttura in bambù si combina perfettamente con il risultato visivo contemporaneo che ne emerge. Il bambù funge da rivestimento esterno e da supporto strutturale.

La realización artesanal de la estructura en bambú combina a la perfección con el contemporáneo aspecto visual resultante. El bambú funciona como cerramiento exterior y como apoyo estructural.

Bamboo Gateway

Bamboo Gateway was commissioned for the 2009 Electric Picnic Festival with a dual purpose. From September 3 through 5, the project served as one of the main entry gates for the 20,000 people who attended. During the rest of the year, it serves as a shelter from the rain on this 500-year-old estate. *Guadua angustifolia*, a variety of bamboo native to South America, is the dominant building material, which enabled a high enough roof to be built for horses to pass underneath.

Bamboo Gateway wurde für das 2009 stattgefundene Electric Picnic Festival mit doppelter Absicht in Auftrag gegeben. Zum einen diente das Projekt zwischen dem 3. und 5. September als eines der Haupteingänge für die 20.000 Besucher. Zum anderen fungiert es das restliche Jahr über als Zuflucht vor Regen auf diesem 500 Jahre alten Anwesen. Die *Guadua angustifolia*, eine in Südamerika heimische Bambusart, ist das Hauptbaumaterial, das die Schaffung der hohen Dächer für das Durchreiten von Pferden gestattet hat.

Bamboo Gateway, construite pour le Electric Picnic Festival de 2009, est une arche à double fonction. Du 3 au 5 septembre, elle couvrait une des entrées principales qu'ont empruntées les quelque 20 000 participants à la manifestation. Le reste de l'année, elle offre un lieu où s'abriter de la pluie dans cette propriété vieille de 500 ans. Originaire d'Amérique du sud, la *Guadua angustifolia*, variété de bambou surnommée « acier végétal », est le matériau principal de cette construction. Ses propriétés physiques ont permis la création de toits suffisamment hauts pour laisser passer un cheval et son cavalier.

Bamboo Gateway was voor het Electric Picnic Festival van 2009 verantwoordelijk voor een project met een tweedelig doel: enerzijds werd het, tussen 3 en 5 september gebruikt als een van de hoofdingangen voor de 20.000 bezoekers en anderzijds fungeert het de rest van het jaar als schuilplaats voor de regen in het 500 jaar oude landhuis. De *Guadua angustifolia*, een uit Zuid-Amerika afkomstige bamboesoort is het belangrijkste bouwmateriaal, waarmee hoge plafonds werden gebouwd waar de paarden onderdoor konden.

Bamboo Gateway ha ricevuto l'incarico di realizzare il progetto per l'Electric Picnic Festival del 2009 con un doppio scopo. Da una parte, tra il 3 e il 5 settembre il progetto è stato utilizzato come uno degli ingressi principali per i 20.000 partecipanti. Dall'altra parte, per il resto dell'anno, serve da riparo per la pioggia nell'antica fattoria che vanta 500 anni di storia. La *Guadua angustifolia*, una specie di bambù originaria del Sud America, è il principale materiale da costruzione che ha consentito la creazione di soffitti alti per il passaggio dei cavalli.

Bamboo Gateway fue encargado para el Electric Picnic Festival celebrado en 2009 con un doble propósito. Por un lado, entre los días 3 y 5 de septiembre, el proyecto sirvió como una de las entradas principales para los 20.000 asistentes. Por otro lado, durante el resto del año, funciona como refugio de la lluvia en la antigua finca de 500 años. La *Guadua angustifolia*, una especie de bambú originario de Sudamérica, es el principal material de construcción que permitió la creación de techos altos para el paso de caballos.

Gerard Minakawa/Bamboo DNA
Strandbally, Ireland, 2009
© Gerard Minakawa

This project is considered to be the first permanent bamboo structure of its kind in Ireland. The building has stone foundations and a corrugated metal roof.

Dieses Projekt gilt als die erste permanente Bambusstruktur dieses Typs in Irland. Das Bauwerk wurde auf Steinfundierungen errichtet und die Dächer sind gewellt.

Cette entrée est réputée comme la première structure permanente de bambou de ce type jamais construite en Irlande. Elle repose sur des blocs de pierres cimentées. Les toits sont en acier rouillé.

Dit project wordt beschouwd als de eerste permanente bamboestructuur van zijn soort in Ierland. Het bouwwerk rust op een stenen fundering en de daken zijn golvend.

Questo progetto è considerato la prima struttura permanente di bambù di questo tipo in Irlanda. La struttura si eleva sopra delle fondazioni di pietra e i soffitti sono corrugati.

Este proyecto está considerado como la primera estructura permanente de bambú de este tipo en Irlanda. La construcción se ha levantado sobre unos cimientos de piedra y los techos son corrugados.

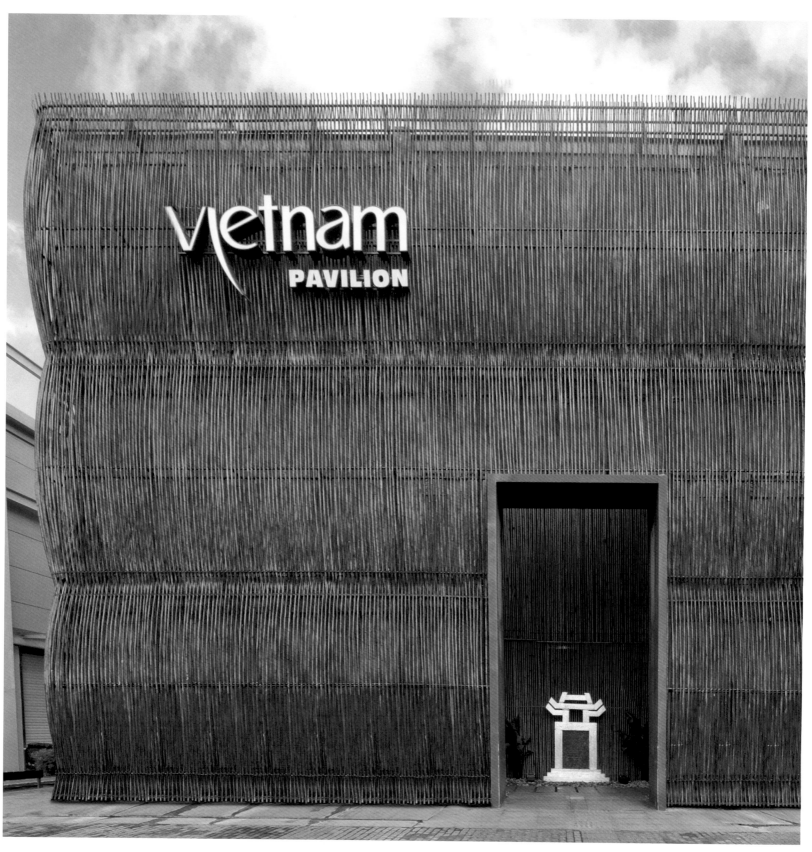

Vietnam Pavilion

The challenge of the architects was to transform an existing warehouse into an attractive pavilion for Expo Shanghai 2010 where cultural exchanges would take place. Bamboo was chosen as the main material for the remodeling and as a symbol to express Vietnam's friendship, in addition to architectural durability and sustainability. The undulating façade and the vertical bamboo structures installed inside the pavilion give visitors the impression of being in a bamboo forest.

Die Herausforderung der Architekten war es, einen bestehenden Keller in einen attraktiven Pavillon für die Weltausstellung in Shanghai 2010 zu verwandeln, in dem kulturelle Austausche stattfinden sollten. Bambus war das gewählte Hauptmaterial für diese Renovierung, ist es doch das beste Element, um den Gastfreundschaftsgeist von Vietnam sowie die architektonische Beständigkeit und Nachhaltigkeit zum Ausdruck zu bringen. Die gewellte Fassade und die im Inneren installierten senkrechten Bambusstrukturen rufen beim Besucher das Gefühl hervor, sich in einem Bambuswald zu befinden.

Les architectes ont relevé le défi qui consistait à transformer une boutique préexistante en un séduisant pavillon destiné à accueillir les échanges culturels à l'Exposition Universelle de Shanghai 2010. Le bambou fut le principal matériau choisi pour cette rénovation, car il exprime à merveille l'esprit de l'amitié avec le Vietnam, la pérennité et les qualités environnementales de son architecture ancestrale. La façade ondulée et les structures verticales de bambou placées à l'intérieur donnent aux visiteurs l'impression d'être dans une bambouseraie.

De uitdaging voor de architecten was om een bestaand magazijn om te bouwen tot een aantrekkelijk paviljoen voor de Wereldtentoonstelling van Shanghai van 2010, waar culturele uitwisselingen plaatsvonden. Bamboe is gekozen als belangrijkste materiaal voor de renovatie en als element dat de vriendschappelijke aard van Vietnam en de architectonische bestendigheid en duurzaamheid het beste tot uitdrukking brengt. De golvende gevel en de verticale structuren van bamboe die in het interieur zijn geïnstalleerd geven de bezoekers het gevoel dat ze in een bamboebos zijn beland.

La sfida degli architetti era quella di trasformare un magazzino preesistente in un accattivante padiglione per l'Esposizione Universale di Shanghai 2010 dedicato agli scambi culturali. Il bambù è stato scelto come materiale principale per la ristrutturazione, il miglior elemento per esprimere lo spirito di amicizia del Vietnam, la durata nel tempo e la sostenibilità. La facciata ondulata e le strutture verticali in bambù che si trovano all'interno creano nel visitatore la sensazione di trovarsi in un bosco di bambù.

El reto de los arquitectos era transformar una bodega existente en un pabellón atractivo para la Exposición Universal de Shanghái 2010 donde tuvieran lugar los intercambios culturales. El bambú fue elegido el material principal para la renovación, el mejor elemento para expresar el espíritu de la amistad de Vietnam, la durabilidad y la sostenibilidad arquitectónicas. La fachada ondulada y las estructuras verticales de bambú instaladas en el interior crean en el visitante la sensación de estar en un bosque de bambú.

Vo Trong Nghia (principal architect),
 Shunri Nishizawa (associate architect)
Pudong, China, 2010
© Vo Trong Nghia

The design made use of bamboo
for the exterior and interior. It was
installed over an arched structure on
the façade to produce the effect of an
undulating surface.

Das Design ist durch den Einsatz
von Bambus innen und außen
gekennzeichnet. An der Fassade wurde
er über einer Struktur in Bogenform
installiert, um den Effekt einer
gewellten Oberfläche zu erzeugen.

Le projet se caractérise par l'utilisation
du bambou à l'intérieur comme à
l'extérieur. Pour la façade, le bambou
a été monté sur une structure en arc
de cercle afin de donner l'impression
d'une surface ondulée.

Het ontwerp wordt gekenmerkt
door het gebruik van bamboe, zowel
binnen als buiten. De gevel is op een
boogvormige structuur geïnstalleerd,
zodat er een golvend effect ontstaat.

Il progetto è caratterizzato dall'uso del
bambù, sia all'interno che all'esterno
della struttura. Sulla facciata questo è
stato inserito su una struttura a forma
di arco per produrre l'effetto di una
superficie ondulata.

El diseño se caracteriza por el uso del
bambú en el interior y en el exterior.
En la fachada se instaló sobre una
estructura en forma de arco para
producir el efecto de una superficie
ondulada.

Plan / Plan

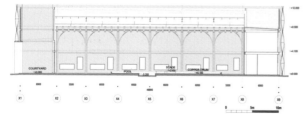

Section / Coupe

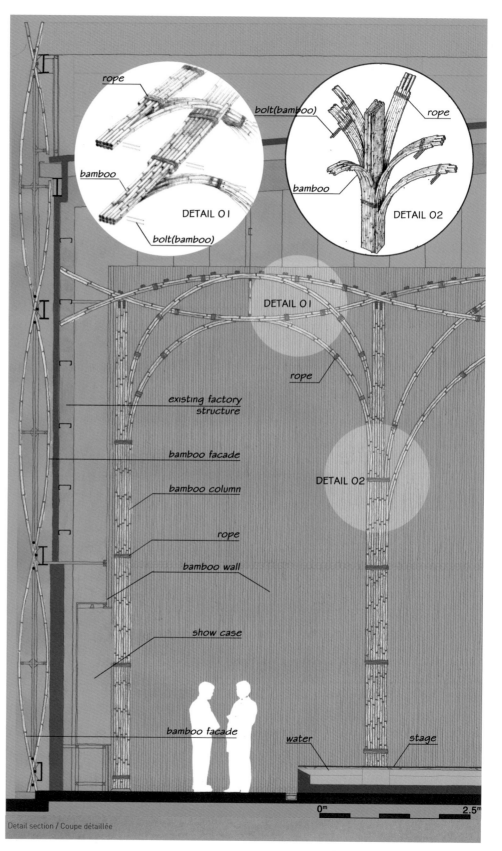

rope

bolt(bamboo)

rope

bamboo

bamboo

DETAIL 01

DETAIL 02

bolt(bamboo)

DETAIL 01

rope

existing factory structure

bamboo facade

bamboo column

DETAIL 02

rope

bamboo wall

show case

bamboo facade

water

stage

0ᵐ

2.5ᵐ

Detail section / Coupe détaillée

German-Chinese House

Designed by Markus Heinsdorff in collaboration with MUDI, this pavilion built for Expo Shanghai is the only two-story building where bamboo was used. This highly-renewable and fast-growing material was used for the load-bearing structure. Strong and light bamboo posts were attached to the structure with steel joints, providing easy assembly and dismantling. The furniture for the interior was made from laminated bamboo.

Entworfen durch Markus Heinsdorff in Zusammenarbeit mit MUDI, ist dieser für die Weltausstellung in Shanghai gebaute Pavillon das einzige zweistöckige Gebäude der Welt, das Bambus einsetzt. Dieses extrem erneuerbare und rasch nachwachsende Naturmaterial wird als Lasttragwerk verwendet. Die leichten und zugleich starken Bambusstäbe werden mit Stahldichtungen an die Struktur befestigt, was einen leichten Auf- und Abbau ermöglicht. Desgleichen kamen Bambuslamellen für die Innenausstattung zum Einsatz.

Œuvre de l'architecte Markus Heinsdorff en collaboration avec MUDI, le pavillon sino-allemand construit pour l'Exposition Universelle de Shanghai est le seul bâtiment de deux étages à utiliser le bambou. Ce matériau, des plus renouvelables puisqu'il pousse très vite, a été employé dans la structure de soutènement et dans la structure porteuse. Les tiges de bambou, légères et résistantes, sont fixées à la structure avec des colliers d'acier, ce qui assure la rapidité du montage et du démontage. Le mobilier intérieur est également en bambou laminé.

Dit door Markus Heinsdorff in samenwerking met MUDI ontworpen paviljoen, dat gebouwd werd voor de Wereldtentoonstelling van Shanghai, is het enige gebouw met twee verdiepingen waarin bamboe verwerkt is. Dit uiterst hernieuwbare en snel groeiende materiaal wordt gebruikt als draagstructuur. De lichte en sterkte bamboe staanders worden aan de structuur bevestigd door middel van stalen verbindingstukken, waardoor deze eenvoudig kan worden gemonteerd en gedemonteerd. Het meubilair is ook gemaakt van bamboe laminaat.

Progettato da Markus Heinsdorff in collaborazione con MUDI, il padiglione costruito per l'Esposizione Universale di Shanghai è l'unico edificio a due piani in cui viene utilizzato il bambù. Questo materiale estremamente rinnovabile e a rapida crescita viene utilizzato come struttura di sostegno del carico. Gli steli di bambù, leggeri e forti, vengono fissati alla struttura tramite dei giunti in acciaio; il montaggio e lo smontaggio risultano quindi semplificati. Anche gli arredi interni sono realizzati in bambù laminato.

Diseñado por Markus Heinsdorff en colaboración con MUDI, el pabellón construido para la Exposición Universal de Shanghái es el único edificio de dos pisos donde se emplea el bambú. Este material extremadamente renovable y de rápido crecimiento se utiliza como estructura de soporte de carga. Los postes de bambú, ligeros y fuertes, se fijan a la estructura con juntas de acero, con lo que se consigue un fácil montaje y desmontaje. El mobiliario del interior también fue construido en bambú laminado.

MUDI
Shanghai, China, 2010
© MUDI

The design of the pavilion roof and façade are reminiscent of a traditional Chinese paper parasol. The building was designed following environmental criteria.

Das Design des Pavillons mit seinem Dach und der Fassade aus Bambus erinnert an die Details der traditionellen chinesischen Schirme aus Papier. Das Gebäude wurde nach Maßgabe umweltverträglicher Kriterien konzipiert.

La structure de la couverture et de la façade en bambou du pavillon évoque celles des parapluies traditionnels chinois. L'édifice a été conçu dans le respect des normes environnementales.

Het ontwerp van het paviljoen doet, voor wat betreft de details van het dak en de gevel van bamboe, denken aan de traditionele Chinese papieren paraplu's. Het gebouw is ontworpen volgens milieuvriendelijke criteria.

Il progetto del padiglione sul tetto e la facciata in bambù ricordano, per i dettagli, il tradizionale ombrello cinese di carta. L'edificio è stato concepito seguendo criteri ecologici.

El diseño del pabellón en la cubierta y la fachada de bambú recuerda en los detalles al tradicional paraguas chino de papel. El edificio fue concebido siguiendo criterios medioambientales.

Site plan / Plan du site

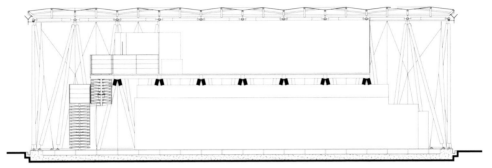

Longitudinal section / Coupe longitudinale

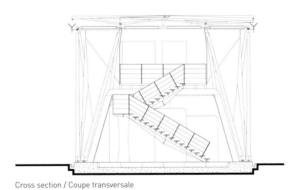

Cross section / Coupe transversale

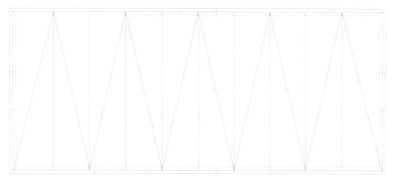

Roof plan / Plan du toit

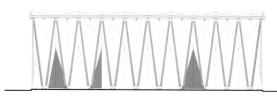

East elevation / Élévation est

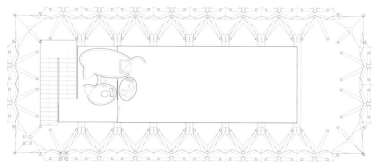

Second floor plan / Plan du second niveau

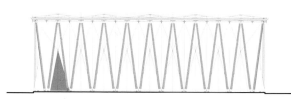

West elevation / Élévation ouest

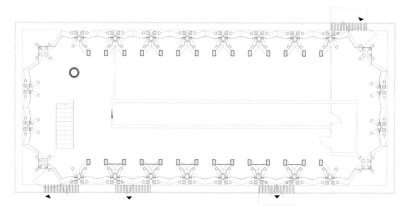

Ground floor plan / Plan du premier niveau

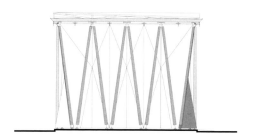

Noth elevation / Élévation nord

The Weaving Project Pavilion

This pavilion is an experimental project resulting from years of research that began with a visit to Japan to learn weaving techniques. Tests were carried out and scale models made in the studio during the design process. The structure can be made in bamboo or plywood, meaning that it is 100% recyclable. It can be unraveled and its components reused. The pavilion was presented at the NOTCH 10 Art & Culture Festival and was positioned at the center of The Village Plaza.

Der Pavillon ist ein experimentelles Projekt, das aus einer jahrelangen Forschung resultierte, die auf einer Reise nach Japan begann, um Webtechniken zu erlernen. Im Architektenbüro wurden dann Versuche durchgeführt und eine Attrappe für die Schaffung des Tragwerks gebaut. Dieses Tragwerk wird aus Bambus bzw. Furnierholz gebaut, also 100% wiederverwertbar, was ein Entweben und die Wiederverwendung der Bauteile ermöglicht. Der Pavillon wurde auf dem Festival NOTCH 10 Art & Culture vorgestellt und in der Mitte des The Village Plaza aufgestellt.

Une expérience conduite sur plusieurs années a abouti à cette structure cylindrique ouverte. Tout a commencé au Japon, lors d'un voyage d'études pour approfondir notre connaissance des cloisons tissées. Avant la construction, leurs structures ont été modélisées et des maquettes réalisées. Pouvant être tissé en bambou ou en contreplaqué, le pavillon est entièrement recyclable. Il suffit de défaire les panneaux pour en réutiliser les éléments. Il a été présenté au festival NOTCH 10 Art & Culture, puis placé au centre de The Village Plaza.

Het paviljoen is een experimenteel project dat het resultaat is van een jarenlang onderzoek, dat begon tijdens een studiereis naar Japan voor het leren van vlechttechnieken. Terug in de studio werden er tests uitgevoerd en maquettes van de structuur gemaakt. Die structuur is in bamboe of gelaagd hout vervaardigd en is dus voor 100% recyclebaar. Het kan worden ontvlochten en alle onderdelen kunnen worden hergebruikt. Het paviljoen werd gepresenteerd tijdens het NOTCH 10 Art & Culture festival en staat midden op het The Village Plaza.

Il padiglione è un progetto sperimentale risultante da una ricerca lunga vari anni, iniziata in occasione di un viaggio in Giappone per apprendere le tecniche di lavorazione del materiale. Tornati nello studio, gli architetti hanno realizzato prove e modellini per la creazione della struttura. Questa è costruita in bambù o legno compensato, quindi è riciclabile al 100%; ciò consente di suddividere e riutilizzare tutti i componenti. Il padiglione è stato presentato in occasione del festival NOTCH 10 Art & Culture al centro del Village Plaza.

El pabellón es un proyecto experimental resultante de una investigación de años iniciada en un viaje a Japón para aprender las técnicas de tejido. Una vez en el estudio, se realizaron procesos de prueba y maquetas para la creación de la estructura. Dicha estructura se fabrica en bambú o madera contrachapada; por lo tanto, es 100% reciclable, lo que permite destejer y volver a utilizar todos sus componentes de nuevo. El pabellón se presentó en el festival NOTCH 10 Art & Culture y se ha ubicado en el centro de The Village Plaza.

David A. García
Beijing, China, 2009
© David A. Garcia, Max Gerthel

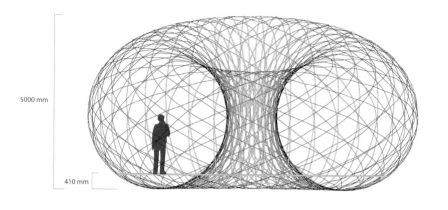

5000 mm

410 mm

8000 mm

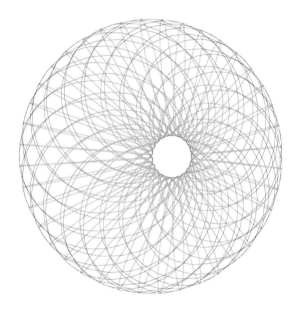

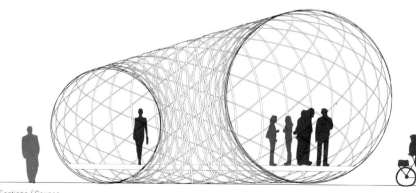

Sections / Coupes

The woven structure of the pavilion, which provides stability without the need for adhesives, nails, or other joints, can serve as a façade, roof, column, or foundation.

Die gewobene Struktur des Pavillons, welche Stabilität ohne Leimen, Nägel oder andere Verbindungstypen bietet, kann als Fassade, Dach, Säule oder Fundierung dienen.

La structure tissée du pavillon est parfaitement stable sans qu'il soit nécessaire d'utiliser adhésif, clou ou quelque autre procédé d'assemblage. Les panneaux sont à leur place dans les façades, les toitures, les colonnades ou les fondations.

De gevlochten structuur van het paviljoen, dat stabiel is zonder verlijming, spijkers of andere verbindingen, kan dienen als gevel, dak, zuil of fundering.

La struttura lavorata del padiglione, che offre stabilità senza necessità di colle, chiodi o altro tipo di giunti, può funzionare come facciata, soffitto, colonna o basamento.

La estructura tejida del pabellón, que ofrece estabilidad sin pegamento, clavos u otro tipo de unión, puede funcionar como fachada, techo, columna o cimiento.

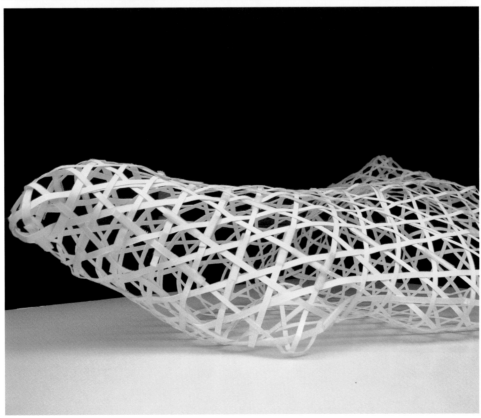

Canopy

This temporary structure was built in the courtyard of the PS1, as part of the summer activities program organized by MoMA for young architects. The architects considered bamboo to be an ideal material to create a metaphoric wooded landscape. Bamboo arches were used to form a vaulted canopy, leaving spaces to regulate humidity and temperature, in order to create four different environments: an open zone with a wading pool, a moisture zone, a living bamboo forest, and a dry zone with a sandy beach area.

Diese vorübergehende Struktur wurde im Innenhof des Kunstzentrums PS1 im Rahmen des Sommeraktivitätenprogramms des MoMA für Nachwuchsarchitekten aufgestellt. Die Architekten sahen Bambus als ideales Material zum Nachempfinden einer Waldlandschaft-Metapher. Es wurden Bambusbögen eingesetzt, die ein Gewölbe bilden, das Lichtungen lässt, um die Feuchtigkeit und Temperatur zu regeln. So wurden vier verschiedene Ambiente geschaffen: eine großzügige Fläche mit Teich, eine Feuchtzone, ein lebendiger Bambuswald und eine Trockenzone mit Sandstrand.

Cette structure éphémère fut construite dans la cour du PS1 Contemporary Art Center, dans le cadre du programme d'activités estivales du MoMA pour les jeunes architectes. Le bambou leur a apparu comme le matériau idéal pour être l'expression métaphorique d'un paysage boisé. Les arcs de bambou forment une voûte aérienne. Sous cette canopée, la régulation de l'humidité et de la température a permis la création de quatre milieux distincts : un vaste espace avec un bassin, une zone humide, une bambouseraie et une zone sèche avec une plage de sable.

Deze tijdelijke structuur werd gebouwd op de binnenplaats van het kunstcentrum PS1 in het kader van het zomeractiviteitenprogramma van het MoMA voor jonge architecten. De architecten vonden bamboe het ideale materiaal om een metafoor van een boslandschap te creëren. Er werd gebruik gemaakt van bamboebogen die een gewelf vormen waarin lichtopeningen zijn openlaten voor de vocht- en temperatuurregeling. Er zijn vier verschillende entourages gecreëerd: een ruime zone met vijver, een vochtige zone, een bos van levend bamboe en een droge zone met zandstrand.

Questa struttura temporanea è stata realizzata nel cortile del centro d'arte PS1 nell'ambito del programma di attività estive del MoMA per i giovani architetti. Gli architetti hanno pensato al bambù come materiale adatto per creare la metafora di un paesaggio boschivo. Sono stati utilizzati degli archi di bambù che formano una cupola e lasciano alcuni punti scoperti per regolare l'umidità e la temperatura, dando vita a quattro ambienti diversi: un'ampia zona arricchita da uno stagno, una zona umida, un bosco di bambù vivente e una zona secca con sabbia di spiaggia.

Esta estructura temporal se construyó en el patio del centro de arte PS1, dentro del programa de actividades de verano del MoMA para jóvenes arquitectos. Los arquitectos pensaron en el bambú como material idóneo para crear la metáfora de un paisaje boscoso. Se emplearon unos arcos de bambú, que forman una bóveda y dejan claros para regular la humedad y la temperatura, para generar cuatro ambientes distintos: una amplia zona con estanque, una zona húmeda, un bosque de bambú vivo y una zona seca con arena de playa.

nARQUITECTS
Long Island City, NY, United States, 2004
© nARQUITECTS

In order to achieve the best result for the installation, the architects studied that maximum curvature the bamboo could support and the degree of moisture necessary to be able to shape it.

Um eine Installation mit optimalem Ergebnis zu erreichen, haben die Architekten eruiert, welches die maximale Biegung ist, die Bambus aushalten kann, sowie den notwendigen Feuchtigkeitsgrad für dessen Behandlung.

Pour créer une installation avec un résultat optimal, les architectes calculèrent l'incurvation maximum qu'il était possible d'imposer au bambou, ainsi que le niveau d'humidité nécessaire pour le manipuler.

Voor het creëren van een installatie met een optimaal resultaat hebben de architecten onderzocht wat de maximale kromming was die bamboe kon verdragen en welke vochtigheidsgraad nodig was om die te bewerkstelligen.

Per creare un'installazione che garantisse un ottimo risultato, gli architetti hanno identificato la curvatura massima che può sopportare il bambù, oltre al grado di umidità necessario per manipolarlo.

Para crear una instalación con un óptimo resultado, los arquitectos estudiaron cuál era la curvatura máxima que podía soportar el bambú, así como el grado de humedad necesario para manipularlo.

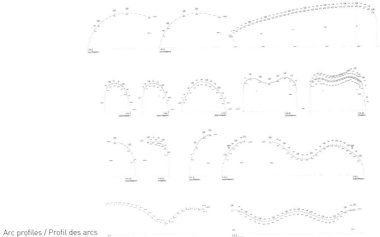

Arc profiles / Profil des arcs

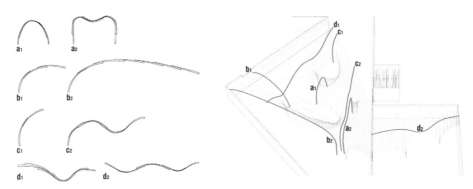

Splice types / Types d'épissure

a1-a2
Structural: ring beam to ring beam / Éléments structuraux : d'un soubassement à un autre

b1-b2
Structural: ring beam to wall strap / Éléments structuraux : du soubassement à un anneau

c1-c2
Structural cantiveler: ring beam to canopy edge / Éléments de saillie : de l'anneau au bord de la marquise

d1-d2
Non-structural / Éléments non structuraux

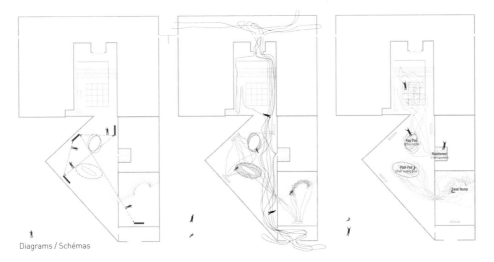

Diagrams / Schémas

landscape   weather

CANOPY

A canopy built with freshly cut green bamboo turns from green to tan over the summer /
Marquise construite en bambou vert fraîchement coupé qui devient marron durant l'été

Sand Hump　　Pool Pad　　Fog Pad　　Rainforest

100 deg 5% humidity   90 deg 15% humidity   80 deg 90% humidity   70 deg 100% humidity

Dips in the canopy provoke different modes of lounging in four distinct environments / Des inclinaisons dans la canopée plongent
les différents salons en quatre ambiances bien distinctes

July 21st: 11:00...　　　　*... 2:00*　　　　*... 6:00*

Pinches in the canopy produce a range of shadow densities / Les fluctuations dans la canopée produisent des effets d'ombres
de densités variées

Conceptual diagram / Schéma de conception

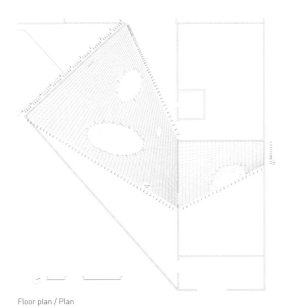

Floor plan / Plan

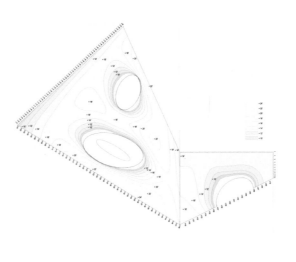

Topography / Topographie

Bamboo Dome Europe 2004

This project was built to mark the 4U international scout camp held in Luxembourg in 2004. The dome structure, symbolizing the world, was raised at the center of the campsite. This dome was built using bamboo rods measuring 8 m (26 ft) in length to reach a height of 11 m (36 ft), a diameter of 13 m (42.5 ft), and a base of 130 m² (1,400 sq ft). Engineer Christoph Tönges was the inventor of the CONBAM joining technique used in this project, which makes economical and large-scale bamboo construction possible.

Das Projekt wurde als Meilenstein für das internationale Pfadfinderlager 4U 2004 in Luxemburg geschaffen. Die Kuppelstruktur stellt symbolisch die Welt dar und wurde in der Mitte des Zeltlagers aufgestellt. Dieses Gewölbe wurde mit 8 m langen Bambusstäben gebaut, die eine Höhe von 11 m, einen Durchmesser von 13 m und eine Grundfläche von 130 m² erreichten. Der Ingenieur Christoph Tönges ist der Erfinder dieser CONBAM-Anschlusstechnik, die erstmals auf dieses Projekt Anwendung fand und eine ökonomische, großdimensionierte Tragkonstruktion aus Bambus ermöglicht.

Ce projet avait pour vocation de donner une visibilité au campement international scout 4U qui s'est tenu en 2004 au Luxembourg. La structure de la coupole symbolise le monde et occupe le centre du campement. Cette voûte a été construite avec des tiges de bambou de 8 m de long, qui permettent d'obtenir une hauteur de 11 m, un diamètre de 13 m et une base de 130 m². L'ingénieur Christoph Tönges est l'inventeur de la structure CONBAM utilisée pour ce projet. Ce type d'assemblage permet d'élever des constructions économiques de grandes dimensions en bambou.

Het project werd ontworpen als een mijlpaal voor het internationale scout 4U kamp dat in 2004 in Luxemburg werd gehouden. De structuur van de koepel staat symbool voor de wereld en is in het midden van het kamp geplaatst. Dit gewelf werd gebouwd met 8 m lange bamboestengels die 11 m hoog worden en heeft een diameter van 13 m en een grondvlak van 130 m². Ingenieur Christoph Tönges is de bedenker van de verbindingstechniek CONBAM die in dit project werd toegepast en waarmee met bamboe een economische constructie van grote afmetingen kon worden opgebouwd.

Il progetto è stato realizzato trasformandosi nel simbolo del campo scout internazionale 4U tenutosi nel 2004 in Lussemburgo. La struttura della cupola simboleggia il mondo ed è stata sistemata al centro del campo. Sono stati impiegati steli di bambù di 8 m di lunghezza che raggiungono un'altezza di 11 m, un diametro di 13 m e una base di 130 m². L'ingegniere Christoph Tönges è colui che ha inventato la tecnica di giunzione CONBAM applicata a questo progetto, che consente di realizzare una struttura economica e di grandi dimensioni con il bambù.

El proyecto se erigió como un hito para el campamento internacional scout 4U celebrado en 2004 en Luxemburgo. La estructura de la cúpula simboliza el mundo y se ubicó en el centro del campamento. Esta bóveda se construyó con cañas de bambú de 8 m de longitud que alcanzan una altura de 11 m, un diámetro de 13 m y una base de 130 m². El ingeniero Christoph Tönges fue el creador de la técnica de unión CONBAM aplicada en este proyecto, que permite una construcción económica y de grandes dimensiones con el bambú.

Christoph Tönges/CONBAM
Luxembourg, Luxembourg, 2004
© Christoph Tönges

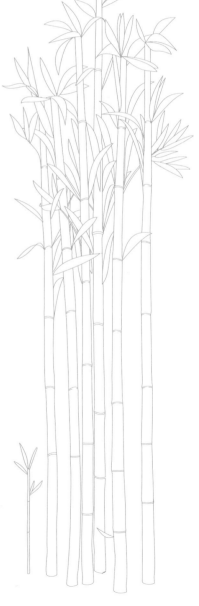

The bamboo dome is the result of combining two geometric structures: an icosahedron and a pentagonal dodecahedron. The number of poles were reduced as much as possible to make the structure lightweight.

Das Tragwerk der Bambus-Kuppel ist eine Kombination zweier geometrischer Strukturen: ein Ikosaeder und ein pentagonales Dodekaeder. Die Anzahl der Stangen wurde auf ein Minimum reduziert, um Leichtigkeit zu vermitteln.

Cette coupole de bambou est le fruit de l'union de deux structures géométriques : un icosaèdre et un dodécaèdre pentagonal. Le nombre de tiges est réduit au minimum pour alléger la structure.

De bouw van de bamboe koepel is een combinatie van twee geometrische structuren: een icosaëder (of regelmatig twintigvlak) en een vijfhoekig twaalfvlak. Het aantal staanders wordt tot een minimum beperkt zodat het geheel lichter lijkt.

La struttura della cupola di bambù combina due elementi geometrici: un icosaedro e un dodecaedro pentagonale. Il numero di canne viene ridotto al minimo per conferire leggerezza.

La construcción de la cúpula de bambú es una combinación de dos estructuras geométricas: un icosaedro y un dodecaedro pentagonal. El número de postes se reduce al mínimo para aportar ligereza.

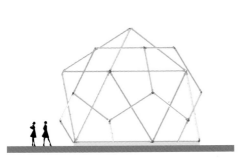
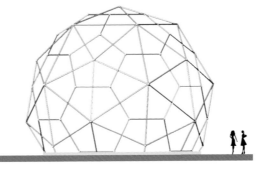
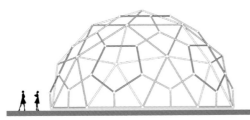
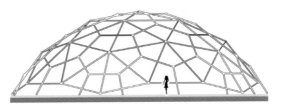

Construction process of evolution of the dome / Processus de l'évolution et de la construction de la coupole

Boo Tech

Boo Tech is a prototype consisting of a geodesic dome built with bamboo members, fabric, steel joints, and glass panes. The base of the dome rests on a steel plate located inside the tanks, stabilized to prevent the structure from overturning. The bamboo was used to form bars that were mechanically installed with special equipment. It was assembled following a complex geometry to demonstrate the static properties, lightness, versatility, and modernity of this material.

Boo Tech ist ein Prototyp aus einer geodätischen Kuppel, die aus Bambus- und Stoffelementen sowie Stahlfugen und Glaspaneelen besteht. Ihre Basis ruht auf einem Stahlblech im Inneren der Tanks, die so stabilisiert werden und ein Umkippen der Struktur verhindern. Bambus wurde in der Form von Latten verwendet und mechanisch durch Sonderausrüstung eingesetzt. Er wurde nach Maßgabe einer komplexen Geometrie verlegt, um die statischen Eigenschaften, die Leichtigkeit, Vielseitigkeit und Modernität dieses Materials unter Beweis zu stellen.

Boo Tech est le prototype d'une coupole géodésique construite avec des éléments en bambou, des tissus, des colliers d'acier et des plaques de verre. La base de la coupole repose sur une plaque d'acier située à l'intérieur des réservoirs, stabilisés pour éviter que la structure se renverse. Le bambou a été transformé en baguettes installées mécaniquement avec des palans spécialement conçus. Le montage fait appel à une géométrie complexe destinée à prouver la stabilité, la légèreté, la polyvalence et la modernité du matériau.

Boo Tech is een prototype van een geodesische koepel die is opgebouwd uit elementen van bamboe, textiel, stalen verbindingsstukken en glasplaten. De basis van de koepel steunt op een stalen plaat, gelegen binnenin tanks die gestabiliseerd zijn om te voorkomen dat de structuur kantelt. Het bamboe is gebruikt in de vorm van latten en wordt mechanisch geïnstalleerd met speciale apparatuur. Het is gemonteerd volgens een complexe geometrie die de statische eigenschappen, lichtheid, veelzijdigheid en moderniteit van dit materiaal laat zien.

Boo Tech è un prototipo composto da una cupola geodesica realizzata con elementi di bambù, tessuti, giunti di acciaio e lastre di vetro. La base della cupola poggia su una lastra di acciaio posta all'interno dei serbatoi, stabilizzati per evitare il rovesciamento della struttura. Il bambù è stato utilizzato sotto forma di listoni e installato meccanicamente con delle apposite pale. È stato montato seguendo una geometria complessa per dimostrare le proprietà statiche, la leggerezza, la versatilità e la modernità di questo materiale.

Boo Tech es un prototipo consistente en una cúpula geodésica construida con elementos de bambú, tejidos, juntas de acero y placas de vidrio. La cúpula apoya su base en una placa de acero situada en el interior de los tanques, estabilizados para evitar que vuelque la estructura. El bambú ha sido utilizado en forma de listones y se ha instalado mecánicamente con palas especiales. Se montço siguiendo una geometría compleja para demostrar las propiedades estáticas, la ligereza, la versatilidad y la modernidad de este material.

Mauricio Cárdenas, Roberto Banfi, Giacomo Schirru/Studio Cárdenas
Milan, Italy, 2009
© Studio Cárdenas

Section and plan / Coupe et plan

The structure was created from prefabricated triangular bamboo elements. This micro-architecture prototype is based on a methodology of fast and simple assembly combining traditional crafts and mass production.

Das Tragwerk wurde aus dreieckigen Elementen aus vorgefertigtem Bambus geschaffen. Dieser Prototyp der Mikroarchitektur basiert auf einer einfachen und raschen Montageweise, die Handwerk und Massenproduktion verbindet.

Cette structure est un assemblage d'éléments triangulaires préfabriqués en bambou. Ce prototype de micro-architecture demande une méthode de montage aussi simple que rapide qui associe procédés artisanaux et production de masse.

De structuur is opgebouwd uit geprefabriceerde driehoekige bamboe elementen. Dit prototype van micro-architectuur is gebaseerd op een methodologie van eenvoudige en snelle montage waarin ambachtswerk en massaproductie gecombineerd zijn.

La struttura è stata realizzata partendo da elementi triangolari prefabbricati in bambù. Questo prototipo di microarchitettura si basa su un metodo di montaggio semplice e veloce che integra produzione artigianale e di massa.

La estructura se creó a partir de elementos triangulares prefabricados de bambú. Este prototipo de microarquitectura se basa en un método de montaje sencillo y rápido que aúna artesanía y producción en masa.

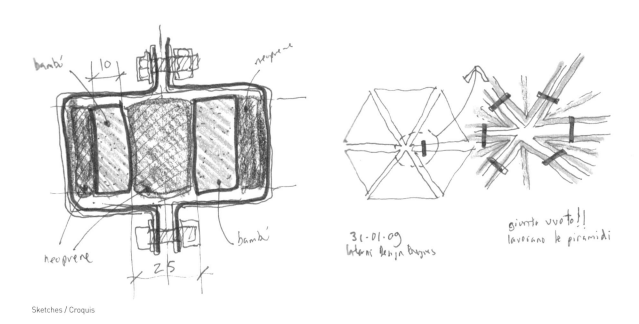

Sketches / Croquis

31-01-09
laterni Benja Bugnes

giunto vuoto!!
lavorano le piramidi

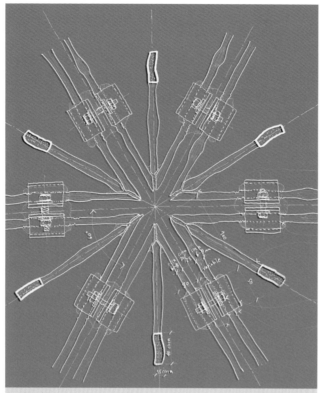

Floor plan / Plan

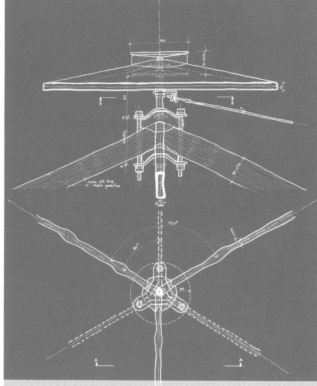

Plan-section B-B and section A-A / Plan-coupe B-B et coupe A-A

Drawing of the internal energy / Dessin de l'énergie interne

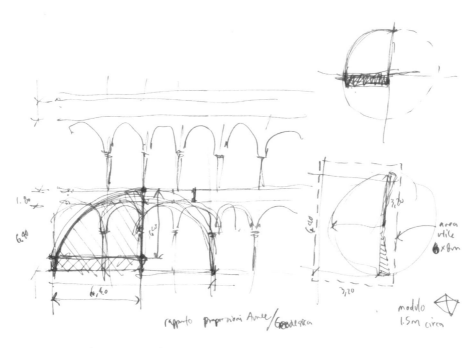

Conceptual sketches / Dessins de conception

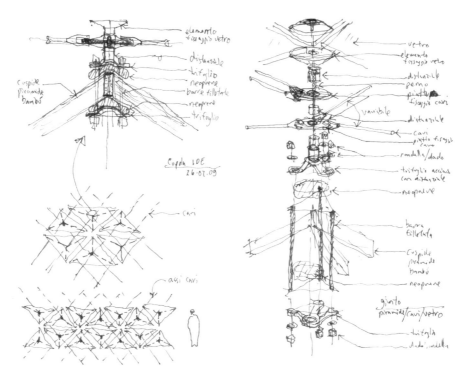

Construction drawings / Dessins de construction

Bamboo Starscraper

The name of this project comes from the geometry of the six-pointed star characterizing its floor plan. The structure was finished with six bamboo poles in the center lashed together to form simple but elegant transversal bars; if visitors stands below them, they can see the star they form. From this point, a series of concentric bamboo columns are tensed with a synthetic rope made from aramid, which is stronger than steel.

Das Projekt verdankt seinen Namen der Geometrie des sechszackigen Sterns, auf dem sein Strukturplan basiert. Die Struktur war mit sechs Bambushalmen in der Mitte abgeschlossen, die aneinander gebunden waren, um einfache aber elegante Längsstangen zu bilden; setzte sich der Betrachter darunter, so konnte er den Stern erkennen, den diese bildeten. An diesem Punkt wurde eine konzentrische Reihe an Bambussäulen durch ein synthetisches Aramidfaser-Seil in Spannung gehalten, das stärker als Stahl ist.

Cette structure doit son nom à son plan géométrique en forme d'étoile à six branches. L'assemblage des six mâts qui se rapprochent en son centre crée un motif transversal aussi simple qu'élégant. En passant en dessous, le visiteur découvrait l'étoile ainsi formée. De ce point, les mâts faits de tiges de bambou placés tout autour étaient maintenus en tension par une corde en polyamide aromatique, plus résistante que l'acier.

De naam van het project is afgeleid van een geometrie met zes punten waarop het structurele grondplan is gebaseerd. De structuur was afgewerkt met zes bamboestokken in het midden, die onderling waren vastgebonden zodat ze eenvoudige maar elegante dwarsbalken vormden; van onderaf gezien leken ze een ster te vormen. Vanaf dat punt werd een concentrische serie bamboe zuilen gespannen met synthetische vezel touw van aramidevezel dat sterker is dan staal.

Il nome del progetto si deve alla geometria della stella a sei punte sulla quale si basa il piano strutturale. La struttura era rinforzata da sei travi di bambù situate al centro e fissate tra loro per creare delle semplici ma eleganti barre trasversali; se lo spettatore si posizionava al di sotto di questa poteva contemplare la stella che si formava. Da questo punto una serie concentrica di colonne di bambù veniva mantenuta in tensione con una corda in fibra sintetica aramidica, più forte dell'acciaio.

El nombre del proyecto se debe a la geometría de la estrella de seis puntas sobre la que se basa su plan estructural. La estructura está rematada por seis varas de bambú situadas en el centro y atadas entre sí para crear unas sencillas pero elegantes barras transversales; si el espectador se sitúa debajo, puede contemplar la estrella que formaban. Desde este punto, una serie concéntrica de columnas de bambú se mantiene en tensión con cuerda de fibra sintética de aramida, más fuerte que el acero.

Gerard Minakawa/Bamboo DNA
Indio, CA, United States, 2009
© Jeff Clark

The bamboo structure was designed to withstand the strong gusts of wind that are typical of the region. At the tip of the central spire, a combustion system was installed to produce a gas-fired flame.

Bambus wurde als Tragwerk entworfen, um den starken Windböen in dieser Gegend zu trotzen. Oberhalb der Hauptturmspitze wurde eine Verbrennungsanlage installiert, die Gasflammen ausspuckte.

Le bambou a été utilisé dans la structure pour résister aux fortes bourrasques de vent habituelles dans cette région. Un système de combustion installé au sommet générait de grandes flammes de gaz.

Het bamboe vormt onderdeel van de structuur, om de windstoten, kenmerkend voor het gebied, het hoofd te kunnen bieden. Helemaal bovenaan de spits was een verbrandingssysteem geïnstalleerd waaruit een gasvlam brandde.

Il bambù è stato pensato strutturalmente per sostenere le forti raffiche di vento tipiche della zona. Nella parte alta della guglia centrale è stato inserito un sistema di combustione a gas.

La estructura de bambú se diseñó para soportar las fuertes rachas de viento típicas de la zona. En lo alto de la aguja central se instaló un sistema de combustión que emitía llamaradas de gas.

Microclimatico Pavilion

This pavilion was presented in the Fabbrica del Vapore for the Milan International Furniture Fair. This technically advanced structure basically comprises a frame assembled in steel (advanced technology) and bamboo (traditional technology). The design is for a floating deck with a metal and woven bamboo frame with steel joints. It is completed by a crosspiece that supports the polycarbonate panels and which works as a thermal buffer, owing to the water sprinking system that lowers the roof temperature.

Dieser Pavillon wurde auf der Internationalen Möbelmesse in Mailand in der Fabbrica del Vapore präsentiert. Diese technisch fortschrittliche Konstruktion besteht im Wesentlichen aus einem auf Stahl montierten Tragwerk (Hightech) und Bambus (traditionelle Technik). Das Design ist ein schwimmender Boden mit Metallgerüst und Bambus, der in Stahlfugen eingewebt ist. Das ganze wird durch einen Kreuzbalken gekrönt, der die Polykarbonatlamellen stützt und als Wärmepuffer dient, dank eines Wassersprenkelsystems, das die Deckentemperatur senkt.

Ce pavillon fut présenté au Salon international du meuble de Milan, dans la Fabbrica del Vapore. Cette construction innovante associe des éléments complexes en acier pour les assemblages (technologie de pointe) à une structure traditionnelle en bambou. Cette pièce flottante est construite comme une vannerie mais les ligatures classiques sont ici remplacées par des colliers d'acier. L'assemblage en croix supporte les feuilles de polycarbonate du toit. Le système d'aspersion d'eau fait baisser la température de la toiture et réduit les échanges thermiques.

Dit paviljoen werd gepresenteerd op de Internationale Meubelbeurs van Milaan, in de Fabbrica del Vapore. Deze technologisch geavanceerde constructie is opgebouwd uit een gemonteerde staalstructuur (geavanceerde technologie) en bamboe (traditionele techniek). Het ontwerp is een drijvende woning met een metalen draagconstructie en gevlochten bamboe met stalen verbindingsstukken. Het loopt uit in een kruisbalk die de policarbonaat laminaten ondersteunt en die dienst doet als thermische buffer. Dankzij een besproeiingssysteem wordt de temperatuur van het dak verlaagd.

Questo padiglione è stato presentato in occasione del Salone Internazionale del Mobile di Milano, nella Fabbrica del Vapore. Si tratta di una costruzione tecnicamente avanzata, composta sostanzialmente da una struttura in acciaio (tecnologia di avanguardia) e bambù (tecnica tradizionale). Il progetto prevede un piano flottante con telaio in metallo e bambù intrecciato con giunti d'acciaio. La struttura culmina in un transetto che supporta le lastre in policarbonato e funziona da ammortizzatore termico grazie al sistema ad aspersione di acqua che riduce la temperatura del tetto.

Este pabellón fue presentado en el Salón Internacional del Mueble de Milán, en la Fabbrica del Vapore. Esta construcción técnicamente avanzada se compone de una estructura montada en acero (tecnología avanzada) y bambú (técnica tradicional). El diseño es un piso flotante con armazón de metal y bambú tejido con juntas de acero. Culmina en un crucero que soporta las láminas de policarbonato y que funciona como amortiguador térmico gracias al sistema de aspersión de agua, que reduce la temperatura de la cubierta.

Mauricio Cárdenas/Studio Cárdenas
Milan, Italy, 2006
© Studio Cárdenas

The design is transparent and elegant in order to adapt to different uses in urban or rural sttings. The modular structure makes it easy to assemble, and it adapts well to its surroundings.

Das Design ist transparent und elegant und wurde so konzipiert, um sich verschiedenen Nutzungen in städtischen oder ländlichen Umgebungen anzupassen. Einfach zu montieren, dank seiner Modulstruktur, passt es sich auch gut in sein Umfeld ein.

Transparent et élégant, ce volume a été conçu pour de multiples usages dans des contextes urbains et ruraux. D'un montage facile grâce à sa structure modulaire, il s'adapte bien à son environnement.

Het ontwerp is transparant en elegant en is toepasbaar voor verschillende gebruiken, zowel in de stad als op het platteland. Het is eenvoudig te monteren dankzij de modulaire structuur en is aanpasbaar aan de omgeving.

Il progetto è trasparente ed elegante, concepito per adattarsi a usi diversi, sia nei contesti urbani che rurali. Facile da montare grazie alla sua struttura modulare, si adatta bene al contesto circostante.

El diseño es transparente y elegante, y ha sido concebido para adaptarse a usos diferentes en contextos urbanos o rurales. Fácil de montar gracias a su estructura modular, se adapta bien al entorno.

Section B-B / Coupe B-B

Floor plan / Plan

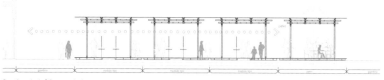

Section A-A / Coupe A-A

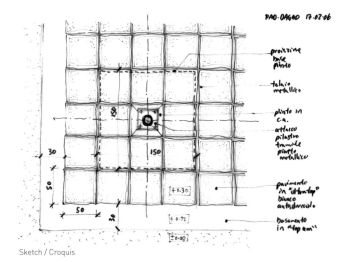

Sketch / Croquis

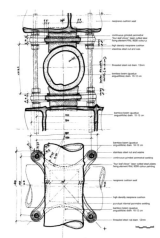

Construction drawing / Dessin de construction

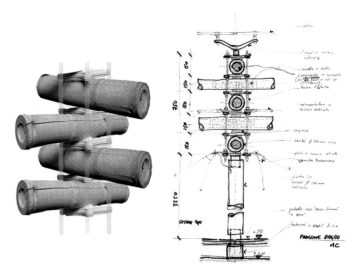

Rendering and sketch / Représentation en 3D et croquis

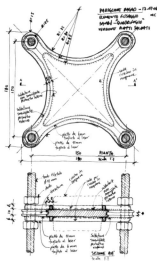

Sketch / Croquis

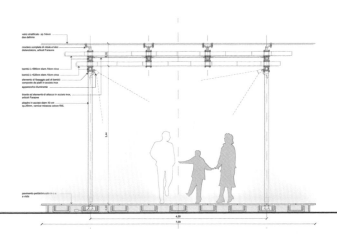

Side view / Vue latérale

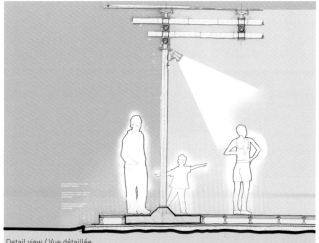

Detail view / Vue détaillée

Ideale Stadt – Reale Projekte
Architekten von Gerkan, Marg
und Partner in China

Bamboo Sculpture
Pinakothek

This sculpture was designed for the "Ideale Stadt – Reale Projekte, Architekten von Gerkan, Marg and Partner in China" exhibition, held at the Pinakothek der Moderne in Munich. This bamboo sculpture, standing 8 m (26 ft) tall has the structure of a traditional Chinese scaffold. It was designed as a gesture of friendship and as a demonstration of the physical application of local technical knowledge in the Chinese construction sector. The bamboo canes were tied with an original Chinese technique using plastic strips from Hong Kong.

Diese Skulptur wurde für die Ausstellung „Ideale Stadt – Reale Projekte, Architekten von Gerkan, Marg and Partner in China" entworfen und in der Pinakothek der Moderne in München aufgestellt. Die 8 m hohe Bambus-Skulptur besitzt die Gestalt eines in China üblichen Baugerüstes und steht als Willkommensgeste und als Dokumentation der regional geprägten handwerklichen und technologischen Kenntnisse im chinesischen Baugewerbe. Die Bambus-Rohre wurden mit chinesischen Bindetechniken und Kunststoffbändern aus Hong Kong verbunden.

Réalisée pour l'exposition « Ideale Stadt – Reale Projekte, Architekten von Gerkan, Marg and Partner in China », cette sculpture tout en bambou, de 8 m de haut, a été présentée à la Pinakothek der Moderne de Munich. Sa structure est celle des échafaudages traditionnels chinois. En même temps qu'un geste d'amitié entre les peuples, c'est surtout une preuve tangible de la validité des connaissances techniques mises en œuvre dans le secteur de la construction en Chine. Les tiges de bambou sont attachées par une ligature originale chinoise réalisée avec des bracelets de plastique importés de Hong Kong.

Deze sculptuur is ontworpen voor de tentoonstelling "Ideale Stadt – Reale Projekte, Architekten von Gerkan, Marg and Partner in China" die in de Pinakothek der Moderne te München werd gehouden. Deze 8 m hoge bamboe sculptuur heeft de structuur van een traditionele Chinese steiger. Hij is ontworpen als teken van vriendschap en tegelijkertijd als fysiek bewijs van de plaatselijke technische kennis van de Chinese bouwsector. De bamboestengels zijn door middel van een oorspronkelijke Chinese techniek met plastic stroken uit Hong Kong aan elkaar verbonden.

Questa scultura è stata progettata per la mostra «Ideale Stadt – Reale Projekte, Architekten von Gerkan, Marg and Partner in China», tenutasi nella Pinakothek der Moderne di Monaco. La scultura di 8 m di bambù ha la struttura di un'impalcatura tradizionale cinese. Progettata per simboleggiare un gesto di amicizia, è nello stesso tempo una «prova di fisica applicata» delle conoscenze tecniche locali dell'ingegneria costruttiva cinese. Le canne di bambù sono state legate con una tecnica originale cinese con tiranti in plastica di Hong Kong.

Esta escultura de 8 m de bambú fue diseñada para la exposición «Ideale Stadt – Reale Projekte, Architekten von Gerkan, Marg and Partner in China», celebrada en la Pinakothek der Moderne de Múnich. Tiene la estructura de un andamio tradicional chino y se diseñó como un gesto de amistad y, al mismo tiempo, como prueba física de la aplicación de los conocimientos técnicos locales del sector chino de la construcción. Las cañas de bambú se ataron con una técnica original china de tiras de plástico de Hong Kong.

Christoph Tönges / CONBAM (detailed design and execution), GMP – Architeketen von Gerkan, Marg und Partner (idea)
Munich, Germany, 2005
© Christoph Tönges

This project is a tribute to Chinese scaffolding, which is built entirely of bamboo. It can be made to reach extreme heights of up to 80 stories and its appearance is handcrafted. They are very stable and are easy to assemble.

Dieses Projekt ist eine Hommage an die mit Bambus gebauten leichten chinesischen Baugerüste. Mit diesen handwerklich aussehenden Gerüsten können extreme Höhen von 80 Stöcken erreicht werden. Sie sind sehr stabil und leicht zusammenzufügen.

Cette œuvre rend hommage aux échafaudages chinois entièrement en bambou. Ils peuvent être très hauts puisqu'ils font jusqu'à 80 étages. D'apparence artisanale, ils sont très stables et faciles à monter.

Dit project is een eerbetoon aan de Chinese steigers die helemaal uit bamboe zijn opgebouwd. Ze kunnen extreme hoogtes van wel 80 verdiepingen bereiken en zien er ambachtelijk uit. Ze zijn zeer stabiel en kunnen eenvoudig worden gemonteerd.

Questo progetto vuole rendere omaggio alle impalcature cinesi realizzate interamente in bambù. Possono raggiungere altezze estreme, fino a 80 piani, mantenendo un aspetto artigianale. Sono molto stabili e facilmente assemblabili.

Este proyecto es un homenaje a los andamios chinos construidos íntegramente con bambú. Pueden alcanzar alturas extremas (hasta 80 pisos) y su apariencia es artesanal. Son muy estables y de fácil ensamblaje.

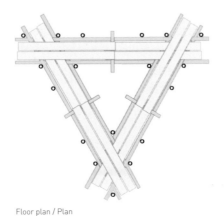

Floor plan / Plan

Bamboo Block House

Three greenhouses built with the Bamboo Block House system were presented at the 2010 Milan International Furniture Fair. This construction system is based on the transformation of each bamboo cane in a traditional and waste-free way. Each cane is split vertically into two equal sections and positioned vertically to form a module comprising four members. The strips leftover from the initial splitting process are used to make the beams form part of the roof.

Während der Internationalen Möbelmesse in Mailand 2010 wurden drei Wintergärten vorgestellt, die als sogenannte Bamboo Block House ausgeführt waren: ein Bausystem, das aus der Veränderung eines jeden Bambusrohrs auf traditionelle Weise und frei von Rückständen entsteht. Jedes Rohr wird senkrecht in zwei gleiche Hälften zerschnitten und diese werden dann asymmetrisch angebracht, um ein Modul aus vier Elementen zu bilden. Die beim ursprünglichen Zurechtschneiden übrigbleibenden Bambusstäbe werden zur Erzeugung von Balken genutzt, die für die Decke eingesetzt werden.

Ces trois serres construites avec le système Bamboo Block House ont été présentées au Salon international du meuble de Milan en 2010. Ce système de construction exploite la transformation de chaque tige de bambou, selon les méthodes traditionnelles, qui les débarrasse de tout résidu. Chaque tige est coupée verticalement en deux sections égales qui sont ensuite positionnées de manière asymétrique pour former un module composé de quatre éléments. Les éclisses restantes de la première coupe sont utilisées pour la fabrication des fermes de la charpente.

Tijdens de Internationale Meubelbeurs van Milaan van 2010 zijn drie serres gepresenteerd die opgebouwd zijn met het zogenaamde Bamboo Block House: een bouwsysteem dat voortkomt uit het op traditionele en afvalvrije wijze omvormen van bamboestengels. Iedere stengel wordt verticaal in twee gelijke delen gesneden en wordt asymmetrisch geplaatst, zodat er een module ontstaat die bestaat uit vier elementen. De stroken die na de aanvankelijke snede zijn overgebleven worden benut voor de vervaardiging van de balken die onderdeel zijn van het dak.

In occasione del Salone Internazionale del Mobile del 2010 sono state presentate tre serre costruite con il cosiddetto Bamboo Block House: un sistema costruttivo che nasce dalla trasformazione di ogni stelo di bambù in modo tradizionale e senza produrre rifiuti. Ogni stelo viene tagliato verticalmente in due sezioni uguali, che vengono sistemate in modo asimmetrico per formare un modulo composto da quattro elementi. Le strisce inutilizzate dopo il taglio iniziale servono per la produzione delle travi che andranno a costituire il tetto.

Durante el Salón Internacionaldel Mueble de Milán de 2010 se presentaron tres invernaderos construidos con el sistema Bamboo Block House, que surge de la transformación de cada tallo de bambú de la manera tradicional y libre de residuos. Los tallos se cortan verticalmente en dos secciones iguales y se colocan de manera asimétrica para formar un módulo compuesto de cuatro elementos. Las tiras sobrantes del corte inicial se aprovechan para la producción de las vigas que formarán parte de la cubierta.

Mauricio Cárdenas, Salma Abarro/ Studio Cárdenas
Milan, Italy, 2010
© Studio Cárdenas

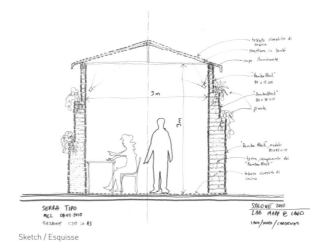

Sketch / Esquisse

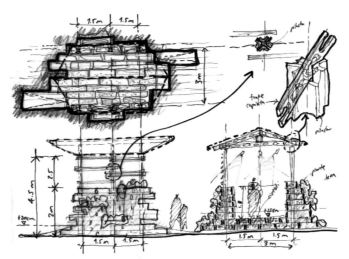

Conceptual sketches / Dessins de conception

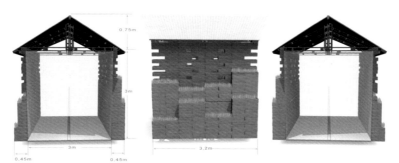

Front elevation / Élévation avant   Side elevation / Élévation latérale   Rear elevation / Élévation arrière

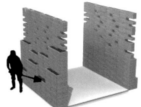

Installing the carpet and walls with the inclusion of bamboo / Installation du tapis et des parois avec l'inclusion de tiges de bambou

Including land within blocks of bamboo / Inclusion de la terre à l'intérieur des blocs de bambou

Insertion of the plants and the roof structure / Insertion des plantes et de la structure du plafond

Closing of the roof with cloth and resin / Fermeture du toit avec une toile et de la résine

Assembly diagram / Schéma d'assemblage

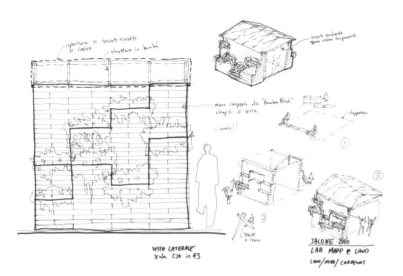

Conceptual sketches / Dessins de conception

Installing of the green carpet (10 × 2,5 m) and bamboo blocks / Installation du tapis vert (10 × 2,5 m) et des blocs de bambou

Insertion of cement in the blocks / Insertion du ciment dans les blocs

Walls assembling / Montage des parois

Including land in sacks and installation of the roof structure / Inclusion de sacs de terre et pose de la structure du toit

Planting and installation of communication and roofing material / Installation des plantes, du matériel de communication et de la couverture du toit

Completed structure / Structure montée

Sketch / Croquis

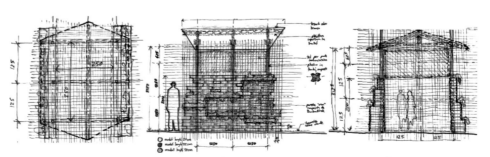

Floor plan / Plan   Side elevation / Élévation latérale   Front elevation / Élévation frontale

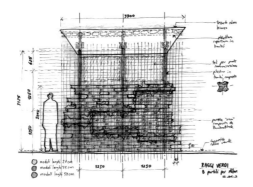

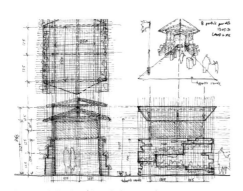

Conceptual sketches / Croquis de conception

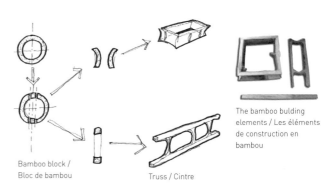

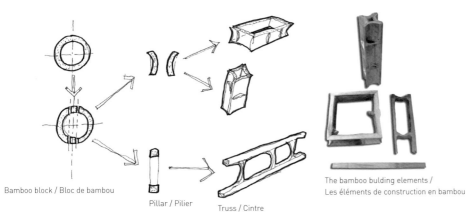

Bamboo block / Bloc de bambou

Pillar / Pilier

Truss / Cintre

The bamboo bulding elements /
Les éléments de construction en bambou

Drawing elements 1 / Dessins des éléments 1

Bamboo block /
Bloc de bambou

Truss / Cintre

The bamboo bulding
elements / Les éléments
de construction en
bambou

Drawing elements 2 / Dessins des éléments 2

In this case, the structure is formed by two dry-assembled side walls 1.20 m (4 ft) in height, and six pillars that support the bamboo roof. The modules were filled with soil and plants.

In diesem Fall besteht die Struktur aus zwei Seitenwänden, die trocken 1,20 m hoch gezogen wurden, und sechs Säulen, auf denen das Bambusdach ruht. Die Module wurden mit Erde und Pflanzen gefüllt.

Cette structure comprend deux murs latéraux de 1,20 m de haut montés à sec. Le toit en bambou repose sur six piliers. Les modules jardinières seront remplis de terre et de plantes.

In dit geval bestaat de structuur uit twee zijwanden van 1,20 m hoog die zonder mortel zijn opgebouwd en zes pilaren die het bamboedak ondersteunen. De modules zijn gevuld met grond en planten.

In questo caso la struttura è composta da due pareti laterali realizzate a secco di 1,20 m di altezza e sei pilastri che sorreggono il soffitto di bambù. I moduli sono stati riempiti di terra e piante.

En este caso, la estructura se compone de dos paredes laterales montadas en seco de 1,20 m de alto y seis pilares que sostienen el techo de bambú. Los módulos se llenaron con tierra y plantas.

The DROP

The project design was commissioned for the Boom Festival held in Portugal in 2010. The building is actually three spaces in one: a visionary art gallery, a space for performing arts creation, and a projection room-workshop. The structure consists of different materials: bamboo posts, sand, locally-sourced stones, fabric, and red clay. The different spaces make up an area of 4,800 m² (51,700 sq ft). The bamboo was sloped to form different landscapes, which act as tunnels.

Der Entwurf dieses Projekts wurde vom Boom Festival in Auftrag gegeben, das 2010 in Portugal stattfand. Das Bauwerk besteht in Wirklichkeit aus drei Räumen, die einen einzigen bilden: eine Galerie visionärer Kunst, ein Bereich für die Kreation von Bühnenkünsten und eine Kinowerkstatt. Die Struktur besteht aus verschiedenen Materialien: Bambuspfetten, Sand, örtliche Steine, Stoff und rote Tonerde. Die verschiedenen Räume bilden einen 4.800 m²-großen Komplex. Bambus wurde geneigt aufgestellt, um die verschiedenen Gänge, die als Tunnel angelegt waren, zu formen.

Commandé pour l'édition 2010 du Boom Festival, au Portugal, ce tunnel à ciel ouvert consiste en trois espaces qui n'en font qu'un : une galerie d'art visionnaire, une zone de création réservée aux arts de la scène et un ciné-atelier. La structure fait appel à plusieurs matériaux : tiges de bambou, sable, pierre locale, toiles et argile rouge. Les différentes zones forment un ensemble de 4 800 m². Les éclisses recourbées créent des passages qui ressemblent à des tunnels.

Het ontwerp voor dit project is opgedragen door het Boom Festival dat in 2010 in Portugal werd gehouden. De constructie bestaat in werkelijkheid uit drie ruimtes die samen een geheel vormen: een galerie voor visionaire kunst, een creatieve ruimte voor podiumkunsten en een filmwerkplaats. De structuur is opgebouwd uit verschillende materialen: bamboe staanders, zand, plaatselijke natuursteen, stof en rode klei. De verschillende ruimtes vormen samen een totaaloppervlak van 4.800 m². Het bamboe is schuin geïnstalleerd om verschillende landschappen te creëren die dienst doen als tunnels.

La fase progettuale di questo lavoro è stata incaricata dal Boom Festival tenutosi in Portogallo nel 2010. La struttura si compone in realtà di tre spazi che creano una sola unità: una galleria di arte visionaria, una zona di creazione di arti sceniche e un cine-laboratorio. La struttura è composta da diversi materiali: aste di bambù, sabbia, pietra locale, stoffa e argilla rossa. I vari spazi creano un insieme di 4.800 m². Il bambù è stato montato inclinato per creare i diversi paesaggi, che funzionano come gallerie.

El diseño de este proyecto fue encargado por el Boom Festival celebrado en 2010 en Portugal. La construcción son en realidad tres espacios que forman uno solo: una galería de arte visionario, una zona de creación de artes escénicas y una sala de proyección-taller. La estructura se compone de diversos materiales: postes de bambú, arena, piedra local, telas y arcilla roja. Los diferentes espacios forman un conjunto de 4.800 m². El bambú se instaló inclinado para crear los distintos pasajes, que funcionan como túneles.

Gerard Minakawa/Bamboo DNA
Idanha-a-Nova, Portugal, 2010
© Gerard Minakawa

The placement of bamboo with different lengths and widths enabled different walls and ceilings to be created. The art gallery features sloping bamboo walls.

Die Anordnung des Bambus mit variablen Höhen und Breiten hat es ermöglicht, verschiedene Wände und Dächer zu schaffen. Besonders ragt die Kunstgalerie hervor, in der das Material durch die Mauern geneigt ist.

En jouant avec la disposition des bambous, de hauteur et de largeur variables, on modifie l'apparence des murs et toits. La galerie d'art, aux murs en bambous recourbés, est particulièrement remarquable.

De plaatsing van het bamboe met variabele hoogte en breedte maakt het mogelijk om verschillende muren en plafonds te creëren. Opvallend is de kunstgalerie, waar het materiaal schuin is geplaatst, waardoor er muren ontstaan.

La disposizione del bambù ad altezze e larghezze variabili consente di creare pareti e soffitti diversificati. Degna di nota è la galleria d'arte, dove il materiale si inclina per dare vita alle pareti.

La disposición del bambú con alturas y anchos variables permite crear diferentes paredes y techos. Destaca la galería de arte, donde el material se inclina para crear los muros.

Bug Dome

The architects of this bamboo structure were inspired by the particular morphology of insects. This space was used during the SZHK Biennale for entertainment events and as a shelter for illegal workers. This original "cocoon" was conceived as a refuge for modern man wanting to escape from the explosive force of urban development in Chinese cities. The bamboo construction methods were based on the local knowledge of rural Guangxi, the province from where the construction workers had emigrated.

Die Architekten haben sich an der besonderen Morphologie der Insekten inspiriert, um diese Bambusstruktur zu bauen. Der Raum wurde während der SZHK Biennale für Unterhaltungs-Events und als Unterschlupf für illegale Arbeiter genutzt. Dieser originelle „Kokon" ist konzeptuell ein Zufluchtsort für den modernen Menschen, der dem Stress des Baubooms der chinesischen Großstädte entfliehen möchte. Die Baumethoden mit Bambus basieren auf dem lokalen und ruralen Wissen aus Guangxi, das die Gastbauarbeiter mitgebracht haben.

La morphologie particulière des insectes a inspiré aux architectes cette structure en bambou. Cet espace a accueilli plusieurs manifestations lors de la SZHK Biennale avant de devenir un abri pour les sans-papiers. Conceptuellement, ce cocon est un refuge pour l'homme moderne qui tente d'échapper à la force explosive de l'urbanisme des villes chinoises. Les méthodes utilisées pour l'assemblage des bambous s'appuient sur les connaissances locales et rurales du Guangxi, transmises par les ouvriers spécialement venus pour monter la construction.

Voor het creëren van deze bamboe structuur lieten de architecten zich inspireren door de opmerkelijke morfologie van insecten. De ruimte werd tijdens de SZHK-biënnale gebruikt voor ludieke evenementen en als schuilplaats voor illegale arbeiders. Deze originele "cocon" is een conceptuele schuilplaats voor de moderne mens die wil ontsnappen aan de explosieve kracht van het urbanisme van de Chinese steden. De bouwmethodes met bamboe zijn gebaseerd op de plaatselijke en rurale kennis van Guangxi, waar de geëmigreerde bouwvakkers vandaan kwamen.

Gli architetti si sono ispirati alla particolare morfologia degli insetti per creare questa struttura di bambù. Lo spazio è stato utilizzato durante la SZHK Biennale per eventi di intrattenimento e come riparo per i lavoratori illegali. Questa sorta di bozzolo originale è concettualmente un rifugio per l'uomo moderno che desidera fuggire dalla forza esplosiva dell'urbanismo della città cinese. I metodi di costruzione con il bambù si sono basati sulle conoscenze locali e rurali di Guangxi, portate dai lavoratori emigrati operanti nel settore edilizio.

Los arquitectos se inspiraron en la particular morfología de los insectos para crear esta estructura de bambú. El espacio se utilizó durante la SZHK Biennale para eventos de entretenimiento y como cobijo para los trabajadores ilegales. Este original «capullo» es conceptualmente un refugio para el hombre moderno que quiere escapar de la fuerza explosiva del urbanismo de la ciudad china. Los métodos de construcción con bambú se basaron en el conocimiento local y rural de la región de Guangxi, de donde habían emigrado los trabajadores de la construcción.

Casagrande Laboratory Taiwan
Shenzhen, China, 2009
© Hsieh Ying-Chun, Marco Casagrande, Roan Ching-Yueh

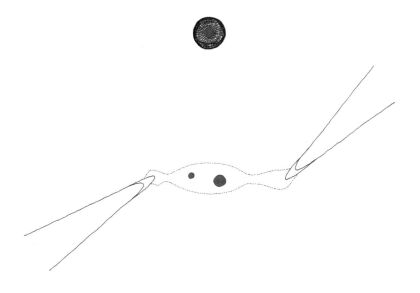

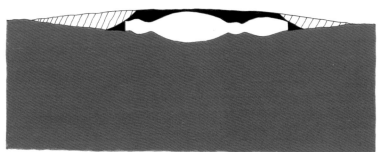

Sketch / Croquis

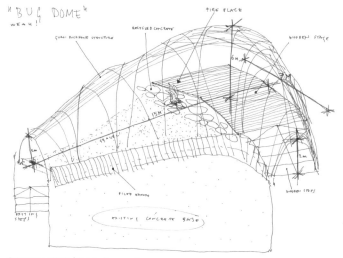

Conceptual sketch / Dessin de conception

The space appears weak and flexible, and its construction was the result of participative planning by the designers and construction with local building knowledge.

Das Gebäude macht einen feingliedrigen und flexiblen Eindruck, sein Bau ist das Ergebnis der Planung, an der Designer und Bauarbeiter beteiligt waren und lokales Bauwissen eingeflossen ist.

D'aspect fragile et flexible, cet édifice est le fruit d'une collaboration entre ses concepteurs, les ouvriers du bâtiment et les techniques de construction traditionnelles chinoises.

Het gebouw ziet er breekbaar en flexibel uit en is het resultaat van de gezamenlijke planning van de ontwerpers en de bouwvakkers en van de plaatselijke kennis van bouwen.

L'edificio ha un aspetto debole e flessibile; la struttura è il risultato della pianificazione partecipativa tra i progettisti, gli operai e le conoscenze costruttive locali.

El edificio es de aspecto débil y flexible, y su construcción es el resultado de la planificación participativa entre los diseñadores, los trabajadores de la construcción y el conocimiento constructivo local.

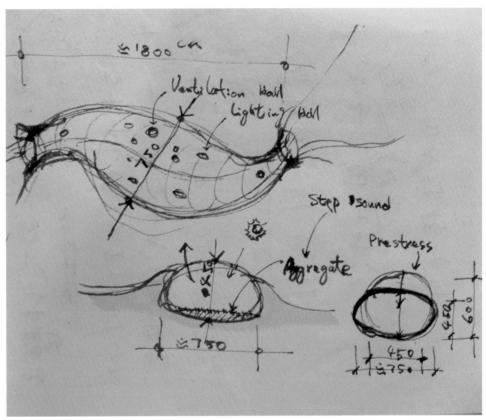

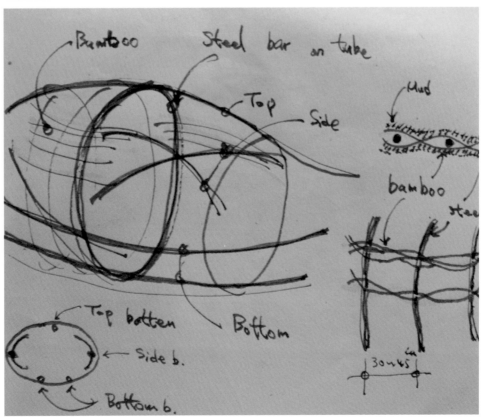

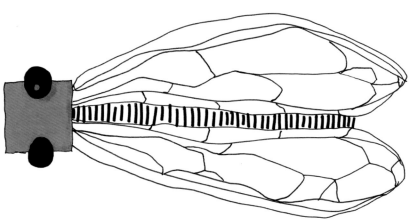

Conceptual sketch / Dessin de conception

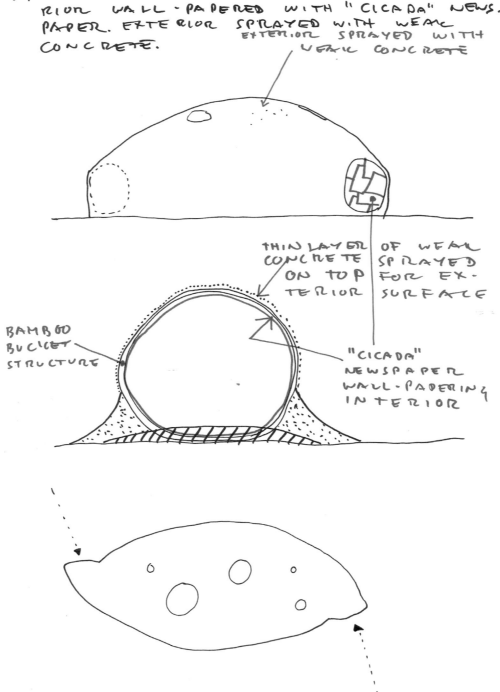

B. BAMBOO STRUCTURE ON TOP OF EARTH. INTE-
RIOR WALL-PAPERED WITH "CICADA" NEWS.
PAPER. EXTERIOR SPRAYED WITH WEAK
CONCRETE.

EXTERIOR SPRAYED WITH
WEAK CONCRETE

THIN LAYER OF WEAK
CONCRETE SPRAYED
ON TOP FOR EX-
TERIOR SURFACE

BAMBOO
BUCKET
STRUCTURE

"CICADA"
NEWSPAPER
WALL-PAPERING
INTERIOR

Conceptual sketch / Dessin de conception

Bamboo Wing

The architectural practice specializes in promoting the use of bamboo as a sustainable and effective building resource. The aim of this project was to demonstrate the potential of this wood as a structural material.The building is a structure made entirely of bamboo, without the use of steel or synthetic materials. The design was inspired by nature: birdwings, forming a 12 m (40 ft) open-air space without vertical columns. The pavilion is used for weddings, concerts, ceremonies, and other events.

Das Architekturbüro ist auf die Förderung von Bambus als nachhaltiger und effizienter Baustoff spezialisiert. Ziel dieses Projekt war es, das Potential dieses Holzes als Strukturmaterial unter Beweis zu stellen. Das Gebäude ist eine rein aus Bambus gebildete Struktur, ohne dass auf andere künstliche Materialien zurückgegriffen wurde. Das Design insipiert sich an der Natur: die Flügel eines Vogels bilden einen 12 m großen Freiluftraum ohne senkrechte Säulen. Der Pavillon wird für Hochzeiten, Musikkonzerte, Zeremonien, usw. genutzt.

Spécialisé dans la promotion de l'utilisation du bambou – une ressource durable et performante pour la construction –, le bureau d'études voulait démontrer le potentiel de ce matériau pour la conception des structures. Cet abri est exclusivement en bambou, et donc sans acier ni autres matériaux transformés. Sa forme naturaliste, les ailes d'un oiseau, se déploie sur un espace de 12 m à l'air libre ne reposant sur aucune colonne. Le pavillon est utilisé pour les noces, les concerts et autres festivités.

Het architectenbureau is gespecialiseerd in het bevorderen van het gebruik van bamboe als duurzaam en efficiënt bouwmateriaal. Dit project had als doel de mogelijkheden van dit soort hout als structuurmateriaal te laten zien. Het gebouw bestaat uit een structuur van pure bamboe waarbij geen gebruik is gemaakt van staal of andere kunstmaterialen. Het ontwerp is geïnspireerd op de natuur – de vleugels van een vogel – en creëert een ruimte van 12 m in de open lucht, zonder verticale zuilen. Het paviljoen wordt gebruikt voor bruiloften, muziekconcerten, ceremonies, etc.

Lo studio di architettura è specializzato nella promozione dell'uso del bambù come risorsa costruttiva sostenibile ed efficace. L'obiettivo di questo progetto era quello di mostrare le potenzialità di questo legno come materiale strutturale. L'edificio è una struttura composta da bambù puro, senza l'impiego di acciaio o di altri materiali artificiali. Il progetto si ispira alla natura: le ali di un uccello che formano uno spazio di 12 m, all'aperto, senza colonne verticali. Il padiglione è utilizzato per matrimoni, concerti di musica, cerimonie, ecc.

Este estudio de arquitectura se especializa en promover el uso del bambú como recurso de construcción sostenible y eficaz. El objetivo de este proyecto era mostrar el potencial de esta madera como material estructural. El edificio es una estructura formada por bambú puro, sin usar acero u otros materiales artificiales. El diseño se inspira en la naturaleza: las alas de un pájaro que forman un espacio de 12 m al aire libre sin columnas verticales. El pabellón se utiliza para bodas, conciertos de música, ceremonias, etc.

Vo Trong Nghia
Phúc Yên, Vietnam, 2009
© Vo Trong Nghia

The spectacular design of this cultural center has two main features: a birdwing shape and the use of bamboo as the only building material.

Dieses Kulturzentrum ist aus zwei Gründen so spektakulär: ein Design basierend auf Vogelflügeln und das Tragwerk aus Bambus als alleiniges Baumaterial.

Ce centre culturel est aussi remarquable pour son plan évoquant les ailes ouvertes d'un oiseau que pour l'usage structurel du bambou comme unique matériau de construction.

Het centrum is om twee redenen spectaculair: het ontwerp dat geïnspireerd is op de vleugels van een vogel en het structurele gebruik van bamboe als enig bouwmateriaal.

La spettacolarità di questo centro culturale risiede in due aspetti: un progetto che si ispira alle ali di un uccello e l'uso strutturale del bambù come materiale costruttivo unico.

La espectacularidad de este centro cultural reside en dos puntos: un diseño basado en las alas de un pájaro y el uso estructural del bambú como material constructivo único.

Site plan / Plan du site

Ground floor Plan / Plan

Section / Coupe

SuperFlex System

Søren Korsgaard arkitekt
Hawaii, HI, United States, 2010
© Søren Korsgaard

The Super Flex system was designed to work as the architectural frame of a house, sports hall, temporary market, and barn, among other uses. It consists of very few easy-to-assemble components for a multitude of solutions. The structure can take on different sizes depending on the use it is given and on users' needs through the addition or removal of roof components and residential units. Bamboo is the most widely used material as it has lower environmental impact and adapts better than others to any climate.

Das SuperFlex wurde als architektonisches Tragwerk eines Hauses, einer Sporthalle, eines temporären Markts, Getreidespeichers, etc. konzipiert. Es besteht aus wenigen, leicht aufzubauenden Bestandteilen mit verschiedenartigen Anwendungen. Die Struktur kann sich an verschiedene Größen und Bedürfnisse des Nutzers anpassen, indem Komponenten der Decke und den Wohneinheiten hinzugefügt bzw. weggenommen werden. Bambus ist das meist zum Einsatz kommende Material, dank seiner geringen Umweltauswirkungen und nicht zuletzt, weil es sich an jedes Klima anzupassen vermag.

Le système SuperFlex a été imaginé pour fournir la structure porteuse d'une maison, d'un pavillon des sports, d'un marché temporaire, d'un grenier à grain, etc. Il comprend un petit nombre de composants, mais offre des solutions multiples, et il est d'une grande simplicité d'assemblage. La structure s'ajuste aux dimensions du projet et aux besoins de ses usagers puisqu'il est possible d'ajouter ou d'enlever des éléments de la couverture et des unités résidentielles. Le bambou est le matériau le plus employé car c'est celui qui a le plus faible impact sur l'environnement et qui s'adapte le mieux à tous les climats.

Het SuperFlex-systeem is ontworpen als bouwstructuur voor een woning, een sporthal, een tijdelijke markt, een graanschuur, etc. Het bestaat uit een klein aantal bestanddelen die talrijke oplossingen bieden en eenvoudig te monteren zijn. De structuur kan verschillende afmetingen hebben, afhankelijk van de toepassing en de behoeftes van de gebruiker, doordat er bestanddelen en wooneenheden kunnen worden toegevoegd of juist weggehaald. Bamboe is het meest gebruikte materiaal doordat het weinig impact op het milieu heeft en het zich aanpast aan ieder willekeurig klimaat.

Il sistema SuperFlex è stato progettato per fungere da struttura architettonica di una casa, un padiglione sportivo, un mercato temporaneo, un granaio, ecc. È formato da pochi elementi che offrono molteplici soluzioni e sono semplici da montare. La struttura può avere diverse dimensioni in funzione dell'uso e delle necessità dell'utente, aggiungendo o eliminando elementi dal tetto e dalle unità residenziali. Il bambù è il materiale maggiormente impiegato dato che genera un minore impatto ambientale ed è quello che meglio si adatta a qualsiasi clima.

El sistema SuperFlex fue diseñado para funcionar como estructura arquitectónica de una casa, un pabellón deportivo, un mercado temporal, un granero, etc. Está formado por pocos componentes con múltiples soluciones y sencillos de montar. La estructura puede adoptar diferentes tamaños en función de las necesidades del usuario añadiendo o quitando componentes de la cubierta y unidades residenciales. El bambú es el material que más se emplea, ya que genera un menor impacto medioambiental y es el que mejor se adapta a cualquier clima.

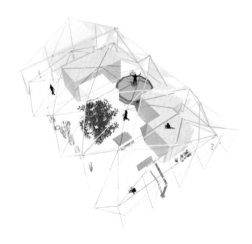

Renderings / Représentation en 3D

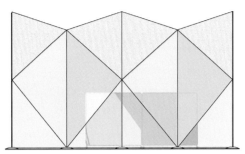

East elevation / Élévation est

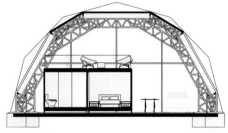

Section B-B / Coupe B-B

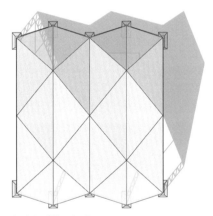

Roof plan / Plan du toit

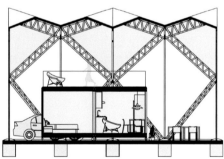

Section A-A / Coupe A-A

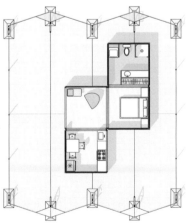

Floor plan / Plan

The project consists of three areas: interior, semi-covered, and open-air space. The geometry of the roof structures is inspired by Japanese *origami* techniques.

Das Projekt setzt sich aus drei Bereichen zusammen: Innenraum, halb überdachter und Freilauft-Raum. Die Geometrie der Dachstrukturen inspiriert sich an den japanischen *Origami*-Techniken.

Le projet se compose de trois zones : fermée, semi-couverte et espace à ciel ouvert. Les triangles de la toiture géométrique s'inspirent des pliages des origamis japonais.

Het project beslaat drie zones: interieur, halfoverdekte ruimte en exterieur. De geometrie van de structuren van het dak is geïnspireerd op de Japanse *origami*-techniek.

Il progetto si articola in tre zone: interno, semicoperto e spazio all'aperto. La geometria delle strutture del soffitto si ispira alle tecniche dell'*origami* giapponese.

El proyecto se compone de tres zonas: interior, semicubierta y espacio al aire libre. La geometría de las estructuras del techo se inspira en las técnicas del *origami* japonés.

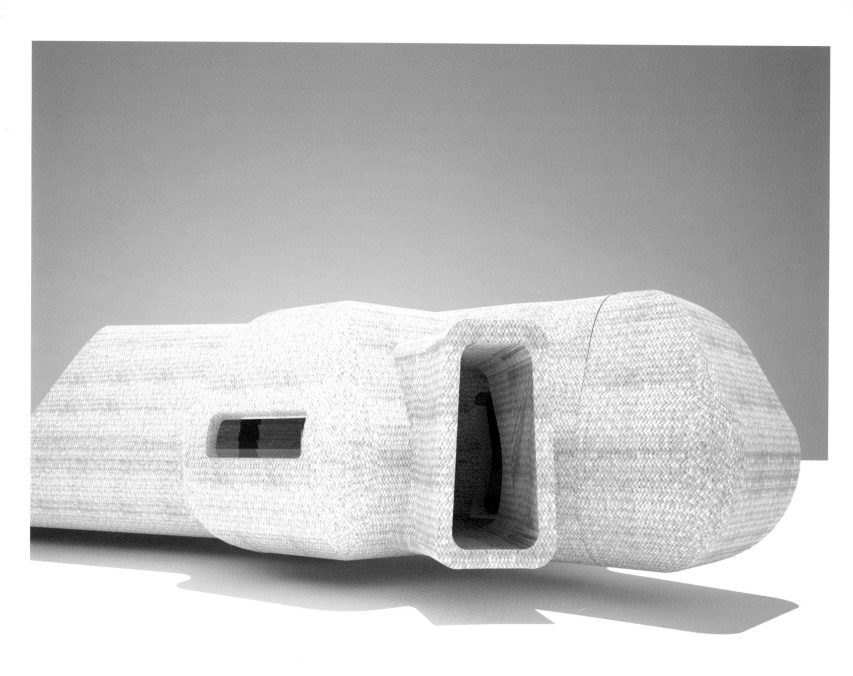

Woven House

This home was built as a showpiece to promote bamboo as a sustainable building material. The design is an attempt to make use of the thousand-year-old building tradition typical in Asian countries for large-scale modern architectural design. The walls, floor, and ceiling form a continuous surface that also incorporate seats and shelves. Woven bamboo is present in most of the building. This prototype can be constructed in any area where there is a tradition of bamboo weaving.

Das Haus wurde als Showcase zur Werbung für Bambus als nachhaltiges Baumaterial entworfen. Das Design ist ein Versuch, die jahrtausendealte Bautradition asiatischer Länder in die moderne Architektur in großem Stil einfließen zu lassen. Die Wände, der Boden und die Decke sind eine kontinuierliche Fläche, aus der auch die Sessel und Regale geschaffen sind. Bambus ist auch im größten Teil der Konstruktion eingeflochten. Der Prototyp kann überall dort eingesetzt werden, wo es die Tradition des Bambusflechtens gibt.

Cette maison a été conçue pour être la vitrine du bambou utilisé comme matériel de construction durable. Le plan tente de capturer l'essence de la tradition architecturale millénaire des pays asiatiques pour la propulser dans l'architecture moderne à grande échelle. Les murs, le sol et le toit forment une surface continue qui se prolonge également dans les soutènements. Murs et cloisons sont en bambou tissé. Ce prototype peut être installé dans n'importe quelle zone où il existe une tradition de tissage du bambou.

Het huis is ontworpen als etalage om het gebruik van bamboe als duurzaam bouwmateriaal te bevorderen. Met dit ontwerp is een poging gedaan om de eeuwenoude traditionele bouwtraditie van Aziatische landen te benutten en deze te projecteren op de moderne architectuur op grote schaal. De muren, vloer en het dak zijn een doorlopend oppervlak waarin ook de zitplaatsen en de planken zijn gevormd. In het grootste deel van de constructie wordt gevlochten bamboe gebruikt. Het prototype kan worden geïnstalleerd in ieder willekeurig gebied waar een traditie van het vlechten met bamboe bestaat.

La casa è stata progettata come una sorta di vetrina per promuovere l'uso del bambù come materiale da costruzione. Il progetto tenta di sfruttare la millenaria tradizione costruttiva dei paesi asiatici per proiettarsi nell'architettura moderna su grande scala. Le pareti, il pavimento e il soffitto sono una superficie continua che costituisce anche le sedute e le scaffalature. Il bambù si presenta intrecciato nella maggior parte della struttura. Il prototipo può essere installato in qualsiasi zona in cui esista la tradizione della lavorazione del bambù.

La casa fue diseñada como escaparate para promover el bambú como material de construcción sostenible. El diseño es un intento de aprovechar la tradición constructiva milenaria de los países asiáticos para proyectarlo en la arquitectura moderna a gran escala. Las paredes, el suelo y el techo son una superficie continua que forma también los asientos y los estantes. El bambú se presenta tejido en la mayor parte de la construcción. El prototipo puede instalarse en cualquier zona donde exista la tradición de tejer bambú.

Søren Korsgaard arkitekt
Philippines, 2010
© Søren Korsgaard

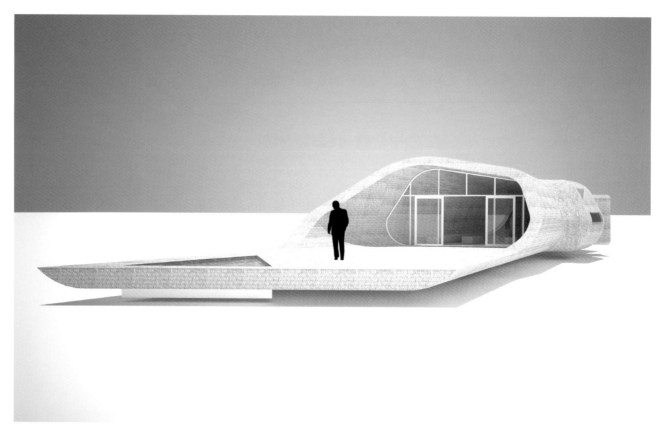

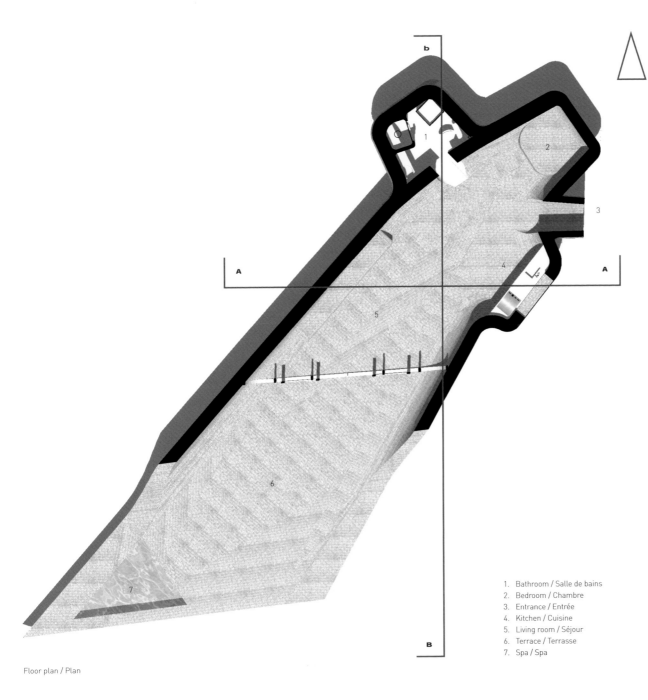

The originality and flexibility offered by bamboo were a basic part of the design for this vacation home. Its futuristic and dynamic style provides a surface that alternates open and closed areas.

Die Originalität und Flexibilität von Bambus waren fundamental für die Schaffung dieses Ferienhauses. Das zukunftsweisende und dynamische Design schafft eine Fläche, auf sich der offene und geschlossene Zonen abwechseln.

L'originalité et la flexibilité du bambou caractérisent cette résidence de vacances. Le plan futuriste et dynamique du volume fait alterner zones ouvertes et fermées.

De originaliteit en flexibiliteit van bamboe zijn fundamenteel geweest bij het ontwerp van deze vakantiewoning. Het futuristische en dynamische ontwerp bestaat uit een oppervlak waarin open en gesloten zones elkaar afwisselen.

L'originalità e la flessibilità che offre il bambù sono state fondamentali per creare questa casa per le vacanze. Il progetto futurista e dinamico offre una superficie che alterna zone aperte ad altre chiuse.

La originalidad y la flexibilidad que ofrece el bambú han sido fundamentales para crear esta casa de vacaciones. El diseño futurista y dinámico ofrece una superficie que alterna zonas abiertas y cerradas.

1. Bathroom / Salle de bains
2. Bedroom / Chambre
3. Entrance / Entrée
4. Kitchen / Cuisine
5. Living room / Séjour
6. Terrace / Terrasse
7. Spa / Spa

Floor plan / Plan

Bamboo Diamonds

This project is a modern interpretation combining the traditional advantages of bamboo with the current needs of sustainable architecture. The structure consists of a skeleton of bamboo panels and posts, which provide strength and stability, and truss beams. The building has a floor area of 120 m² (1,290 sq ft) to hold eight visitors, but it can be enlarged with other modular structures to provide more space. It is also equipped with fire-resistant panels and thermal and acoustic insulation.

Das Projekt ist eine moderne Interpretation, die die traditionellen Vorzüge des Bambus mit den aktuellen Bedürfnissen nachhaltiger Architektur verbindet. Die Struktur besteht aus einem Lamellengestell und Pfosten aus Bambus, die dem Ganzen Kraft und Stabilität verleihen, sowie aus Jalousiehalmen. Das Gebäude umfasst 120 m² für acht Besucher, kann aber durch zusätzliche Modul-Strukturen erweitert werden, falls mehr Raum erforderlich ist. Es ist mit brandfesten Paneelen und Wärme- und Lärmisolierung verkleidet.

Ce projet est une interprétation moderne qui met les avantages traditionnels du bambou au service d'une architecture intégrée au développement durable. La structure consiste en une armature de plaques, poteaux en bambou et poutres en treillis, qui lui donne sa résistance et sa stabilité. L'édifice de 120 m² est conçu pour accueillir huit personnes, mais il suffit d'ajouter des structures modulaires pour agrandir l'espace. Il est muni de panneaux ignifugés et bénéficie d'une isolation phonique et thermique.

Het project is een moderne interpretatie die de traditionele voordelen van bamboe combineert met de huidige behoeften van duurzame architectuur. De structuur is gevormd door een skelet van bamboe platen en staanders, die kracht en stabiliteit bieden, en vakwerk. Het gebouw heeft 120 m² en is bedoeld voor acht bezoekers, maar kan worden uitgebreid met andere modulaire structuren. Het is ook uitgerust met brandwerende panelen en warmte- en geluidsisolatie.

Il progetto è un'interpretazione moderna che combina i vantaggi tradizionali del bambù con le necessità attuali dell'architettura sostenibile. La struttura è composta da uno scheletro a lastre e steli di bambù che garantiscono forza e stabilità, oltre a travi per tralicciatura. L'edificio ha 120 m² e può ospitare otto persone, ma può essere moltiplicato con altre strutture modulari per disporre di maggiore spazio. È inoltre dotato di pannelli antincendio e di isolamento termico e acustico.

El proyecto es una interpretación moderna que combina las ventajas tradicionales del bambú con las necesidades actuales de la arquitectura sostenible. La estructura está formada por un esqueleto de láminas y postes de bambú, que aportan fuerza y estabilidad, y vigas de celosía. El edificio tiene 120 m² y capacidad para ocho visitantes, pero se puede multiplicar con otras estructuras modulares para disponer de más espacio. También está equipado con paneles antiincendios y aislamientos térmico y acústico.

Joseph Cory/Geotectura Studio
Haifa, Israel, 2009
© Geotectura Studio

This self-sufficient and multifunctional building makes use of cost-effective materials, mainly bamboo, in the construction of prefabricated modules to minimize their environmental impact.

Dieses eigenständige und multifunktionale Gebäude setzt vorteilhafte Materialien, vor allem Bambus, beim Bau von vorgefertigten Teilen ein, um so die Auswirkungen für das Ökosystem zu minimieren.

Autonome et polyvalente, cette pyramide inversée a un très faible impact sur l'écosystème car elle est en matériaux économiques, le bambou étant le principal pour la construction des éléments préfabriqués.

Dit zelfvoorzienende en veelzijdige gebouw gebruikt rendabele materialen, met name bamboe, bij de bouw van geprefabriceerde delen, om de impact op het ecosysteem tot een minimum te beperken.

Questo edificio autosufficiente e multifunzionale utilizza materiali economici, principalmente il bambù, nella costruzione di prefabbricati per ridurre al minimo l'impatto sull'ecosistema.

Este edificio autosuficiente y multifuncional utiliza materiales rentables, principalmente el bambú, en la construcción de prefabricados para minimizar el impacto sobre el ecosistema.

Renderings / Représentations en 3D

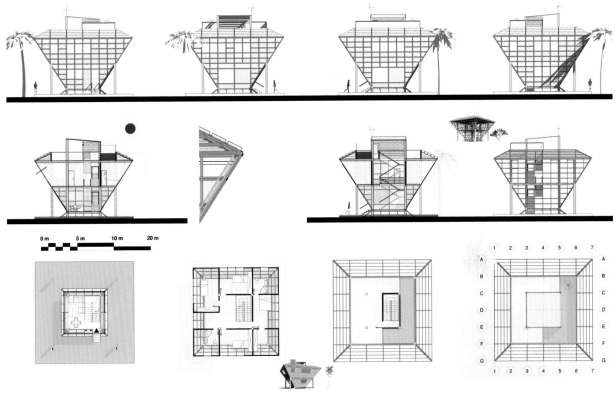

Plans, Sections, Elevations, Diagrams and Construction Details / Plans, coupes, élévations, diagrammes et détails de construction

Caretaker's House

Eric Gartner/SPG Architects
Osa Peninsula, Costa Rica, 2011
© SPG Architects

The design of this small home of 127 m² (1,370 sq ft) was commissioned by the owner of a property on the Osa Peninsula. The base of the structure is made of concrete and stucco as a totally closed and protected area, protected from its surroundings. The main feature is the upper structure made from bamboo, rising from the lower level and imitating the tree forms of the surrounding rainforest.

Dieses 127 m² kleine Haus wurde für den Hausmeister eines Familienanwesens auf der Halbinsel Osa entworfen. Das Fundament des Baus ist aus Beton und Stuck und bildet einen vollkommen abgeschotteten und von der Umgebung geschützten Bereich. Es besticht besonders das obere Tragwerk aus Bambus, das von der unteren Etage emporragt und die Baumformen des umgebenden Walds nachempfindet.

Les plans de cette maison de 127 m² ont été réalisés pour le propriétaire d'un domaine familial situé sur la péninsule d'Osa. Les fondations de la construction, en béton et stuc, sont conçues pour être entièrement fermées et protégées par une isolation totale de l'environnement. On remarque la structure supérieure en bambou, au-dessus du rez-de-chaussée, à l'image des arbres de la forêt environnante.

Het ontwerp van dit kleine huis van 127 m² werd gemaakt voor de huisbewaarder van een familie-eigendom gelegen op het schiereiland Osa. Het is de bedoeling dat het grondvlak van het gebouw bestaat uit beton en pleisterkalk en dat het een helemaal afgesloten en beschermde zone wordt, geïsoleerd van de omgeving. Opvallend is de bovenstructuur van bamboe, die vanaf de benedenverdieping verrijst en de boomvormen van het omringende woud imiteert.

Il progetto di questa piccola casa di 127 m² è stato realizzato per il casiere di una proprietà familiare ubicata nella penisola di Osa. La base della costruzione è realizzata in cemento e stucco ed è destinata a essere una zona totalmente chiusa e protetta, isolata dall'ambiente circostante. Si impone la struttura superiore in bambù che emerge dal piano inferiore e imita le forme arboree del bosco circostante.

Esta pequeña casa de 127 m² se ha diseñado para el casero de una propiedad familiar ubicada en la península de Osa. La base de la construcción, en una zona totalmente cerrada y protegida, aislada del entorno, es de hormigón y estuco. Destaca la estructura superior de bambú, que se alza desde la planta baja e imita las formas arboladas de la selva circundante.

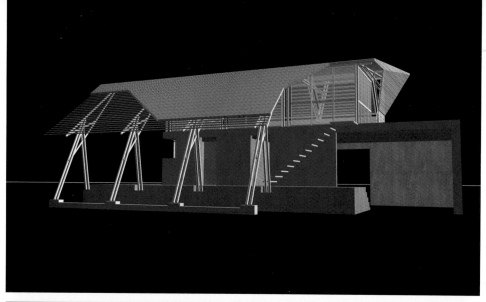

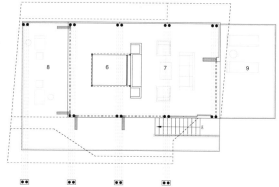

Upper level / Plan du niveau supérieur

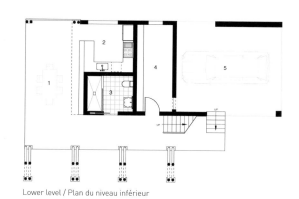

Lower level / Plan du niveau inférieur

The original bamboo structure, rising from the ground towards the upper level like a tree, acts as a filter to protect the interior spaces from the sun and elements.

Die originelle Bambusstruktur, die sich aus dem unteren Bereich nach oben wie ein Baum hochwindet, schützt die Innenräume von der Sonne und den externen Elementen.

Comme un arbre, la superstructure en bambou part du bas et s'élève vers l'étage. Elle filtre les rayons du soleil, protégeant ainsi les espaces intérieurs des agressions de l'extérieur.

De originele bamboestructuur, die vanuit het onderste gedeelte als een boom naar het bovenste gedeelte groeit, filtreert en beschermt de binnenruimtes tegen de zon en externe elementen.

L'originale struttura in bambù che parte dalla zona inferiore fino a raggiungere il primo piano come se si trattasse di un albero, filtra e protegge gli spazi interni dal sole e dagli elementi esterni.

La original estructura de bambú, que parte de la zona inferior hacia la superior como si de un árbol se tratara, filtra y protege los espacios interiores del sol y de los elementos externos.

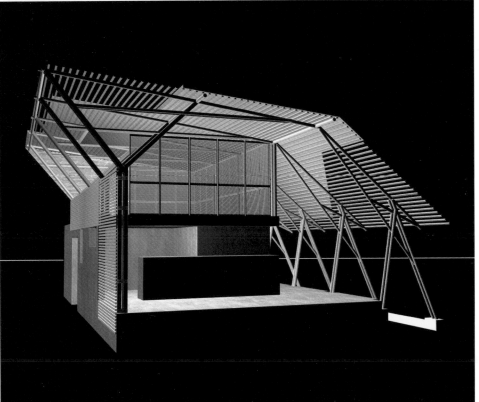

Emerging Ghana

Complying with the conditions of the competition organized by Enviu, the architects designed an eco-affordable and flexible family home for Ghana's emerging middle class. The house is made from modular panels of lightweight bamboo and dahoma wood. The project is based on three principles: integration into the local setting, use of recognizable architecture, and the utilization of sustainable local materials that reduce the need for transport and energy while boosting the development of local industry.

In Erfüllung der Auflagen des von Enviu, einer internationalen Stiftung für nachhaltige Innovation, ausgeschriebenen Wettbewerbs, haben die Architekten ein ökologisches Einfamilienhaus geschaffen, das für die aufstrebende Mittelklasse Ghanas erschwinglich und flexibel ist. Das Haus besteht aus Modulpaneelen aus leichtem Bambus und Dahoma-Holz. Das Projekt basiert auf drei Grundsätzen: Anpassung an die lokalen Verhältnisse, Einsatz einer wiedererkennbaren Architektur und nachhaltiger örtlicher Materialien, die den Transport verkürzen, den Energieverbrauch drosseln sowie das lokale Gewerbe ankurbeln.

Pour répondre au cahier des charges du concours organisé par Enviu, une fondation internationale qui se consacre à l'innovation durable, les architectes dessinèrent une maison écologique et flexible, accessible aux familles de la classe moyenne émergente au Ghana. Elle se compose de panneaux modulaires en bambou léger et en bois de dabéma. Le projet repose sur trois principes : intégration locale, utilisation d'une architecture reconnaissable et emploi de matériaux locaux qui réduisent le coût écologique des transports, limitant ainsi la consommation d'énergie et favorisant l'essor de l'industrie locale en accord avec un développement durable.

In naleving van de vereisten van de aanbesteding die georganiseerd werd door Enviu, een internationale stichting die zich bezig houdt met duurzame innovatie, hebben de architecten een ecologische eengezinswoning ontworpen die flexibel en betaalbaar is voor de opkomende middenklasse van Ghana. Het huis is opgebouwd uit modulaire panelen van licht bamboe en dahoma hout. Het project is uitgegaan van drie basisprincipes: lokale integratie, gebruik van herkenbare architectuur en aanwending van duurzame, plaatselijke materialen waardoor transportkosten en energieverbruik worden teruggebracht en de ontwikkeling van de plaatselijke industrie wordt bevorderd.

Attenendosi ai requisiti previsti dal concorso organizzato da Enviu, gli architetti hanno progettato una casa familiare ecologica, accessibile e flessibile per la classe media emergente del Ghana. La casa è composta da pannelli modulari di bambù leggero e legno dahoma. Il progetto si basa su tre principi: integrazione locale, utilizzo di un'architettura riconoscibile e uso di materiali locali sostenibili che riducono il trasporto e il consumo energetico promuovendo lo sviluppo dell'industria locale.

Cumpliendo los requisitos del concurso organizado por Enviu, los arquitectos diseñaron una casa familiar ecológica, asequible y flexible para la clase media emergente de Ghana. La casa se compone de paneles modulares de bambú ligero y madera dahoma. El proyecto se basa en tres principios: integración local, utilización de una arquitectura reconocible y el uso de materiales locales sostenibles, que reducen el transporte y el consumo energético e impulsan el desarrollo de la industria local.

Blanc Borderless Architecture,
João Caeiro
Cape Coast, Ghana, 2010
© Blanc Borderless Architecture

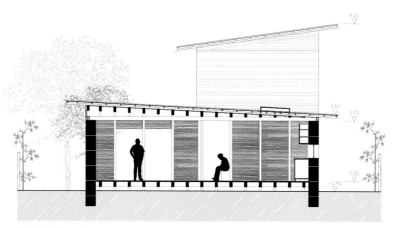

Section A / Coupe A

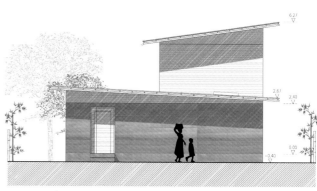

Elevation 1 / Élévation 1

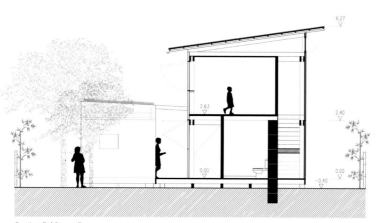

Section B / Coupe B

Elevation 2 / Élévation 2

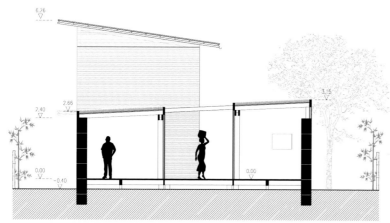

Section C / Coupe C

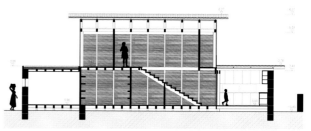

Section D / Coupe D

The design takes advantage of modular bamboo panels to establish a harmonious transition between interior and exterior spaces. The use of local materials means they can be easily maintained, recycled, and reused.

Das Design mit modularen Bambuspaneelen schafft eine harmonische Verbindung zwischen Innen- und Außenräumen. Der Gebrauch lokaler Werkstoffe erleichtert die Instandhaltung, das Recycling und die Wiederverwertung.

L'utilisation de panneaux modulaires en bambou dans le projet assure une relation harmonieuse entre les espaces intérieurs et extérieurs. L'usage de matériaux locaux facilite l'entretien, le recyclage et le réemploi.

Het ontwerp met modulaire bamboepanelen zorgt voor een harmonieuze verhouding tussen de binnen- en buitenruimtes. Het gebruik van plaatselijke materialen vereenvoudigt het onderhoud, de recyclage en het hergebruik.

Il progetto che vede l'utilizzo di pannelli modulari in bambù definisce una relazione armonica tra gli spazi interni ed esterni. L'uso di materiali locali facilita la manutenzione, il riciclaggio e il riutilizzo.

El diseño con paneles modulares de bambú establece una relación armoniosa entre los espacios interiores y exteriores. El uso de materiales locales facilita el mantenimiento, el reciclaje y la reutilización.

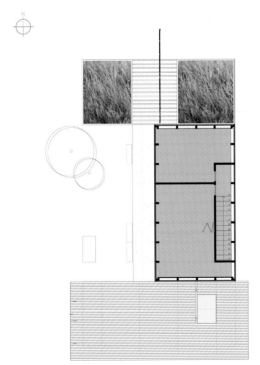

Upper level / Plan du niveau supérieur

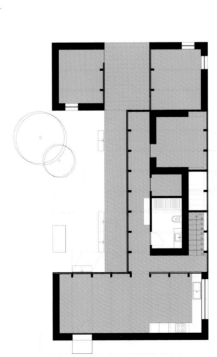

Lower level / Plan du niveau inférieur

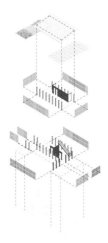

Axonometric / Axonométrie

Living areas /
Zones de jour

Kitchen and bathroom /
Cuisine et Salle de bains

Sleeping areas /
Zones de nuit

Circulation and storage /
Circulation et magasin

Lower level / Niveau inférieur

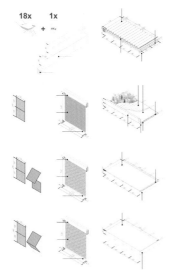

18x   1x

Construction details / Détails de construction

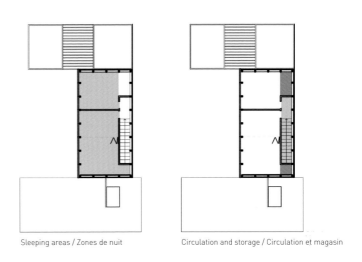

Sleeping areas / Zones de nuit

Circulation and storage / Circulation et magasin

Upper level / Niveau supérieur

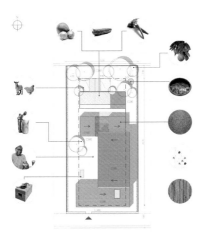

Plot layout / Schéma de la parcelle

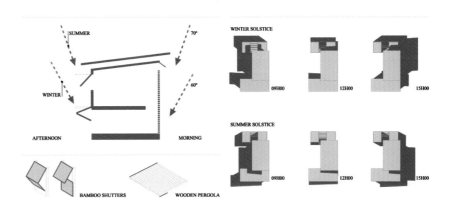

SUMMER   70°

WINTER   60°

AFTERNOON   MORNING

BAMBOO SHUTTERS   WOODEN PERGOLA

WINTER SOLSTICE

09H00   12H00   15H00

SUMMER SOLSTICE

09H00   12H00   15H00

Solar schemes / Schémas solaires

Sustainable Bamboo Pavilion

Esan Rahmani
India, 2011
© Esan Rahmani

This building is meant for use by underprivileged inhabitants of the Indian Ocean coast as a way of improving their lives through architecture and homes. The design principle involved is a synthesis of sustainable architecture that expresses beauty and efficiency with the the positive qualities of bamboo. The interior contains a common living area, several bedrooms, and rest areas. The rational use of space, light requirements, and the flexibility offered by bamboo resulted in an umbrella-like design.

Der Pavillon soll über Baukunst und Wohnqualität das Leben der am meisten benachteiligten Bevölkerungsgruppen an der Küste des Indischen Ozeans verbessern. Das Design ist eine Synthese nachhaltiger Architektur, in der Schönheit, Effizienz und die positiven Eigenschaften des Bambus voll zum Ausdruck kommen. Im Inneren werden das gemeinsame Wohnzimmer, mehrere Schlafzimmer und Erholungsbereiche untergebracht. Der räumliche Rationalismus, die Lichtanforderungen und die Flexibilität von Bambus haben zu einem Entwurf in Form eines Regenschirms geführt.

Destiné aux populations défavorisées de l'océan Indien, ce pavillon vise à améliorer leur qualité de vie par l'architecture et l'habitat. Le concept présidant à l'élaboration des plans fait la synthèse d'une architecture respectueuse de l'environnement qui exprime les remarquables qualités du bambou, dont la beauté et l'efficacité. À l'intérieur, il y aura une salle de séjour collective, plusieurs chambres et des zones de repos. L'utilisation rationnelle de l'espace, les exigences en matière de lumière et la flexibilité du bambou ont abouti à ce volume en forme de parapluie.

Het paviljoen is bestemd om de levenskwaliteit van kansarme bevolkingsgroepen aan de kust van de Indische Oceaan te verbeteren door middel van architectuur en woning. Het concept van het ontwerp is een synthese van duurzame architectuur die blijk geeft van schoonheid, efficiëntie en van de positieve kwaliteiten van bamboe. In het interieur zullen een gemeenschappelijke woonkamer, meerdere slaapmakers en rustruimtes worden ingericht. Het rationalisme van de ruimte, de vereisten voor licht en de flexibiliteit van bamboe leidden tot dit ontwerp in de vorm van een paraplu.

Il padiglione è destinato alle popolazioni in difficoltà della costa dell'Oceano Indiano e ha l'obiettivo di migliorare la loro qualità della vita tramite interventi architettonici e una casa in cui vivere. Il concetto alla base del progetto è una sintesi di architettura sostenibile che esprime bellezza, efficienza e le qualità positive del bambù. L'interno ospiterà un salotto comune, varie camere e zone relax. Il razionalismo spaziale, i requisiti di luce e la flessibilità del bambù hanno portato a questo progetto che, nelle forme, ricorda un ombrello.

El pabellón está destinado a las poblaciones desfavorecidas de la costa del océano Índico para mejorar su calidad de vida a través de la arquitectura y la vivienda. El concepto de diseño es una síntesis de arquitectura sostenible que expresa belleza, eficiencia y las cualidades positivas del bambú. En el interior se ubicarán una sala de estar común, varios dormitorios y áreas de descanso. El racionalismo espacial, los requisitos lumínicos y la flexibilidad del bambú condujeron al diseño con forma de paraguas.

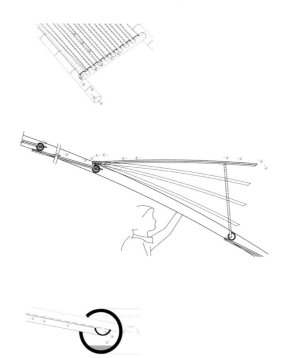

Construction details / Détails de construction

Exploded view drawing / Vue en éclaté

Floor plan / Plan

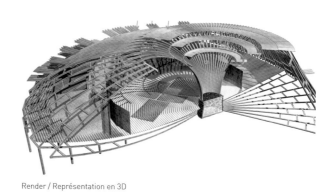

Render / Représentation en 3D

Bamboo is used not only in floors and roof tiles, but also in the structure. Large bamboo curtains permit a flexible room layout

Bambus wird nicht nur für den Boden und als Ziegel eingesetzt, sondern auch zum Bau des Tragwerks. Große Bambuswandschirme gestatten eine flexible Disposition der Zimmer.

Le bambou n'a pas seulement fourni les sols et les tuiles mais aussi l'ossature. Les grands rideaux de bambou permettent une distribution modulaire des pièces.

Bamboe is niet alleen gebruikt voor de vloer en de dakpannen maar ook voor de structuur. Grote bamboe schermen maken een flexibele inrichting van de slaapkamers mogelijk.

Il bambù non solo viene utilizzato per i pavimenti e le tegole, ma anche per la struttura. Grandi tende di bambù consentono una distribuzione flessibile delle camere.

El bambú no solo se utiliza para el suelo y las tejas, sino también para la construcción de la estructura. Grandes cortinas de bambú permiten la distribución flexible de las habitaciones.

Moving Meshes

An exhibition held in Eindhoven gave designer Maria Blaisse the idea of researching the possbilities offered by bamboo's flexibility. She contacted the Advanced Geometry Unit at Arup and went to work on the design of multi-purpose pavilions without the use of a computer. Her research was based on human movement and material flexibility. Nautilus, the pavilion created for a traveling exhibition of Dutch design in 2011, will be mobile, flexible, and, above all, flexible.

Ausgehend von einer in Eindhoven stattgefundenen Ausstellung hat die Designerin Maria Blaisse die Flexibilitätsfähigkeiten von Bambus eingehend untersucht. Sie setzte sich mit dem Advanced Geometry Unit von Arup in Verbindung und nahm ihre Arbeit am Entwurf von Mehrzweck-Pavillons auf, ohne sich dabei auf den Computer zu stützen. Die menschliche Bewegung und die Biegsamkeit des Materials waren die Schlüsselelemente ihrer Forschung. Der Nautilus, ein für eine Wanderausstellung des niederländischen Designs 2011 bestimmter Pavillon, wird demnach mobil, faltbar und vor allem flexibel sein.

C'est pour une exposition, qui s'est tenue à Eindhoven, que la styliste Maria Blaisse a entrepris l'exploration des possibilités offertes par la flexibilité du bambou. Après avoir pris contact avec la Advanced Geometry Unit de Arup, elle s'est mise à dessiner des pavillons polyvalents sans avoir recours à l'ordinateur. Ses recherches portaient sur le mouvement humain et la flexibilité du matériau. Elles ont abouti à la création du Nautilus, pavillon mobile, pliable et, surtout, flexible présenté en 2011 lors d'une exposition itinérante consacrée au design hollandais.

Naar aanleiding van een tentoonstelling in Eindhoven onderzocht ontwerpster Maria Blaisse de mogelijkheden die bamboe voor wat betreft flexibiliteit biedt. Zij raakte in contact met de Advanced Geometry Unit van Arup en begon te werken aan het ontwerp voor polyvalente paviljoens zonder gebruik te maken van de computer. De menselijke beweging en de flexibiliteit van het materiaal waren de elementen die centraal stonden in haar onderzoek. De Nautilus, het paviljoen dat is bestemd voor een reizende expositie over Nederlands ontwerp in 2011, zal mobiel, opbouwbaar en bovenal flexibel zijn.

Partendo da una mostra tenutasi a Eindhoven, la progettista Maria Blaisse ha studiato il grado di flessibilità offerto dal bambù. Ha così contattato la Advanced Geometry Unit di Arup e ha iniziato a lavorare alla progettazione di padiglioni polivalenti senza l'utilizzo del computer. Il movimento urbano e la flessibilità del materiale sono stati gli elementi su cui si è basato il lavoro di ricerca. Il Nautilus, il padiglione pensato per una mostra itinerante del design olandese nel 2011, sarà mobile, «pieghevole» e, soprattutto, flessibile.

A partir de una exposición celebrada en Eindhoven, la diseñadora Maria Blaisse investigó las posibilidades de flexibilidad que ofrece el bambú. Se puso en contacto con la Advanced Geometry Unit de Arup y empezó a trabajar en el diseño de pabellones polivalentes sin utilizar el ordenador. El movimiento humano y la flexibilidad del material fueron los elementos en los que se basó la investigación. El Nautilus, el pabellón previsto para una exposición itinerante del diseño holandés en 2011, será móvil, plegable y, sobre todo, flexible.

Maria Blaisse
Amsterdam, The Netherlands, 2008
© Maria Blaisse

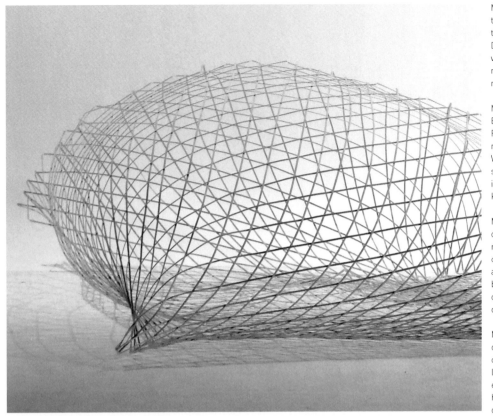

Maria Blaisse discovered that bamboo takes on different forms in response to the movement of the human body. During the project, she experimented with dancers who improvised their movements in order to achieve a large number of configurations.

Maria Blaisse hat entdeckt, dass Bambus verschiedene Formen als Reaktion auf die Bewegungen des menschlichen Körpers annimmt. Während des Projekts experimentierte sie mit Tänzern, die Bewegungen improvisierten, um so zahlreiche Konfigurationen zu erhalten.

Maria Blaisse a travaillé avec des danseurs qui improvisèrent des mouvements afin d'obtenir des configurations multiples. C'est ainsi qu'elle s'est aperçue que le bambou réagit aux mouvements du corps humain en prenant des formes diverses.

Maria Blaisse ontdekte dat bamboe diverse vormen aanneemt als reactie op de bewegingen van het menselijke lichaam. Tijdens haar project experimenteerde zij met dansers die hun bewegingen improviseerden om diverse configuraties te verkrijgen.

Maria Blaisse ha scoperto che il bambù adotta diverse forme come reazione al movimento del corpo umano. Durante il progetto ha studiato questo aspetto con dei ballerini che hanno improvvisato dei movimenti per ottenere molteplici configurazioni.

Maria Blaisse descubrió que el bambú adopta diversas formas como reacción al movimiento del cuerpo humano. Durante el proyecto, experimentó con bailarines, que improvisaron sus movimientos para obtener múltiples configuraciones.

DESIGN

Urban Picnic
Jason Carlow/C:A+D Carlow Architecture
and Design
www.carlow-ad.com
Hong Kong, China, 2007
© Thomas Fasting

This flexible and multi-purpose furniture
system made in Corian® and laminated bamboo
was designed for use in public spaces.

Flexibles und vielfältig einsetzbares Möbelsystem
aus Corian® und laminiertem Bambus, für
den Einsatz in öffentlichen Räumen konzipiert.

Gamme de mobilier flexible et polyvalent
fabriqué en Corian® et bambou laminé,
conçu pour les espaces publics.

Systeem van flexibel en veelzijdig meubilair,
vervaardigd uit Corian® en gelaagd bamboe,
ontworpen voor openbare ruimtes.

Sistema di arredi flessibile e multiuso
prodotto in Corian® e bambù laminato,
pensato per gli spazi pubblici.

Sistema de mobiliario flexible y multiusos
fabricado con Corian® y bambú laminado,
diseñado para los espacios públicos.

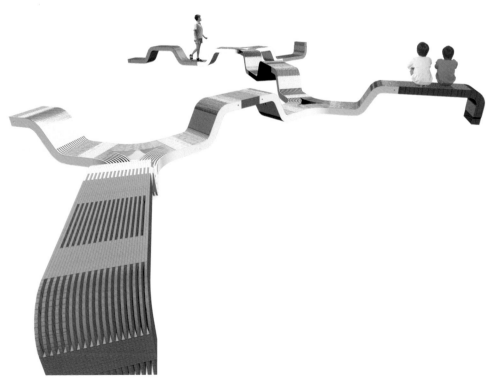

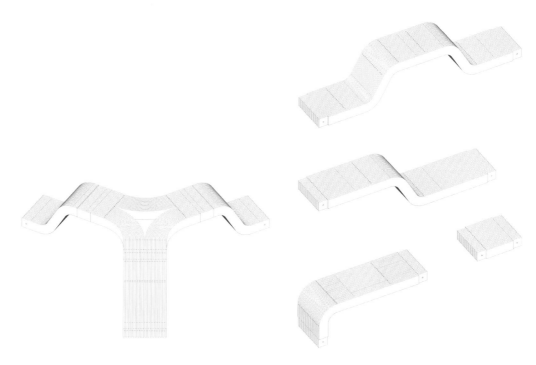

Pile Isle
Elena Goday, Christoph Tönges/CONBAM
www.conbam.de
www.bambus-conbam.de
Amsterdam, The Netherlands, 2010
© Christoph Tönges

Charred bamboo (*Phyllostachys pubescens*)
bench measuring 3 m (10 ft) in length
and ties with metal strips without the
need for screws or adhesive.

3 m lange Bank aus karbonisiertem Bambus
(*Phyllostachys pubescens*), die mit vier
Metallbändern ohne Schrauben oder Leim
zusammengehalten wird.

Banc en bambou (*Phyllostachys pubescens*)
carbonisé, de 3 m de long assemblé, sans vis
ni colle, par quatre bracelets métalliques.

Bank van verkoolde (*Phyllostachys pubescens*)
bamboe van 3 m lang, zonder schroeven of
lijm verbonden met vier metalen banden.

Panca di bambù (*Phyllostachys pubescens*)
carbonizzato, lungo 3 m e fissato con quattro
cinghie di metallo senza viti né incastri.

Banco de bambú (*Phyllostachys pubescens*)
carbonizado, de 3 m de longitud y atado con
cuatro correas de metal sin tornillos ni colas.

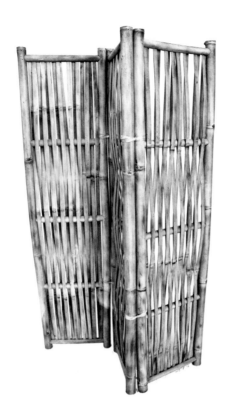

Three-Panels Screen
Marjolain Poulin
www.maobamboo.blogspot.com
San Salvador, El Salvador, 2008–2010
© Jianca Lazrus

This screen was hand made entirely from bamboo. The frame is made from cylinders and the screen uses only strips.

Manuell und ausschließlich aus Bambus hergestellter Wandschirm. Für die Rahmen wurden Zylinderstangen und für den Schirm nur Streifen eingesetzt.

Paravent fabriqué à la main et réalisé entièrement en bambou. Les cadres sont faits avec les tiges et les écrans avec des bandelettes.

Handgemaakt kamerscherm, helemaal van bamboe. Voor de omlijstingen zijn cilinders gebruikt en voor de schermen alleen stroken.

Paravento realizzato a mano, interamente in bambù. Per le cornici sono stati utilizzati dei cilindri e sulle superfici solo strisce.

Biombo construido a mano y realizado íntegramente en bambú. En los marcos se han utilizado cilindros y en las pantallas sólo tiras.

Nobu Table
Marjolain Poulin
www.maobamboo.blogspot.com
San Salvador, El Salvador, 2008-2010
© Marjolain Poulin

This table measuring 76 × 52 × 112 cm (30 x 20.5 × 44 in) was made by hand combining large bamboo cylinders with the walnut tabletop and base.

76 × 52 × 112 cm großer Tisch, der manuell gefertigt wurde, indem lange Bambuszylinder mit der Tischauflage und der Nussbaumholzbasis verbunden wurden.

Table de 76 × 52 × 112 cm faite à la main en associant de grosses tiges de bambou au plateau et au pied en noyer.

Handgemaakte tafel van 76 × 52 × 112 cm, waarin grote bamboe cilinders worden gecombineerd met een notenhout tafelblad.

Tavolo di 76 × 52 × 112 cm realizzato a mano combinando grandi cilindri di bambù con il ripiano e la base in legno di noce.

Mesa de 76 × 52 × 112 cm realizada a mano combinando grandes cilindros de bambú con la madera de nogal del tablero y la base.

All Black Bamboo Bike
Craig Calfee, Danilo Masuelli/RAW Bamboo
Bikes
www.rawbamboobikes.co.uk
West Yorkshire, United Kingdom, 2010
© Rachel Hammond

This road and mountain bike has a frame
made entirely in bamboo and finishings in
hemp to make them strong and flexible.

Fahrrad oder Mountainbike mit einem
vollkommen aus Bambus hergestelltem
Rahmen und Finishs aus Hanf, die
dieses robust und flexibel machen.

Vélo de route ou de montagne avec cadre
intégralement en bambou et finitions en
chanvre qui assurent résistance et souplesse.

Racefiets of mountainbike met een helemaal
uit bamboe gemaakt frame, met afwerkingen
in hennep, waardoor hij sterk en flexibel is.

Bicicletta da strada o mountain bike con telaio
interamente realizzato in bambù e finiture in
canapa che la rendono forte e flessibile.

Bicicleta de carretera o montaña con cuadro
construido totalmente en bambú con acabados
en cáñamo que la hacen fuerte y flexible.

The Dale Bamboo Bike
Craig Calfee, Danilo Masuelli/RAW Bamboo Bikes
www.rawbamboobikes.co.uk
West Yorkshire, United Kingdom, 2010
© Steve Phipps

High performance road and mountain bike. The natural qualities of bamboo make it more flexible and enable it to resist vibration better.

Hochleistungsfahrrad für die Straße und querfeldein. Dank der natürlichen Eigenschaften des Bambus ist es flexibler und hält Stößen besser stand.

Vélo très aérodynamique pour route et montagne. Du fait des propriétés naturelles du bambou, cette bicyclette est plus flexible et résiste mieux aux vibrations.

Fiets met hoog rendement voor op de weg en in de bergen. Dankzij de natuurlijke eigenschappen van bamboe is hij flexibeler en beter bestand tegen trillingen.

Bici ad alto rendimento da strada e mountain bike. Grazie alle qualità naturali del bambù, è più flessibile e resiste meglio alle vibrazioni.

Bicicleta de alto rendimiento para carretera y montaña. Debido a las propiedades naturales del bambú, es más flexible y resiste mejor la vibración.

Biomega RIO
Ross Lovegrove (designer), Flavio Deslandes (bamboo technique), Biomega (company)
www.biomega.com
Copenhagen, Denmark, 2009
© Kenny Viese

This top of the range eco-bike has a frame made entirely of bamboo has a gentle pedal motion. It is low maintenance and highly durable.

Hochwertiges Ökofahrrad mit gesamtem Rahmen aus Bambus, der eine sanfte Achse beinhaltet, wenig wartungsanfällig und langlebig ist.

Bicyclette écologique haut de gamme très durable avec cadre intégralement en bambou et axe très souple, qui demande peu d'entretien.

Deze eco-fiets van het hoge segment, met geïntegreerd bamboe frame, vereist weinig onderhoud en is zeer duurzaam.

Ecobici di alto livello con telaio interamente di bambù e asse morbido; richiede poca manutenzione e dura nel tempo.

Ecobicicleta de gama alta con cuadro íntegro de bambú que contiene un eje suave, necesita poco mantenimiento y tiene una gran durabilidad.

B²O

Antoine Fritsch/Fritsch-Associés
www.fritsch-associes.com
Conflans-Sainte-Honorine, France, 2009
© Christoph Tönges

This design is for an eco-bike with a bamboo-fiber frame. All the sealants and finishes used are organic-based products.

Das Design zeigt ein Ökofahrrad dessen Rahmen aus Bambusfasern ist und mit Sessel und Finishs aus reinen organischen Produkten.

Vélo écologique avec cadre en fibre de bambou revêtu d'une finition à base de produits naturels.

Het ontwerp is een eco-fiets met een bamboevezel frame, met afdichtingen en afwerkingen op basis van organische producten.

Ecobici con telaio in fibra di bambù, giunzioni e finiture a base di prodotti organici.

El diseño es una ecobicicleta cuyo cuadro es de fibra de bambú, con sellados y acabados a base de productos orgánicos.

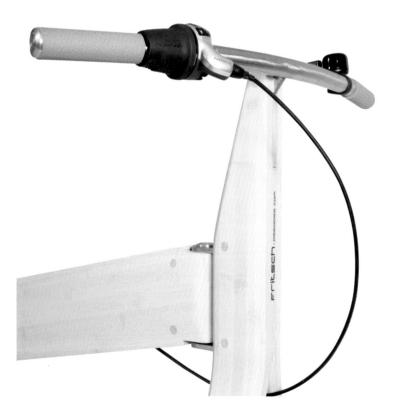

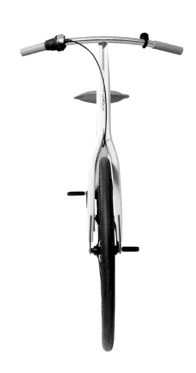

Shellcase for iPad

Vers Audio
www.versaudio.com
Wayland, MA, United States, 2008
© Vers Audio

This handmade iPad case has a metal foot that allows the different applications to be used with a comfortable viewing angle.

Diese Hülle für iPads schützt nicht nur das Gerät, sondern wird auch mit einem Metallsockel geliefert, mit dem man die verschiedenen Anwendungen aus einem bequemen Sichtwinkel bedienen kann.

Cette coque pour iPad a une fonction protectrice. Elle dissimule un pied métallique qui permet de se servir des diverses applications en disposant d'un angle de vision pratique.

Naast het beschermen van het apparaat is in deze handgemaakte beschermcase voor de iPad een metalen voet ingebouwd waarmee de verschillende toepassingen kunnen worden gebruikt, met een comfortabele invalshoek.

Questa custodia per iPad realizzata a mano, dispone di una base metallica che consente di utilizzare le varie applicazioni da un comodo angolo visivo.

Esta carcasa para iPad hecha a mano, incorpora un pie metálico que permite utilizar las distintas aplicaciones con un ángulo visual cómodo.

Vers 1E Earphones

Vers Audio
www.versaudio.com
Wayland, MA, United States, 2008
© Vers Audio

This noise-canceling headset with microphone for iPhones and iPods were handmade from bamboo following sustainability criteria.

Diese Kopfhörer zur Lärmisolierung mit Mikrofon für iPhones und iPods wurden handwerksmäßig aus Bambus unter Einhaltung von Nachhaltigkeitskriterien gefertigt.

De fabrication artisanale, ces écouteurs en bambou avec micro pour iPhone et iPod satisfont aux critères du développement durable.

Deze geluidsisolerende koptelefoon met microfoon voor iPhone en iPod is ambachtelijk gemaakt met bamboe en voldoet aan de duurzaamheidscriteria.

Questi auricolari con sistema di isolamento sonoro dotati di microfono per iPhone e iPod sono stati realizzati artigianalmente con il bambù secondo criteri di sostenibilità.

Estos auriculares de aislamiento de sonido con micrófono para iPhone y iPod fueron elaborados artesanalmente con bambú siguiendo criterios de sostenibilidad.

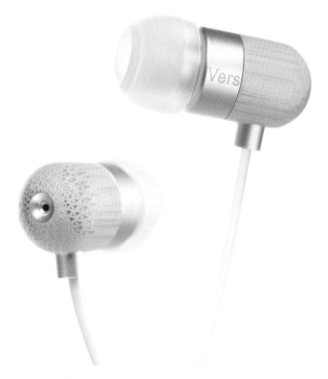

Vers 2X Sound System
Vers Audio
www.versaudio.com
Wayland, MA, United States, 2008
© Vers Audio

Designed to adapt to small spaces, these earbuds offers excellent quality sound owing to its bamboo shell.

Entworfen, um sich an kleinere Räume anzupassen, bietet dieses Gerät einen hervorragenden Sound, dank des Resonanzkastens aus Bambus.

Conçue pour s'adapter à des espaces réduits, cette enceinte offre un son de qualité supérieure grâce à sa caisse de résonance en bambou.

Dit systeem is ontworpen voor kleine ruimtes en geeft een uitstekend geluid, dankzij de bamboe klankkast.

Pensato per adattarsi a piccoli spazi, offre un suono eccellente grazie alla cassa di risonanza in bambù.

Diseñado para adaptarse a espacios pequeños, ofrece un sonido excelente gracias a la caja de resonancia de bambú.

Shellcase for iPhone
Vers Audio
www.versaudio.com
Wayland, MA, United States, 2008
© Vers Audio

The design of this iPhone case combines the toughness and renewable qualities of bamboo with strengthened steel.

Bei dem Design dieser Hülle für iPhones wurde die Widerstandsfähigkeit von verstärktem Stahl und die erneuerbare Eigenschaft des Bambus kombiniert.

Le design de cette coque pour iPhone mise sur le bambou parce que c'est une matière renouvelable. Sa résistance s'associe à celle de l'acier renforcé.

Bij het ontwerp voor deze opbergcase voor de iPhone is de degelijkheid en de kwaliteit van hernieuwbaarheid van het bamboe gecombineerd met versterkt staal.

Nel progetto di questa custodia per iPhone sono state combinate resistenza e qualità di rinnovamento del bambù con l'acciaio rinforzato.

En el diseño de esta carcasa para iPhone se ha combinado la resistencia y la cualidad de renovable del bambú con el acero reforzado.

Vers 1.5R Radio/Alarm
Vers Audio
www.versaudio.com
Wayland, MA, United States, 2008
© Vers Audio

The 1.5R is the result of hybrid design: an alarm clock, radio, and speaker for an iPhone. Handmade, it is easily carried.

Der 1.5R wurde als „hybrides" Design konzipiert: Wecker, Radio und Lautsprecher fürs iPhone. Dieses handwerklich hergestellt Gerät ist besonders leicht tragbar.

Les enceintes iPod/iPhone et Radio réveil 1.5R sont un modèle d'éco-design. De fabrication artisanale, elles voyagent bien.

De 1.5R is bedacht als een "hybride"-ontwerp: nachtalarm, radio en luidspreker voor de iPhone. Ambachtelijk vervaardigd en eenvoudig te vervoeren.

La 1.5R è nata come un progetto «ibrido»: allarme notturno, radio e altoparlante per iPhone. Realizzato artigianalmente, è facilmente trasportabile.

La 1.5R fue concebida con un diseño «híbrido»: alarma de noche, radio y altavoz para iPhone. Se fabricó de manera artesanal y es fácilmente transportable.

Safe Radio
Elise Berthier (designer), Design Republic
(distributor)
www.thedesignrepublic.com
Shanghai, China, 2009
© Lexon/Design Republic

Made in renewable bamboo and eco-friendly
PLA, this radio operates by winding or with an
electrical adapter.

Aus erneuerbarem Bambus und
umweltfreundlichem PLA-Kunststoff hergestellt,
lässt sich dieser Radioapparat mit einer Wicklung
oder einem Stromadapter speisen.

Fabriquée en bambou renouvelable et plastique
recyclable PLA (Poly Acide Lactique) respectueux
de l'environnement, cette radio se recharge avec
une dynamo ou un transformateur.

Deze met recyclebaar bamboe en
milieuvriendelijk PLA-plastic vervaardigde radio
kan worden gevoed met een spoel of met een
stroomadapter.

Prodotta con bambù rinnovabile e plastica PLA
ecologicamente compatibile, questa radio può
essere alimentata da una bobina o un adattatore
di corrente.

Fabricada con bambú renovable y plástico PLA
respetuoso con el medio ambiente, esta radio
se puede alimentar con una bobina o con un
adaptador de corriente.

Bamboo Radio
Elise Berthier (designer), Design Republic
(distributor)
www.thedesignrepublic.com
Shanghai, China, 2009
© Lexon/Design Republic

Clearly inspired by classic styles and made in
natural bamboo and aluminum, this radio has a
telescopic antenna and incorporates an amplifier.

Klar klassisch inspiriert und mit natürlichem
Bambus und Aluminium gefertigt, besteht dieser
Radioapparat aus einer Teleskopantenne und
eingebautem Verstärker und funktioniert mit
Batterien.

D'inspiration classique assumée, cette radio
en bambou naturel est munie d'une antenne
télescopique et d'enceintes incorporées.
Elle fonctionne avec des piles.

De duidelijk klassiek geïnspireerde en in
natuurlijk bamboe en aluminium vervaardigde
radio heeft een telescopische antenne en een
ingebouwde versterker en werkt op een batterij.

Di chiara ispirazione classica e realizzata in
bambù naturale e alluminio, questa radio
dispone di antenna telescopica e amplificatore
incorporato.

De clara inspiración clásica y construida en
bambú natural y aluminio, la radio consta de
antena telescópica y amplificador incorporado.

Bamboo Lamp
Committee (designer), Design Republic
(distributor)
www.thedesignrepublic.com
Shanghai, China, 2007
© Moooi/Design Republic

This minimalist hybrid lamp with stylized curves and sharp silhouette was made using organic material and bamboo, and given a high-quality finish.

Hybride, minimalistische Lampe mit stilisierten Kurven und betonter Silhouette, aus organischen Werkstoffen und Bambus gefertigt, mit einem edlen Finish.

De silhouette élancée, cette lampe hybride minimaliste aux courbes stylisées est entièrement en matériaux naturels, bambou et finition de haut de gamme.

Hybride, minimalistische lamp met stijlvolle lijnen en een slank silhouet, vervaardigd uit organische materie, bamboe en een afwerking van het hoge segment.

Lampada ibrida minimalista dalle curve stilizzate e la linea snella, realizzata con materiali organici, bambù e con finiture esclusive.

Lámpara híbrida minimalista de curvas estilizadas y silueta afilada, elaborada con materia orgánica, bambú y con un acabado de alta gama.

HP Rapelli
Matthias/HAPPY TOYS
www.happy-puzzle.com
www.hape-international.com
Ningbo, China, 2009
© www.happy-puzzle.com

The stability and flexibility of bamboo, together
with non-toxic water-based paint, were a basic
in creating this game.

Die Stabilität und Flexibilität von Bambus
waren neben den nicht toxischen Wasserfarben
fundamental bei der Herstellung dieses
Gesellschaftsspiels.

La stabilité et la flexibilité du bambou ont permis
la conception de ce jouet. Les peintures à l'eau
ne sont pas toxiques.

De duurzaamheid en flexibiliteit van bamboe zijn,
naast de gifvrije waterverf, essentieel geweest
voor dit gezelschapsspel.

La stabilità e la flessibilità del bambù, oltre
alle vernici ad acqua non tossiche, sono state
fondamentali.

La estabilidad y la flexibilidad del bambú, además
de las pinturas al agua no tóxicas, han sido
fundamentales para construir este juego social.

HP Sunshine Dollhouse
Markus and Yang Guokai/HAPPY TOYS
www.happy-puzzle.com
www.hape-international.com
Ningbo, China, 2009
© www.happy-puzzle.com

This eco-friendly dollhouse was designed in
birch veneer plywood and bamboo. It also has
a working solar panel.

Das Öko-Puppenhaus wurde mit
Furnierbirkenholz und Bambus gebaut.
Außerdem hat es eine Solarzelle,
die tatsächlich funktioniert.

Cette maison de poupée écologique a été
réalisée en contreplaqué de bouleau et de
bambou. Le panneau solaire est vrai,
il fonctionne.

Het milieuvriendelijke poppenhuis is ontworpen
met gelaagd berkenhout en bamboe. Het heeft
bovendien een zonnepaneel dat echt werkt.

La casa delle bambole ecologica è stata
progettata con l'impiego di compensato di
betulla e bambù. Inoltre, ha un pannello solare
funzionante.

La casa de muñecas ecológica fue diseñada con
contrachapado de abedul y de bambú. Además,
tiene un panel solar con funcionamiento real.

HP E-Racer Monza, HP E-Racer Le Mans,
HP E-Racer Suzuka
Adam Schillito/HAPPY TOYS
www.happy-puzzle.com
www.hape-international.com
Ningbo, China, 2009
© www.happy-puzzle.com

The body of the E-Racer is made from a carved
bamboo stem. The wheels are lined with rubber.

Das Gestell dieser Autoserie E-Racer wird auf
der Grundlage einer geteilten Bambusstange
gebaut, die Räder sind mit Kautschuk überzogen.

Les voitures de la gamme E-Racer sont taillées
dans une tige de bambou coupée et leurs roues
revêtues de caoutchouc.

Het hoofdsbestanddeel van de E-Racer autoreeks
is gemaakt uit een stuk van een bamboestengel
en de wielen zijn bekleed met rubber.

La struttura della linea di auto di E-Racer
è realizzata partendo da uno stelo di bambù
e le ruote vengono rivestite in caucciù.

El cuerpo de la gama de coches de E-Racer
se construye a partir de un tallo cortado de
bambú y las ruedas se revisten de caucho.

HP E-Truck Yellow
Adam Schillito/HAPPY TOYS
www.happy-puzzle.com
www.hape-international.com
Ningbo, China, 2009
© www.happy-puzzle.com

The actual shape of natural bamboo was made use of in the solid and contemporary design of this toy truck.

Die ganz eigene und natürliche Form des Bambus wurde genutzt, um das robuste und moderne Design dieses Spielzeug-Lasters zu schaffen.

Les formes naturelles du bambou ont été exploitées pour imaginer cette maquette solide d'un camion moderne.

De vorm en aard van bamboe zijn benut voor dit robuuste en moderne ontwerp van deze speelgoedvrachtauto.

La forma tipica naturale del bambù è stata utilizzata per creare il progetto robusto e moderno di questo camion giocattolo.

La forma propia y natural del bambú se ha aprovechado para crear el diseño robusto y moderno de este camión de juguete.

HP E-Offroader
Adam Schillito/HAPPY TOYS
www.happy-puzzle.com
www.hape-international.com
Ningbo, China, 2009
© www.happy-puzzle.com

The body of this SUV is made from a carved bamboo stem. The wheels are lined with rubber so as not to scratch the floor.

Das Gestell des Geländewagens besteht aus zurechtgeschnittenen Bambusstangen. Die Räder sind mit Kautschuk überzogen, um den Boden nicht zu verkratzen.

Ce véhicule tout-terrain est fait dans une tige de bambou coupée. Ses roues, revêtues de caoutchouc, ne rayent pas les sols.

Het hoofdbestanddeel van deze terreinwagen is vervaardigd uit een stuk bamboestengel. De wielen zijn bekleed met rubber zodat ze geen krassen maken op de vloer.

La struttura del fuoristrada è realizzata partendo da uno stelo tagliato di bambù. Le ruote vengono rivestite in caucciù affinché non graffino il pavimento.

El cuerpo del todoterreno está hecho de un tallo cortado de bambú. Las ruedas se revisten de caucho para que no rayen el suelo.

HP E-Plane
Adam Schillito/HAPPY TOYS
www.happy-puzzle.com
www.hape-international.com
Ningbo, China, 2009
© www.happy-puzzle.com

The properties of bamboo, such as
flexibility and stability, enable this toy
plane to fly for many hours of play.

Die Eigenschaften von Bambus, wie
Flexibilität und Stabilität führen dazu,
dass das Spielzeugflugzeug viele
Stunden Flugspiele aushält.

Les propriétés du bambou, sa flexibilité
et sa stabilité, assurent des heures de vol
à cette maquette d'avion et des heures
de jeux à ses heureux propriétaires.

Dankzij de eigenschappen van
bamboe, zoals flexibiliteit en stabiliteit,
kan dit speelgoedvliegtuig tijdens
het spel lange tijd vliegen.

Le proprietà del bambù, come la flessibilità
e la stabilità, fanno sì che l'aereo giocattolo
sia in grado di volare per lunghe ore di gioco.

Las propiedades del bambú, como la flexibilidad
y la estabilidad, hacen que este avión de juguete
sea capaz de volar durante muchas horas
de juego.

Chair Jun Zi
Jeff Dah-Yue Shi (designer), Kao-Ming Chen
(craftsman)/Dragonfly Gallery
www.dragonfly.com.tw
Taipei, Taiwan, 2010
© Dragonfly Gallery

This chair with an elegant and noble design has
a structure consisting of a rounded box made
from bamboo frames.

Elegante und edler Designersessel, dessen
Struktur aus einem abgerundeten Kasten in
Form von Bambushalmen besteht.

Siège aux formes élégantes et nobles dont la
structure se compose d'une caisse arrondie en
forme de cadre en bambou.

Stoel met elegant en nobel ontwerp waarvan de
structuur is opgebouwd uit een ronde vorm met
een omlijsting van bamboestokjes.

Sedia dal design elegante e nobile, la cui
struttura è composta da una cassa stondata
che riprende la forma degli steli di bambù.

Silla de diseño elegante y noble, cuya estructura
se compone de una caja redondeada formada por
varillas de bambú.

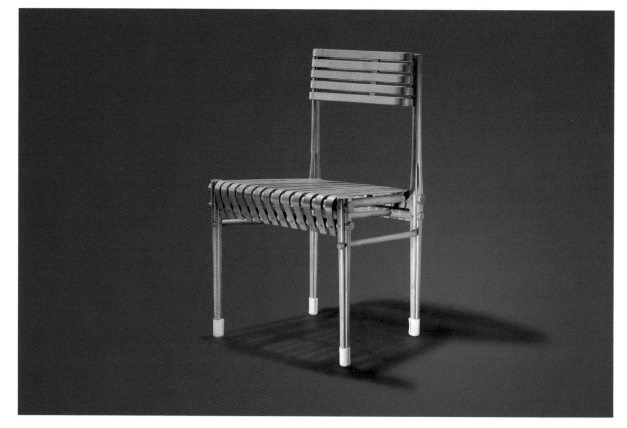

Bentboo Tripod
Chen-Hsu Liu (designer), Kao-Ming Chen
(craftsman)/Yii Design
www.yiidesign.com
Taipei, Taiwan, 2010
© William Chen

This stool was made with a traditional craft
technique and is an example of a new possibility
for using bamboo in mass production.

Dieses Objekt ist mit den beiden Enden eines in
lange Streifen geschnittenen Bambushalms, die
um einen Mittelkern gewoben werden, gefertigt.

Ce tabouret, qui reprend une structure artisanale
traditionnelle, montre une nouvelle utilisation du
bambou pour la production industrielle.

Deze kruk is gefabriceerd met een traditionele
ambachtelijke techniek en vormt een bewijs van
een nieuwe gebruiksmogelijkheid van bamboe
in massaproductie.

Questo sgabello prodotto con una tecnica
artigianale e tradizionale è la dimostrazione di
una nuova possibilità di impiego del bambù nella
produzione di massa.

Este taburete, fabricado con una técnica
artesanal y tradicional, es una demostración
de una nueva posibilidad de uso del bambú
en la producción en masa.

Bambool Barstool and Bambool Stool
Yu Jui Chou (designer), Su-Jen Su (craftsman)/
Yii Design
www.yiidesign.com
Taipei, Taiwan, 2010
© William Chen

Three bamboo canes had their tops split and
woven with bamboo strips to form the seat
of this stool.

Drei Bambusstämme wurden am oberen Teil
durchgeschnitten und mit Bambusfasern
verwoben, um die Sitzfläche dieses Hockers zu
bilden.

Trois tiges de bambou ont été coupées dans leur
partie supérieure, puis ligaturées avec des bandes
de bambou pour former l'assise de ce tabouret.

Drie bamboestammen zijn aan de bovenkant
gespleten en zijn met stroken bamboe gevlochten
om de zitting van deze kruk te vormen.

Tre tronchi di bambù sono stati sezionati nella
parte superiore e intrecciati con strisce di bambù
per dare vita alla seduta di questo sgabello.

Tres troncos de bambú se han seccionado en la
parte superior y se han tejido con tiras de bambú
para formar el asiento de este taburete.

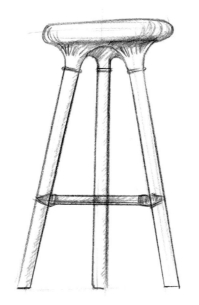

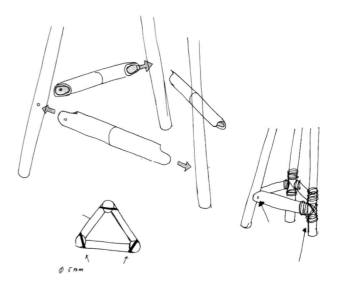

Bamboo Squeeze
Ching-Ting Hsu (designer), Kao-Ming Chen
(craftsman)/Yii Design
www.yiidesign.com
Taipei, Taiwan, 2010
© William Chen

Inspired by a childhood memory, this stool
reinterprets the Taiwanese tradition of using
a cushion as the seat for bamboo chairs.

Inspiriert an Kindererinnerungen auf dem
Lande, wird hier die taiwanesische Tradition
aufgegriffen, ein Kissen als Sitzfläche auf einen
Bambusstuhl zu legen.

Inspiré d'un souvenir d'enfance campagnarde,
ce pouf en bambou est dans la plus pure tradition
taïwanaise.

Deze bamboe kruk is geïnspireerd op een
herinnering uit de kinderjaren op het platteland
en volgt de Taiwanese traditie van een kussen
als zitplaats in een bamboe stoel.

Ispirandosi ai ricordi rurali d'infanzia, viene
ripresa la tradizione taiwanese di mettere un
cuscino come seduta in una sedia di bambù.

Inspirada en un recuerdo rural infantil, se recoge
la tradición taiwanesa de poner un cojín como
asiento en una silla de bambú.

Cocoon Plan-Sofa and Twin Stool
Rock Wang (designer), Kao-Ming Chen
(craftsman)/Yii Design
www.yiidesign.com
Taipei, Taiwan, 2010
© William Chen

Shaped like silkworm cocoons, one was made
by interlacing bamboo strips and the other
has a plain silky surface.

In Form eines Kokons einer Seidenraupe.
Gefertigt aus geflochtenen Bambusstreifen.
Die andere Seite weist eine glatte, seidige
Oberfläche auf.

En forme de cocon de vers à soie, ces objets
se tissent en alternant bandes de bambou
et de matière lisse et soyeuse.

Een van deze stoelen die de vorm van de cocon
van een zijderups hebben, is gemaakt door het
vervlechten van stroken bamboe en de andere
heeft een vlak, zijdeachtig oppervlak.

Una forma che ricorda i bozzoli dei bachi da
seta... uno è realizzato intrecciando strisce di
bambù e l'altro è caratterizzato da una superficie
liscia e setosa.

En forma de capullo de gusanos de seda, uno se
construye entrelazando tiras de bambú y el otro
con una superficie lisa sedosa.

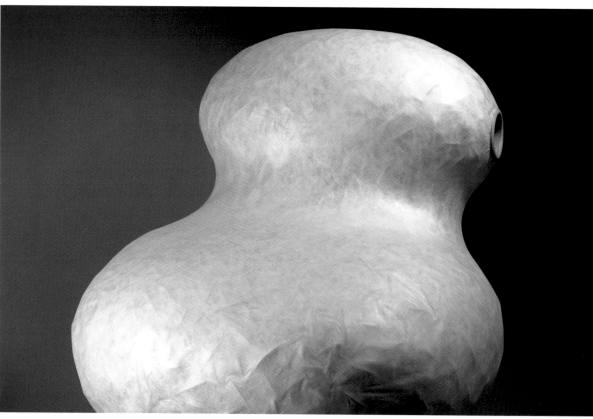

Bamboo Heart
Yu Jui Chou (designer), Su-Jen Su (craftsman)/
Yii Design
www.yiidesign.com
Taipei, Taiwan, 2010
© William Chen

This object was made from the two ends of a bamboo cane cut into long strips and woven around a central piece.

Dieses Objekt ist mit den beiden Enden eines in lange Streifen geschnittenen Bambushalms, die um einen Mittelkern gewoben werden, gefertigt.

Objet construit avec les deux extrémités d'une tige de bambou débitée en larges bandes que l'on tisse autour d'une pièce centrale.

Voorwerp met aan de uiteinden een bamboestam die in lange repen is gesneden, die rondom een centraal onderdeel zijn gevlochten.

Oggetto realizzato con due estremità di un tronco di bambù tagliate a strisce lunghe intrecciate intorno a un elemento centrale.

Objeto construido con dos extremos de un tronco de bambú cortados en tiras largas que se tejen en torno a una pieza central.

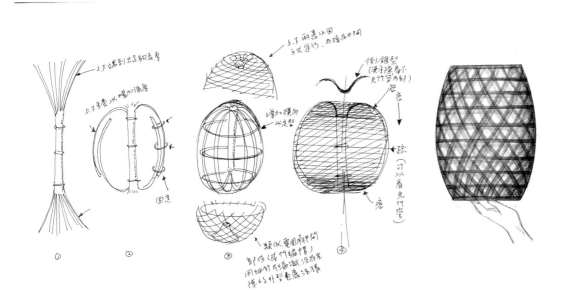

THE STRENGTH OF THE STOOL IS FROM THE LAYERS OF WEAVING.
IT REQUIRES "LAYER BY LAYER" STEP.
IT'S LIKE BOTTLE IN BOTTLE.

Meow
Yu-fen Lo (designer), Su-Jen Su (craftsman)/
Yii Design
www.yiidesign.com
Taipei, Taiwan, 2010
© William Chen

This lamp imitates a pet lying on a sofa. It is
made from bamboo strips that leave small
openings for light to pass.

Lampe, die ein auf einem Sofa sitzendes
Haustierchen nachahmt. Aus Bambushalmen
gefertigt, die kleine Öffnungen bieten, um Licht
durchzulassen.

Luminaire qui imite une mascotte lovée sur
un canapé. Ce luminaire fait de bandelettes de
bambou laisse filtrer la lumière.

Lamp die lijkt op een huisdier dat op de bank
ligt. Gemaakt van stroken bamboe met kleine
lichtdoorlatende openingen.

Lampada che ricorda un cucciolo sdraiato su
un divano. È realizzata con strisce di bambù con
piccole aperture per lasciare passare la luce.

Lámpara que imita a una mascota tumbada en
un sofá. Construida con tiras de bambú que dejan
pequeñas aberturas para dejar pasar la luz.

The Cradle
Chia-en Lu (designer), Kao-ming Chen
(craftsman)/Yii Design
www.yiidesign.com
Taipei, Taiwan, 2010
© William Chen

The precise placement and interlacing
of bamboo strips gives the gentle
movements of a rocking crib.

Die genaue und verflochtene Anordnung
der Bambusstreifen ermöglicht
die sanften Bewegungen, die einer
Kinderwiege zu Eigen sind.

C'est le positionnement précis des bandes
de bambou entrelacées qui assure le doux
balancement séant à un berceau à bascule.

De uitgekiende manier waarop de stroken
bamboe zijn vervlochten maken de rustige
bewegingen van een schommelwieg mogelijk.

La disposizione precisa e l'intreccio delle
strisce di bambù consentono i movimenti
morbidi della culla.

La disposición precisa y entrelazada de las tiras
de bambú permiten los movimientos suaves de
una cuna mecedora.

World Cups: Bamboo Waves
Idee Liu (designer), Chun-han Lin (craftsman)/
Yii Design
www.yiidesign.com
Taipei, Taiwan, 2010
© William Chen

The recognizable circular logo on Starbucks
cups are combined with traditional Taiwanese
bamboo craft.

Der runde, leicht wiedererkennbare Logotyp
der Gefäße von Starbucks wird hier mit dem
traditionellen Bambuskunsthandwerk aus Taiwan
verbunden.

Le logotype rond bien reconnaissable des verres
de Starbucks s'associe à l'artisanat traditionnel
taïwanais en bambou.

Het circulaire logotype dat bekend is van
de Starbucks glazen is gecombineerd met
traditioneel Taiwanees bamboe ambachtswerk.

Il logo circolare riconoscibile dei bicchieri
di Starbucks si combina con l'artigianato
tradizionale taiwanese del bambù.

El logotipo circular reconocible de los vasos
de Starbucks se combina con la artesanía
tradicional taiwanesa del bambú.

Bamboo Chair
Tejo Remy & Rene Veenhuizen/Atelier Remy
Veenhuizen
www.remyveenhuizen.nl
Utrech, The Netherlands, 2010
© Nathan King Photography

Dutch architects utilized a braiding technique
for laminated bamboo strips to create exclusive
chair designs.

Die niederländischen Architekten haben die
Flechttechnik von laminierten Bambusstreifen
genutzt, um exklusive Sesseldesigns zu schaffen.

Les architectes hollandais utilisèrent la structure
des bandes tressées en bambou laminé pour
créer une gamme de sièges exclusifs.

De Nederlandse architecten hebben voor dit
exclusieve stoelontwerp de techniek van het
vlechten van bamboestroken gebruikt.

Gli architetti olandesi hanno impiegato la tecnica
dell'intreccio di strisce di bambù laminato per
creare sedie esclusive.

Estos arquitectos holandeses emplearon la
técnica del trenzado de tiras de bambú laminado
para crear diseños exclusivos de sillas.

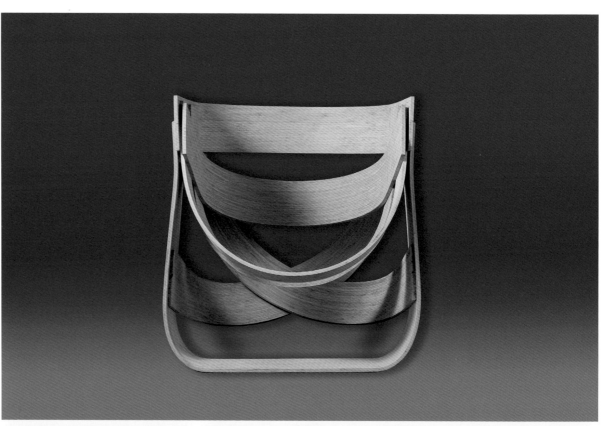

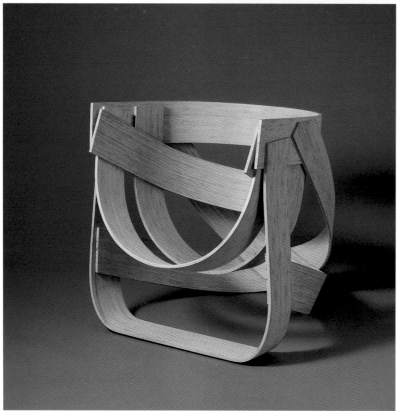

Counter Stool
David N. Ebner
www.davidnebner.com
Brookhaven, NY, United States, 2005
© Steven Amiaga

Solid bamboo stool with plywood core. It represents the Chinese "tree" character', which means peace, calm, and harmony.

Solider Bambushocker mit Furnierholzkern. Stellt das chinesische Schriftzeichen für „Baum" dar, das zugleich auch Friede, Stille und Harmonie bedeuten kann.

Tabouret en bambou très résistant sur un socle en bois contreplaqué. Il reproduit l'idéogramme chinois représentant l'arbre, symbole de paix, calme et harmonie.

Solide bamboe kruk met een kern van gelaagd hout. Het beeldt het Chinese karakter voor "boom" uit, hetgeen vrede, kalmte en harmonie betekent.

Solido sgabello di bambù con nucleo di legno compensato. Rappresenta il carattere cinese dell'albero, che significa pace, calma e armonia.

Taburete de bambú sólido con núcleo de madera contrachapada. Representa el carácter chino de «árbol», que significa paz, calma y armonía.

Side Table I
David N. Ebner
www.davidnebner.com
Brookhaven, NY, United States, 2005
© Steven Amiaga

Side table in bamboo with a plywood core. It has simple and classic styling with Oriental influence.

Beistelltisch aus Bambus auf einem Kern aus Furnierholz. Klassisches und einfaches Design mit asiatischer Note.

Petite table dont le dessus en bambou repose sur un socle de contreplaqué. De facture classique et sobre, ce meuble rappelle l'Orient qui l'a inspiré.

Bamboe bijzettafeltje op een gelaagd houten ondervlak. Klassieke en eenvoudige uitvoering met oriëntaalse invloeden.

Tavolo aggiuntivo di bambù su un nucleo di legno compensato. Fattura classica e semplice, di ispirazione orientale.

Mesa auxiliar de bambú sobre un núcleo de madera contrachapada. De factura clásica y sencilla con inspiración oriental.

Bench
David N. Ebner
www.davidnebner.com
Brookhaven, NY, United States, 2005
© Steven Amiaga

Clearly Asian in inspiration, the functionality
and amber finish of this bench are features
of its design.

Klar asiatisch inspiriert in ihrer Struktur,
Funktionalität und Endbearbeitung in Bernstein:
dies sind die Hauptdesigneigenschaften dieser
Sitzbank.

D'inspiration résolument asiatique, la structure,
la fonctionnalité et la finition ambre de ce banc
soulignent la beauté des lignes.

De structuur, functionaliteit en amber afwerking
van deze bank, met een duidelijke Aziatische
invloed, zijn de belangrijkste kenmerken van
het ontwerp.

Di chiara ispirazione asiatica, la struttura, la
funzionalità e la finitura ambra sono le principali
caratteristiche del progetto.

De clara inspiración asiática, la estructura, la
funcionalidad y el acabado ámbar del banco son
las principales características del diseño.

Vanity Piano Bench
David N. Ebner
www.davidnebner.com
Brookhaven, NY, United States, 2005
© Steven Amiaga

Bench in amber and natural bamboo the
combines the bamboo with plywood, used
as a piano stool.

Bänkchen in Bernstein- und natürlicher
Bambusfarbe, welches Bambus mit Furnierholz
kombiniert und als Klavierstuhl dient.

Tabouret de piano de couleurs ambre et bambou
naturel réalisé en bambou et bois contreplaqué.

Bankje, met amberkleuren en natuurlijk bamboe
waarin bamboe gecombineerd is met gelaagd
hout, dat gebruikt kan worden als pianokruk.

Panca colorata ambra e bambù naturale, che
combina il bambù con il legno compensato,
utilizzata come seduta per i pianisti.

Banco de colores ámbar y bambú natural que
combina el bambú con madera contrachapada,
utilizado como asiento para pianistas.

Sideboard
David N. Ebner
www.davidnebner.com
Brookhaven, NY, United States, 2005
© Steven Amiaga

The design of this multi-purpose cabinet
represents a Chinese character symbolizing
nature and a reference to tranquility and
harmony.

Das Design dieser Mehrzweck-Anrichte stellt
ein chinesisches Schriftzeichen in Verbindung
mit der Natur dar, das auf Ruhe und Harmonie
verweist.

Ce buffet ou meuble de rangement reproduit
un idéogramme chinois lié à la nature qui évoque
la tranquillité et l'harmonie.

Het ontwerp van deze veelzijdige servieskast
heeft de vorm van een Chinees karakter dat
verband houdt met de natuur en verwijst naar
rust en harmonie.

Il progetto di questa credenza multiuso
rappresenta il carattere cinese legato alla
natura, che ispira tranquillità e armonia.

El diseño de este aparador de múltiples usos
representa un carácter chino vinculado a la
naturaleza y que remite a la tranquilidad y la
armonía.

Mirror
David N. Ebner
www.davidnebner.com
Brookhaven, NY, United States, 2005
© Steven Amiaga

Dressing table comprising table and mirror with
strong Asian inspiration and amber finishes.
It has a wide variety of uses.

Kommode, die aus Tisch und Spiegel besteht,
und mit seinen Bernsteinfinishs klar asiatisch
inspiriert ist. Lässt sich sehr vielseitig einsetzen.

Coiffeuse formée d'une table surmontée d'un
miroir d'inspiration orientale avec finition ambre.
Ce meuble se prête à de multiples utilisations.

Toilettafel bestaande uit een tafel en een
ingelijste spiegel met Aziatische invloeden,
afgewerkt in amber. Zeer veelzijdig in gebruik.

Toeletta formata da un tavolino e uno specchio
di chiara ispirazione asiatica, con finiture ambra.
Il mobile può avere molteplici usi.

Tocador formado por mesa y espejo de marcada
inspiración asiática y acabados en ámbar. Tiene
una gran variedad de usos.

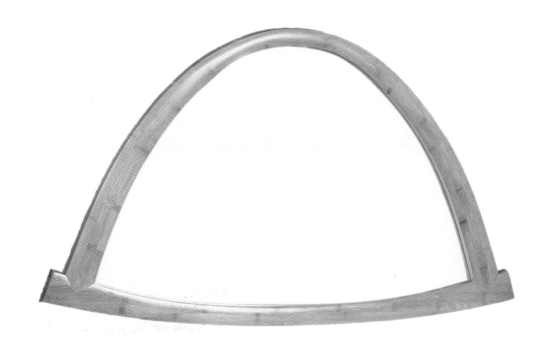

Slatted Bench
David N. Ebner
www.davidnebner.com
Brookhaven, NY, United States, 2005
© Steven Amiaga

Handmade in an amber or natural finish,
the use of slats is an exploration of traditional
furniture design.

Handgefertigt und Endbearbeitung in
Bernstein oder natur. Dieses Designmöbel
aus Bambusstäben basiert auf den
traditionellen Formen des Möbelbaus.

Ouvrage entièrement réalisé à la main,
existant en finition ambre ou naturelle.
Il explore le potentiel du dessin traditionnel
revisité par l'usage des baguettes.

Het handgemaakte en in amber of naturel
afgewerkte ontwerp met latten brengt de
traditionele vormen van meubelontwerp
naar voren.

Realizzato a mano e con finiture ambra o
naturale, il progetto a listoni esplora le forme
tradizionali dei mobili di arredo

Realizado a mano y con acabado en ámbar o
natural, el diseño en listones explora las formas
tradicionales del diseño de muebles.

End Table
David N. Ebner
www.davidnebner.com
Brookhaven, NY, United States, 2005
© Steven Amiaga

Traditional furniture design was inspiration
for this original high table.

Die traditionelle Gestaltungsform von Möbeln
war der ausgehende Inspirationspunkt für die
Kreation dieses originellen und besonders hohen
Tisches.

Les formes traditionnelles du mobilier ont inspiré
cette table très haute d'une grande originalité.

De traditionele vorm van het meubelontwerp is
een inspiratiebron geweest voor de creatie van
deze originele, hoge tafel.

La forma tradizionale degli arredi è stata la fonte
di ispirazione per la creazione di questo originale
tavolo, molto alto.

La forma tradicional del diseño de muebles
ha sido el punto de inspiración para la creación
de esta original mesa de gran altura.

Os Bench
Marjolain Poulin
www.maobamboo.blogspot.com
San Salvador, El Salvador, 2008-2010
© Marjolain Poulin

Thick bamboo canes form the seat and legs of
the bench, which is finished in Holm oak, cypress
and walnut wood.

Großkalibrige Bambusstangen bilden den Sitz und
die Beine der Bank, die mit Eichen-, Zypressen-
und Nussbaumholz abgeschlossen wird.

Des tiges de bambou de large diamètre forment
l'assise et les pieds de ce banc dont les finitions
en bois sont en chêne vert, cyprès et noyer.

Bamboestengels van groot kaliber vormen
deze zitplaats en de poten van de bank, die is
afgewerkt met eikenhout, cipres en notenhout.

Canne di bambù di grande calibro compongono
la seduta e le gambe della panca, ribattuta con
legno di quercia, cipresso e noce.

Cañas de bambú de gran calibre constituyen
el asiento y las patas del banco, que se remata
con madera de encina, ciprés y nogal.

Delsol Chair
Marjolain Poulin
www.maobamboo.blogspot.com
San Salvador, El Salvador, 2008-2010
© Marjolain Poulin

Bamboo has a starring role in the foot a
nd head rest of this beach chaise lounge.

Strandliege, bei der Bambus in Form großer
Zylinder die Hauptrolle bei der Fußstütze und
Kopfstütze spielt.

Chaise longue où le bambou a servi à
la fabrication du repose-pieds et du repose-tête
en forme de grands cylindres.

Standstoel waar bamboe een belangrijke rol
speelt in de voetsteun en de hoofdsteun in de
vorm van grote cilinders.

Sdraio da spiaggia dove il bambù è protagonista,
nel poggiapiedi e nel poggiatesta, sotto forma
di grandi cilindri.

Tumbona de playa donde el bambú cobra
protagonismo en el reposapiés y el reposacabezas
en forma de grandes cilindros.

Corset Chair
Marjolain Poulin
www.maobamboo.blogspot.com
San Salvador, El Salvador, 2008-2010
© Jianca Lazrus

Pine and bamboo were used for this handmade
chair. Small bamboo canes make up the body
of the back and seat.

Pinie und Bambus kamen bei der handwerklichen
Fertigung dieses Stuhls zum Einsatz. Kleine
Bambusstämme bilden die Körper der
Rückenlehne und der Sitzfläche.

Pin et bambou entrent dans la fabrication
de cette chaise de construction artisanale.
De minces tiges de bambou forment le dossier
et l'assise.

Grenenhout en bamboe zijn gebruikt in
deze ambachtelijk gemaakte stoel. Kleine
bamboestengels vormen het hoofdbestanddeel
van de rugleuning en zitting.

Pino e bambù sono utilizzati per la costruzione
artigianale della sedia. Piccole canne di bambù
costituiscono il corpo dello schienale e della
seduta.

Pino y bambú son los materiales utilizados para
la construcción artesanal de esta silla. Pequeñas
cañas de bambú forman el cuerpo del respaldo
y el asiento.

Bookcase End Isle Units
David N. Ebner
www.davidnebner.com
Brookhaven, NY, United States, 2005
© Steven Amiaga

Functional and practical, these elegantly-styled
bookshelves were made entirely of bamboo.

Funktional und praktisch, wurden diese elegant
wirkenden Bücherregale ausschließlich aus
Bambus und per Hand gefertigt.

Fonctionnelles, pratiques et de facture élégante,
ces bibliothèques en bambou ont été réalisées
entièrement à la main.

Deze functionele, praktische en elegante
boekenplanken zijn helemaal met de hand
vervaardigd van bamboe.

Funzionali e pratiche, di fattura elegante, queste
scaffalature di libri sono state realizzate a mano
interamente in bambù.

Funcional y práctica, de factura elegante, estas
estanterías de libros han sido elaboradas a mano
íntegramente en bambú.

Bamboo Bottle
Bamboo Bottle Company
www.bamboobottleco.com
Portsmouth, NH, United States, 2010
© Bamboo Bottle Company

Reusable bamboo (*Phyllostachys pubescens*) and glass bottle. It features an elegant and functional eco-friendly design.

Aus Bambus (*Phyllostachys pubescens*) und Glas hergestellte, wiederverwertbare Flasche, die umweltfreundlich ist und dennoch nicht auf ein elegantes und funktionales Design verzichtet.

Élégante et fonctionnelle, cette bouteille réutilisable fabriquée en bambou géant (*Phyllostachys pubescens*) et verre est respectueuse de l'environnement.

Milieuvriendelijke navulbare fles, gemaakt van (*Phyllostachys pubescens*) bamboe en glas, met een elegant en functioneel ontwerp.

Bottiglia riutilizzabile realizzata in bambù (*Phyllostachys pubescens*) e vetro, rispettosa dell'ambiente e dalle linee eleganti e funzionali.

Botella reutilizable fabricada en bambú (*Phyllostachys pubescens*) y vidrio, respetuosa con el medio ambiente y con un diseño elegante y funcional.

Medio, Gemo, Bo and Solo
Boo Louis/EKOBO Design
www.ekobo.org
Nimes, France 2010
© Boo Louis/EKOBO Design

The bowl, serving dish, and salad servers are
lacquered on the outside, and have an interior
of sanded and treated bamboo.

Tiefer Teller, Platte und Salatbesteck sind aus
gehobeltem und innen behandeltem Bambus,
und wurden außen lackiert.

Plateau creux, grand plat et couverts de service
pour salade en bambou. La face externe est
laquée et la face interne traitée pour contact
alimentaire.

Diep bord, schaal en slabestek, van buiten gelakt
en van binnen van geschuurd en behandeld
bamboe.

Piatto fondo, piatto piano e posate per insalata
laccati all'esterno e in bambù levigato e trattato
all'interno.

Plato hondo, fuente y cubiertos de servir para
ensaladas lacados en su exterior y de bambú
lijado y tratado en su interior.

Maxi Plato
Boo Louis/EKOBO Design
www.ekobo.org
Nimes, France 2010
© Boo Louis/EKOBO Design

This lightweight plate has a large capacity.
It was designed with a solid, raised edge to
prevent spills and to make it easy to hold.

Leichter Teller mit großer Aufnahmefähigkeit,
der mit einem robusten und hohen Rand
konzipiert wurde, um ein Überlaufen zu
vermeiden und ihn bequem festhalten zu können.

Grand plateau léger avec un solide rebord
conçu pour éviter de renverser son chargement
et assurer une bonne prise.

Licht bord met grote inhoud, ontworpen met een
robuuste en hoge rand, om morsen te voorkomen
en waardoor het goed kan worden opgepakt.

Piatto leggero e molto capiente, con un bordo
robusto e alto per evitare di disperderne il
contenuto; comoda impugnatura.

Plato ligero de gran capacidad diseñado
con un borde robusto y alto para evitar derrames
y permitir una sujeción cómoda.

Apero and Copo
Boo Louis/EKOBO Design
www.ekobo.org
Nimes, France 2010
© Boo Louis/EKOBO Design

These small leaf-shaped plates in treated
bamboo were specially designed for serving
sauces, hors d'œuvres, and snacks. Modern
multi-purpose glasses.

Kleine Bambustellerchen, die in Blattform
behandelt wurden, eignen sich besonders
zum Servieren von Saucen, Häppchen oder
Vorspeisen. Mehrzweckgefäß mit modernem
Charakter.

Petits plateaux en bambou traités en forme de
feuille, spécialement conçus pour servir sauces,
tapas et amuse-gueules. Verres contemporains
pour toutes sortes de boisson.

Deze kleine bamboeschoteltjes in de vorm van
een blad zijn speciaal ontworpen om sausen,
borrelhapjes of aperitieven in te serveren.
Veelzijdige kom in een moderne uitvoering.

Piccoli piatti di bambù trattato a forma di foglia,
pensati per la presentazione di salse, stuzzichini
o aperitivi. Bicchiere multiuso dalle linee
moderne.

Pequeños platos de bambú tratado en forma de
hoja, especialmente diseñados para presentar
salsas, tapas o aperitivos. Vaso multiusos de
factura moderna.

Rondo
Boo Louis/EKOBO Design
www.ekobo.org
Nimes, France 2010
© Boo Louis/EKOBO Design

Small easily-stored stackable round plates. The bamboo has been treated so it can be used for serving hot and cold food.

Kleine runde, stapelbare Tellerchen, die sich einfach verstauen lassen. Die Behandlung des Bambus macht es möglich, sowohl warme als auch kalte Speisen auf ihnen zu servieren.

Petits plats ronds empilables faciles à ranger. Le traitement du bambou, agréé pour un usage alimentaire, convient au chaud comme au froid.

Kleine ronde, stapelbare en eenvoudig op te bergen borden. Dankzij het behandelde bamboe kan er zowel warm als koud voedsel in worden opgediend.

Piccoli piatti stondati e impilabili, che possono essere facilmente riposti. Il trattamento del bambù consente di utilizzarli per servire sia piatti caldi che freddi.

Pequeños platos redondos y apilables de fácil almacenamiento. El tratamiento del bambú permite servir alimentos calientes y fríos.

Lotus Leaf
Wong Chi Fung (designer), Design Republic
(distributor)
www.thedesignrepublic.com
Shanghai, China, 2009
© Jia/Design Republic

Bamboo and porcelain stoneware are the
materials used for this plates inspired by lotus
leaves. Their curved design makes them easy
to lift.

Bambus und Sandstein sind die Grundmaterialien
dieser Teller, die von Lotusblättern anregt
wurden. Mit geneigtem Rand, um leichter
gehandhabt zu werden .

Ces assiettes aux formes inspirées par des
feuilles de lotus sont en bambou et grès. Leurs
courbes assurent une bonne prise en main.

Bamboe en keramiek zijn de belangrijkste
materialen van deze borden die geïnspireerd zijn
op lotusbladeren. Met gebogen, ontwerp zodat
ze eenvoudig kunnen worden opgepakt.

Bambù e gres sono i materiali di base di questi
piatti ispirati alle foglie di loto. Il prodotto è
pensato curvo per essere facilmente sollevabile.

Bambú y gres son los materiales básicos de
estos platos inspirados en las hojas de loto.
Diseño curvo para que se puedan levantar
fácilmente.

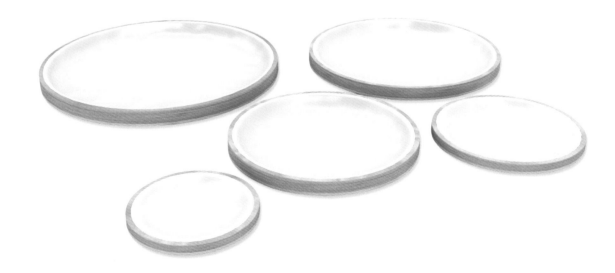

Family Bowl
Wong Chi Feng (designer), Design Republic
(distributor)
www.thedesignrepublic.com
Shanghai, China, 2009
© Jia/Design Republic

These porcelain stoneware and bamboo bowls
feature the homely and elegant design that is
the company's trademark.

Aus Sandstein und Bambus gefertigte Schalen,
die ein Design auf der Grundlage von Wärme
und Eleganz zeigen, das so charakteristisch für
dieses Unternehmen ist.

Bols en grès et bambou dont les formes
chaleureuses et élégantes sont caractéristiques
de l'entreprise.

Kommen van keramiek en bamboe met een
ontwerp waarbij rekening is gehouden met de
warmte en elegantie die kenmerkend zijn voor
het bedrijf.

Ciotole in gres e bambù, con una linea basata
sul calore e l'eleganza caratteristica di questa
azienda.

Boles fabricados con gres y bambú con un diseño
basado en la calidez y la elegancia característica
de la empresa.

Mini Tivo
Boo Louis/EKOBO Design
www.ekobo.org
Nimes, France 2010
© Boo Louis/EKOBO Design

Stackable rectangular trays for one or two persons. They are hand made and varnished, and are stain and odor proof.

Rechteckige, stapelbare Tabletts für ein oder zwei Personen. Handgefertigt, gebeizt und flecken- und geruchsabweisend.

Plats rectangulaires empilables pour une ou deux personnes. Faits à la main, vernis et traités antitaches et anti-odeurs.

Rechthoekige en stapelbare bladen voor een of twee personen. Handgemaakt, gelakt, vlek- en geurbestendig.

Vassoi rettangolari e impilabili per una o due persone. Realizzati a mano, verniciati e resistenti a macchie e odori.

Bandejas rectangulares y apilables para una o dos personas. Construidas a mano, barnizadas y resistentes a manchas y olores.

Mikoto
Martin Robitsch/EKOBO Design
www.ekobo.org
Nimes, France 2010
© Boo Louis/EKOBO Design

This spike-filled knifeholder allows several knives to be inserted in any way. It is hand made entirely of bamboo.

Der Holzblock voller Einkerbungen ermöglicht das Einschieben von Küchenmessern aller Größen. 100% aus handwerklichem Bambus hergestellt.

Ce support rempli de pointes peut recevoir plusieurs couteaux de formes diverses. Il est entièrement en bambou artisanal.

In dit messenblok kunnen verschillende messen met willekeurige vormen worden geplaatst. 100% vervaardigd uit ambachtelijk bamboe.

La struttura traforata consente di inserirvi coltelli di ogni forma. Realizzato al 100% con bambù artigianale.

La tacoma llena de pinchos permite insertar varios cuchillos de cualquier forma. Construido 100% con bambú y de forma artesanal.

Blo
A. Lassalmonie, F. Manzi/EKOBO Design
www.ekobo.org
Nimes, France 2010
© Boo Louis/EKOBO Design

This tissue dispenser has a bright lacquered frame and box made entirely of treated bamboo. It is refillable and can be hung on the wall.

Taschentuchspender mit einem lackierten, glänzenden Rahmen und der vollkommen aus behandeltem Bambus gefertigten Kiste. Nachfüllbar und mit der Möglichkeit, ihn an der Wand aufzuhängen.

Boîte à mouchoirs dont la face externe brillante laquée est en bambou traité. Rechargeable, elle s'accroche au mur.

Tissuedooshouder met een wit gelakte omlijsting van bamboe. Navulbaar en met mogelijkheid om aan de wand te hangen.

Scatola porta-fazzoletti con una cornice laccata brillante e struttura in bambù trattato. Ricaricabile; può essere appesa alla parete.

Caja dispensadora de pañuelos con un marco lacado brillante y la caja íntegra de bambú tratado. Recargable y con opción de colgar en la pared.

Modulo
A. Lassalmonie, F. Manzi/EKOBO Design
www.ekobo.org
Nimes, France 2010
© Boo Louis/EKOBO Design

Bamboo recipient and separate lacquered frame. Adjustable and rotating, it stores brushes, toothpaste, clips, pencils and combs.

Bambusgefäß und separater, lackierter Rahmen. Lässt sich anpassen und drehen, um Zahnbürsten, Zahnpasta, Pinzetten, Stifte und Kämme aufzunehmen.

Nécessaire de salle de bains en bambou et cadre indépendant laqué. Réglable, il tourne et permet de ranger brosses à dents, dentifrice, pinces à épiler, crayons et peignes.

Bamboe opbergdoosje met afneembare gelakte lijst. Afstelbaar en draaibaar, voor het opbergen van borstels, tandpasta, pincet, potloden en kammen.

Recipiente di bambù e cornice separata laccata. Regolabile, girevole, consente di conservare spazzolini, dentifricio, pinzette, trucchi e pettini.

Recipiente de bambú y marco separado lacado. Es ajustable y giratorio para poder almacenar cepillos, pasta de dientes, pinzas, lápices y peines.

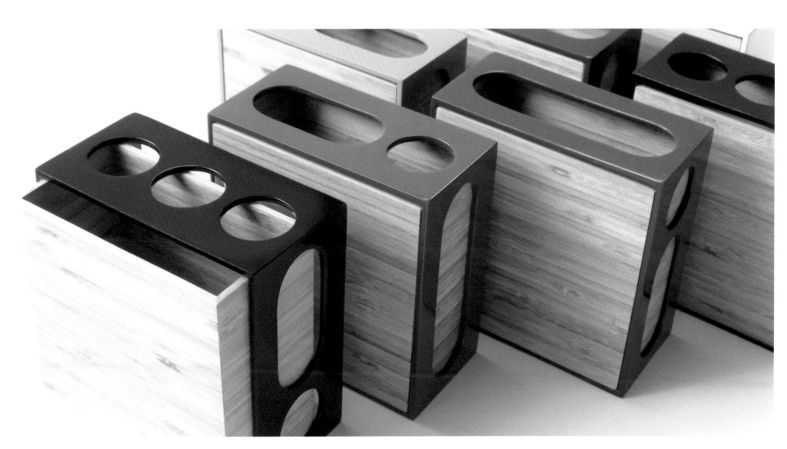

Zig Shelf
Ryan Frank
www.ryanfrank.net
Milan, Italy, 2008
© Ryan Frank

This modular bookcase in solid bamboo is an exclusive eco-friendly design for the 2008 Milan Furniture Fair.

Die Modulregale aus solidem Bambus sind ein exklusives und umweltfreundliches Design für die Mailand Möbelmesse 2008.

Étagère modulaire en bambou, modèle exclusif respectueux de l'environnement présenté au Salon du meuble de Milan en 2008.

Deze uit modules bestaande solide bamboe boekenkast was een exclusief en milieuvriendelijk ontwerp voor de Meubelbeurs van Milaan van 2008.

La scaffalatura modulare in bambù solido è un progetto esclusivo ed ecologico realizzato in occasione del Salone del Mobile di Milano 2008.

La estantería modular de bambú sólido es un diseño exclusivo y respetuoso con el medio ambiente para el Salón del Mueble de Milán 2008.

Chair 1 and Chair 2
Christel Hadiwibawa
www.christelh.com
Sydney, Australia, 2009
© N. Lange, H. Richardson/Intrigue
Photography and Gallery

The fine strips in these chairs were inspired by
the resistance, flexibility, and durability of Asian
bamboo scaffolds.

Die Widerstands- Flexibilitäts- und Lebensdauer-
Eigenschaften von chinesischen Baugerüsten
aus Bambus standen Pate für die feinen
Bambusstreifen des Sitzes.

La résistance, la flexibilité et la longévité des
échafaudages asiatiques en bambou ont inspiré
les fines bandelettes des sièges.

Bestendigheid, flexibiliteit en duurzaamheid
zijn de eigenschappen van de Aziatische
bamboesteigers, waarop de smalle stroken
van de stoelen geïnspireerd zijn.

Le proprietà di resistenza, flessibilità e durata
delle impalcature asiatiche in bambù hanno
ispirato le sottili strisce che caratterizzano
queste sedie.

Las propiedades de resistencia, flexibilidad y
durabilidad de los andamios asiáticos de bambú
inspiraron las finas tiras de las sillas.

ARCHITECTS DIRECTORY / RÉPERTOIRE DES ARCHITECTES

24H > Architecture
Rotterdam, The Netherlands
www.24h-architecture.com
Education Center at Soneva Kiri Resort

Anna Heringer, Eike Roswag/
Ziegert|Roswag|Seiler Architekten Ingenieure
Aga Khan Development Network
Berlin, Germany
www.zrs-berlin.de
www.akdn.org
Hand-Made School

Atelier Tekuto, Fasil Giorgis
Tokyo, Japan
www.tekuto.com
Ethiopia-Japanese Millennium Pavilion

Blanc Borderless Architecture, João Caeiro
Lisbon, Portugal
www.blaanc.com
Emerging Ghana

BUILD LLC
Seattle, WA, USA
www.buildllc.com
Artist's Studio

Casagrande Laboratory Taiwan
Taipei, Taiwan
www.clab.fi
Bug Dome

Christoph Tönges/CONBAM
Geilenkirchen, Germany
www.conbam.de
www.bambus-conbam.de
Bamboo Dome Europe 2004
Bamboo Sculpture Pinakothek

David A. García
Copenhagen, Denmark
www.davidgarciastudio.com
The Weaving Project Pavilion

David Sands/Bamboo Living
Paia, HI, USA
www.bambooliving.com
Pacific Tahitian

De Leon & Primmer Architecture Workshop
Louisville, KY, USA
www.deleon-primmer.com
Mason Lane Farm

Eric Gartner/SPG Architects
New York, NY, USA
www.spgarchitects.com
Caretaker's House

Esan Rahmani
Sydney, Australia
www.esanrahmani.net
Sustainable Bamboo Pavilion

Estudio Lamela Arquitectos
Madrid, Spain
www.lamela.com
Madrid-Barajas Airport

Foreign Office Architects (FOA)
London, United Kingdom
www.f-o-a.net
Carabanchel Social Housing

Gerard Minakawa/Bamboo DNA
New York, NY, USA
www.bamboodna.com
Bamboo Gateway
Bamboo Starscraper
The DROP

GMP – Architekten von Gerkan,
Marg und Partner
Hamburg, Germany
www.gmp-architekten.de
Bamboo Sculpture Pinakothek

Gray Organschi Architecture
New Haven, CT, USA
www.grayorganschi.com
Cottage

John and Cynthia Hardy/PT Bambu
Aga Khan Development Network
Badung, Bali, Indonesia
www.akdn.org
Green School

Jorg Stamm (architect), Bambooroo,
Mark Emery (general contractor)
Koh Kut, Thailand
www.bambooroo.net
Bamboo Bridge at Soneva Kiri Resort

Joseph Cory/Geotectura Studio
Haifa, Israel
www.geotectura.com
Bamboo Diamonds

Karawitz Architecture
Paris, France
www.karawitz.com
Passive House in Bessancourt

Kengo Kuma & Associates
Tokyo, Japan
www.kkaa.co.jp
Great (Bamboo) Wall

Maria Blaisse
Amsterdam, The Netherlands
www.mariablaisse.com
Moving Meshes

MUDI
Shanghai, China
www.mudi.com
German-Chinese House

nARCHITECTS
New York, NY, USA
www.narchitects.com
Canopy

Pasi Aalto, Andreas Grøntvedt Gjertsen, Yashar
Hanstad, Magnus Henriksen, Line Ramstad,
Erlend Bauck Sole/TYIN tegnestue
Trondheim, Norway
www.tyintegnestue.no
Soe Ker Tie House

Ricardo Leyva Cervantes/Ojtat
San Pedro Cholula, Mexico
www.ojtat.org
Aula de Capacitación Flor del Bosque
Casa Cohuatichan
Parque Arboledas Rementería

Richard Rogers Partnership
London, United Kingdom
www.richardrogers.co.uk
Madrid-Barajas Airport

ROEWU architecture
London, United Kingdom
www.roewu.com
Bamboo Forest House

Rocco Yim, William Tam,
Martin Fung/Rocco Design Architects
Hong Kong, China
www.rocco.hk
Bamboo Pavilion in Berlin

Søren Korsgaard arkitekt
Valby, Denmark
www.sorenkorsgaard.com
SuperFlex System
Woven House

Studio Archea
Florence, Italy
www.archea.it
Park Albatros Camping

Studio Cárdenas
Milan, Italy
www.studiocardenas.it
Bamboo Block House
Boo Tech
Microclimatico Pavilion

TreeHouse Company
Wollaston, United Kingdom
www.treehousecompany.com
De Hann TreeHouse

Vo Trong Nghia
Ho Chi Minh City, Vietnam
www.votrongnghia.com
Bamboo Wing
La Vong Restaurant
Vietnam Pavilion
wNw Bar
wNw Café

Zhang Lei/AZL architects
Nanjing, China
www.azlarchitects.com
Showroom in Cross

ZUARQ Arquitectos
Bogotá, Colombia
www.zuarq.co
Chapel
Chinauta House
Garita